A DEVILISH KIND OF COURAGE

ANARCHISTS, ALIENS AND THE SIEGE OF SIDNEY STREET

Andrew Whitehead

REAKTION BOOKS

For Samira and Rohan, with love

Published by
Reaktion Books Ltd
Unit 32, Waterside
44–48 Wharf Road
London N1 7UX, UK
www.reaktionbooks.co.uk

First published 2024
Copyright © Andrew Whitehead 2024

All rights reserved

No part of this publication may be reproduced, stored in a retrieval system, or transmitted, in any form or by any means, electronic, mechanical, photocopying, recording or otherwise, without the prior permission of the publishers

Printed and bound in Great Britain by TJ Books Ltd, Padstow, Cornwall

A catalogue record for this book is available from the British Library

ISBN 978 1 78914 844 2

CONTENTS

Introduction *7*
1 The Tottenham Outrage *18*
2 The 'Alien Invasion' *32*
3 The Worker's Friend *46*
4 Comrades and Lovers *73*
5 Houndsditch *88*
6 100 Sidney Street *110*
7 'A Devilish Kind of Courage' *129*
8 'The Cossacks of Bourgeois Journalism' *154*
9 Acquitted *175*
10 Nina, Luba, Rosa *193*
11 Who Was Peter the Painter? *221*
12 The Anarchist Aftermath *242*
13 Legacy *258*

TIMELINE *268*

Walk: *From Tottenham Police Station to the Marshes 271*
Walk: *From Houndsditch to Sidney Street 275*

REFERENCES *283*
SELECT BIBLIOGRAPHY *301*
ACKNOWLEDGEMENTS *307*
PHOTO ACKNOWLEDGEMENTS *309*
INDEX *311*

Introduction

'Nothing of the sort had been seen within living memory in quiet, law-abiding, comfortable England,' commented Winston Churchill of the Siege of Sidney Street in January 1911.[1] He was Home Secretary at the time and hurried, top-hatted, to the scene, clearly relishing the action and the echo it bore of his army service in Sudan and his work as a correspondent during the Boer War. In a room on the second floor of 100 Sidney Street in the East End of London were two young East European migrants suspected of involvement in a triple police murder the previous month. They saw themselves as revolutionaries – and they had been betrayed by an informer. The two men comprehensively outgunned the police besieging them, who took the astonishing step of calling on the army for help. Rifle-bearing Scots Guards made their way from the Tower of London and took up positions prone on the street on either flank of the besieged house, in a requisitioned house opposite and in the towering bottling plant of a nearby brewery. In all, probably a thousand or more bullets were fired during the stand-off. Tens of thousands of excited East Enders thronged to the spot – many more police were deployed on crowd control duties than in trying to winkle out the gunmen.

The exchange of gunfire at Sidney Street in Stepney lasted more than six hours. This was the first time for almost a century that troops had opened fire in London in support of the police; it was not to happen again until the Iranian embassy siege almost seventy years later. The military brought in machine guns and horse-pulled artillery, though wisely chose not to use them. The besieged building eventually caught fire and was allowed to burn. There were suggestions at the time that the police started the blaze deliberately. Winston Churchill personally ordered the fire brigade not to intervene. It was, in the normally sober words of *The Economist*, 'a pyrotechnic showdown that sparked headlines and manhunts around the world'.[2] Two bodies were found in the rubble – one gunman had been shot and the other died from inhaling smoke.

The Stepney siege was the third and final act in a series of shootings in London that startled and outraged the country. Latvian political émigrés were the principal perpetrators. In all, ten people were killed, four of them policemen. Criminal gangs had guns, but armed robberies at this time were rare. Shoot-outs with the police were just about unknown. On top of the shock, there was the spectacle. An armed robbery at a Tottenham rubber factory in January 1909 led to a two-hour chase across the marshes and beyond involving trams and pony traps, pulling in local kids, street traders, duck hunters and scores of police. It would have been comical but for the fact that four lives were lost. There was nothing light-hearted about the much more sophisticated attempt to burrow into a jeweller's shop at Houndsditch in the City of London a few days before Christmas 1910. The well-equipped gang intended to break into the safe and get away with items worth, in today's prices, almost £1 million. The robbers were interrupted and shot their way out. Three police officers were killed and two others seriously wounded. It was, and remains, the most grievous single incident in the history of London's police. One of the robbers was accidentally shot by his comrades and died within hours; two others were the men who went into hiding in Sidney Street.

Peter the Painter is the name indelibly associated with this spate of armed crime – or what those responsible might have regarded as revolutionary expropriation. In fact, he was not at the site of any of the shootings. By the time of the Siege of Sidney Street, he had fled across the North Sea. But he is not an invention, as has sometimes been suggested. He had been prominent in the Latvian revolution of 1905 and in the rearguard action against a vicious counterrevolution inflicted by the imperial power that then ruled the Baltic states, Russia. Peter the Painter was one of the leading militants in that uprising, organizing armed resistance and staging ambushes, jailbreaks, robberies and assassinations. To some, he was a revolutionary hero; others regarded him as a pistol-toting desperado. The experience of fighting for Latvia (the movement was nationalist as well as leftist) and for social justice, of seeing comrades tortured and killed, of operating underground and being on the run, shaped his political outlook and that of his associates. Thousands of young Latvian men and women were forced into exile, and some brought with them to their new homes a clandestine style of political activity, a hatred of those in uniform and a reliance on semi-automatic pistols that was bred in the Baltic cockpit. A small group among these exiled revolutionaries followed Peter the Painter as he moved from being an active social democrat, which at the time meant Marxist, to an anarchist, with its emphasis on direct action and suspicion of hierarchical politics.

In the popular mythology of London's East End, Peter the Painter has an honoured place in the litany of anti-heroes, and the Siege of Sidney Street is up there with the anti-fascist Battle of Cable Street a quarter of a century later as a compelling political drama played out in public view. Yet myths are just that – folklore that reveals much about the need for a clear and compelling narrative, but less about what actually happened and why. Peter the Painter – whose splendidly alliterative nickname was the creation of the London police – probably only spent a few weeks in London and never throughout that time fired a gun. The intention of this book is to strip back the layers of half-truth and embellishment which have so persistently clouded the retelling of the siege. The aim is explain who the gunmen were and how two of them came to be in a second-floor room of a Stepney boarding house, to detail the three sensational acts of violence undertaken by East European exiles and the ensuing police investigation, and to explore the manner of its reporting and the public and political response.

If the police were responsible for coining the alliterative nickname of Peter the Painter, they also burnished his anti-hero credentials by issuing 'wanted' posters in three languages: English, Yiddish and Russian. The initial poster tended to confirm the popular image of a foreign anarchist: his description included mention of his 'rather old' overcoat and 'rather shabby' boots. But when a new poster was issued with portrait photographs obtained from the French police, it shattered those preconceptions. They show an elegant young man in suit, waistcoat and tie, with a wing collar and a smart hat in his hand. His hair is neatly cut and he has a full goatee beard and a moustache with a stylish upward curve at each end. The photographs were probably taken three or four years before his brief London sojourn. He comes across as confident and suave, unsettlingly so. The reward offered amounted to the equivalent of £60,000 in today's money. Reported sightings came in from across the country and the world, but none were confirmed.

The elusive figure of Peter the Painter has been variously labelled a spy and a provocateur working for the tsarist secret police. The more outlandish theories about his identity have ranged from the Soviet dictator Joseph Stalin to the French bandit Jules Bonnot. In spite of the air of mystery surrounding the name, we know quite a lot about him, including the name he was given at birth (he had at least half a dozen assumed names). Indeed, the London police knew his real name by the close of 1912 as well as the location of the family smallholding in Latvia. But by then they had given up looking. The failure at the Old Bailey trial to secure an enduring conviction against any of those accused of involvement in the Houndsditch police murders led the British authorities to believe that they didn't have a strong enough case to secure Peter the Painter's extradition, let alone a guilty verdict. When, a few years later, the Australian police believed they had tracked the fugitive down, the message from London was: let it be. Better to let a legend grow up of 'the one that got away' than to concede that there was next to no actionable evidence against the man portrayed as the mastermind of a triple police murder.

Peter the Painter is part of a tradition of East End anti-heroes, sandwiched between Jack the Ripper a generation earlier and the Kray brothers half a century later. They all trod the same streets. Jack the Ripper fell upon his victims just a few hundred yards from the site of the Houndsditch shootings; the Kray

Introduction

Police 'wanted' poster with photographs of Peter the Painter issued on 30 January 1911.

brothers' most notorious gangland murder, Ronnie Kray's shooting of George Cornell at the Blind Beggar in March 1966, was carried out just a couple of hundred yards from the site of the Sidney Street siege. Peter the Painter, however, was not an East Ender. The only stay there for which we have hard evidence lasted well under three months. He carried out no murder during his time in London, unlike his partners in the pantheon of the East End underworld. The Latvian could well complain that he doesn't deserve the company he's been consigned to keep.

To respond to the age-old question about Peter the Painter and his associates – were their motives political or criminal? – the answer has to be: a bit of both. The Metropolitan Police at the time sought to suggest that the perpetrators were not politically motivated, perhaps trying to excuse the failure of Special Branch to forestall the attempted robberies and also to frustrate any claim for asylum. But right from the start, the police posters described Peter the Painter and his flatmate Fritz Svaars as anarchists. The anarchist label was sometimes applied by police and in the press – at a time when anarchism was associated in the public mind with assassinations, bombings and 'propaganda by the deed' – to suggest that those so identified were exotic, feral, dangerous. Its use was pejorative more than descriptive. But those involved in the three shootings described in this book saw themselves as insurgents. Several of them were associated with a small anarchist group active in the Latvian diaspora whose name translates as 'flame'. They were not terrorists – they used guns during robberies or to resist arrest rather than to cause panic and foment terror – but they routinely carried sophisticated and powerful weapons. How much of the money they secured was used to buy weapons for the struggle back home or to support the families of Latvian political prisoners is impossible to gauge. But those behind the robberies would probably have regarded resort to crime simply to keep themselves going as a political act. After all, in 1906 the Russian Bolshevik leader, Lenin, endorsed party-approved expropriation and confiscation even when the proceeds were 'partly for the maintenance of persons engaged in the struggle'.[3]

Most of these Latvian émigrés were not Jewish, but the vast majority of Eastern European migrants to Britain at this time were Jews escaping pogroms and religious oppression across the Russian Empire. The Latvians involved in violence in London lived principally in the Jewish East End, had Jewish landlords and workmates, and ate at mainly Jewish cafés and restaurants. Some spoke Yiddish, the language most widely spoken by Jewish immigrants; all had some Russian. They found a congenial meeting place at the Jubilee Street Club, an anarchist venue in Stepney associated with a thriving Yiddish-language weekly paper. The leading figures in the East End's Jewish anarchist movement deplored the use of guns and were deeply alarmed that resort to violence could endanger the right of asylum from which they benefited, but they conceded that some of the perpetrators had attended their meetings, used their reading room and eaten in their canteen.

Part of the narrative of Sidney Street is also that of the remarkable current of immigrant anarchism – with its emphasis on education, labour organization, dignity and social justice – which flourished in the East End in the run-up to the First World War. This account has turned to the Yiddish-language political press to help tell that story. And I have sought particularly to explore the lives and motivations of the three women charged in the aftermath of the Houndsditch police murders. They are sometimes regarded as a footnote to the main story. They weren't. One among them was clearly involved in the preparations for the attempted robbery at Houndsditch; two of the three had been active in some manner in the anarchist movement; all three found their lives changed utterly, in one case tragically, by their association with the group.

In this book, I have referred to the émigrés responsible for the shootings at Tottenham, Houndsditch and Stepney, and their associates, by the names by which they were most widely known at the time. In most cases, these were not the names they were given at birth; in many cases, it was not even how they were known to comrades and friends. Most of the group used multiple assumed names. The difficulties of transliterating from East European languages to English adds to the scope for confusion. As much as possible, I have tried to avoid a blizzard of unfamiliar names clouding the narrative – but it is important to follow the individual stories and aspirations of the fifteen or so exiles and migrants at the heart of the story. Except when quoting directly from newspapers or documents, I have used the names of towns and cities that are current today, making clear as appropriate when the usage at the time was markedly different. I have not included diacritical marks in Latvian names.

Disinformation is a modern concept with a long history. By far the most valuable source to understand the armed encounters are the voluminous records of the City of London Police, the force which was (and remains) responsible for law enforcement in the City of London, the financial district, and is separate from the much larger Metropolitan Police. Many of those who were questioned by the police, especially those complicit in the crimes, were understandably less than candid in their answers. Some had a problem that can further confound the historian – inventing aspects of their testimony because they were boastful or had half an eye on the rewards offered. There are other issues with placing too much reliance on statements taken by the police which often distilled what must have been long interrogations into a few pages of formal prose. Many of those questioned spoke in Yiddish or Russian in the presence of an interpreter who, however competent and assiduous (and they weren't always), would necessarily try to give shape to what was often a confused account. And then the police would mould the account to fit the narrative that they were seeking to develop. While there's no suggestion that there was any attempt to 'verbal' any of the suspects – fitting them up with words they never uttered – there was plenty of leeway to stretch the testimony as most interviewees would not easily have been able to read the statement set down in their name. So while the 113 statements prepared by the police ahead of the trial are the most valuable source of information about who did what at Houndsditch and afterwards, supplemented by the formal trial depositions and the evidence given at the committal hearings and then at the Old Bailey, the watchword has to be: tread carefully.

The Latvian violence came at a turning point for the news media. New halfpenny daily papers, taking advantage of technological innovation, had started to sell in huge numbers, and developed a news agenda with a particular emphasis on crime which proved attractive to their mass readership. News stories increasingly appeared on the front page rather than inside pages; headlines became shorter and sharper; for the first time, action photographs offered readers images that went beyond portraits and artists' sketches and added immensely to the impact of a new, from-the-spot, style of reporting. At the time, papers had almost a monopoly on news. When the evening papers started to land on desks in the Home Office late on the morning of 3 January 1911, top civil servants found out more about what was going on in Stepney than they were being told through Scotland Yard. The Sidney Street siege was close enough to Fleet Street and lasted sufficiently long for leading journalists to get down to Stepney and see a bit of the action. And it was the first breaking news story captured in a format that was then only months old: newsreel cinematographers were able to film the drama as it was happening. Their footage – silent and grainy – was being shown in cinemas just hours later. The Siege of Sidney Street is, in the judgement of the British Film Institute, 'still one of the most spectacular events ever captured on film'.[4]

The handling of the Houndsditch and Sidney Street shootings also offers a vantage point on a deeply discredited movement, Edwardian liberalism. The historian George Dangerfield in *The Strange Death of Liberal England* portrayed a political project that had run out of steam and proved unable to resolve any of the great crises besetting the nation: the issue of women's suffrage, the Irish question, labour militancy and the entrenched power of the landed interest in the House of Lords. He depicted Asquith's Liberal Party as politically and intellectually exhausted by the time of the outbreak of the First World War in 1914. His argument was put forward fully ninety years ago and, while it has been challenged, it retains influence.[5] Yet the Asquith government's response to the sensational crimes committed on London's streets by Latvian revolutionaries was exceptionally liberal. In spite of the hue and cry of the newly powerful popular press, the government refused to be panicked into precipitate action or ill-considered legislation. The political and media chorus of outrage did not lead to a revoking of the right of asylum or stiffer restrictions on the immigrants, 'aliens' as they were described at the time, fleeing antisemitic persecution in tsarist Russia and its empire. The only significant policy change introduced in response to the shootings was the sensible step of making available to the police guns that were a better match for those used by their adversaries.

THE TWO MOST detailed accounts of the Latvian revolutionary violence in London, its practitioners and its consequences are from diametrically different vantage points. Donald Rumbelow is a former City of London policeman who went to great trouble to preserve police documents earmarked for disposal about the attempted robbery in Houndsditch and subsequent shoot-out in Stepney. He came across mounds of these records in Snow Hill Police Station and, having failed to persuade his sergeant that they should be kept, carried them a rucksack-load at a time as he cycled home to Brixton. He then spent years pursuing the story, and his revised account, *The Houndsditch Murders and the Siege of Sidney Street*, published in 1990, is the starting point for all subsequent research. Donald Rumbelow performed the exceptional public service of depositing this huge cache in the London Metropolitan Archives, where the documents are available without restriction to researchers. Philip Ruff is an anarchist and historian who has become an expert on the early twentieth-century revolutionary movement in Latvia and has been tenacious in tracking down the story of Peter the Painter and his comrades. His study *A Towering Flame: The Life and Times of the Elusive Latvian Anarchist Peter the Painter*, published in 2019, is an exemplary work of scholarship and detection. These two accounts dovetail remarkably well, and the two writers have evident respect for each other.

While researching and writing this book, I have often walked through the streets of Tottenham and the East End, communing with the past, making sense of the landscape and taking pleasure in all that has survived from an earlier era. I understand the events related in this book much better because of following in the footsteps of those whose actions I recount. In the hope that others may also enjoy strolling these backstreets, I have devised two self-guided walks. One of these follows the two gunmen who snatched the wages of the Tottenham rubber factory as they headed on foot eastwards towards the marshes. The other traces the route of one of the would-be Houndsditch robbers, George Gardstein, who had been accidentally shot by one of his associates, as he was taken to the room in the East End where he died, and then continues on to Sidney Street and the site of the siege.

So join me as we head to Tottenham High Road.

1

The Tottenham Outrage

A payroll robbery is always risky, but staging such a raid just under the noses of the police is positively reckless. The target, Schnurmann's rubber factory, was almost directly opposite Tottenham Police Station. The two robbers had semi-automatic pistols and after a struggle managed to make off on foot with a large canvas bag containing the wages cash. They were pursued by police officers, on and off duty, who tumbled out of the station. All the police were, initially, unarmed. Factory workers, passers-by and local children all joined in the pursuit, and the cast list expanded to include footballers having a kick-around on the marshes and a posse of duck hunters. Some of those who gave chase showed great courage; others an astonishing lack of caution. The pursuit covered 10 kilometres (6 mi.) and lasted a couple of hours, and the thieves hijacked in turn a tram, a horse-drawn milk float and a vegetable seller's cart. Those following them commandeered cars and bicycles. It was high farce – and tragedy too. Hundreds of bullets were fired. Both robbers suffered fatal injuries. A police constable and a ten-year-old boy were also shot dead; 25 others sustained gunshot wounds and other injuries.

This was not an amateur heist attempt. The refugees responsible, Paul Hefeld and Jacob Lepidus (as with many of those we will encounter, they probably used multiple identities and their names had various spellings), were not only armed but carried a formidable cache of ammunition. Although the robbers failed in their getaway, most of the money was never recovered. All three of the shoot-outs recounted in this book were, from the gunmen's point of view, incidents that had gone wrong. There's every reason to believe that other robberies in London and elsewhere in Britain perpetrated by East European revolutionaries were carried out successfully – with money or valuables secured without shots being fired. The 'expropriators' persisted in staging armed robberies not simply because they were desperate, but because this form of crime had a proven track record in helping to sustain their movement and themselves.

The two men had inside information about the factory. In December 1908, the month before the robbery, Paul Hefeld took a few days' casual work at Schnurmann's, which boasted of being 'the largest rubber buyers in the world'. There were many recent migrants among its workforce. The company's founder, Julius Schnurmann, was himself an immigrant, German-born and Jewish. He established the firm in the mid-1890s, was naturalized as a British citizen a decade later, and a decade after that changed his name to Sherman in the face of wartime anti-German sentiment. The rubber reclamation plant on Chesnut Road, close to Tottenham High Road, was almost directly opposite the local police station, the upper floors of which were a section house that provided sleeping berths for junior policemen.

Hefeld was known to his workmates and recorded on the factory's time sheets as 'Elephant', probably because of his build and a play on the pronunication of his name. He was 21 and from Latvia, a Baltic state then under Russian imperial rule. His work at Schnurmann's was arduous, unskilled and poorly paid and he gave it up a few weeks before the robbery. In the short time he worked there, Hefeld appears to have become aware of the unchanging routine by which the money for the factory's wages was brought from the bank every Saturday morning. Lepidus, the other robber, was also Latvian, some years older and apparently more politically engaged and experienced. He had been working at a timber yard. They both lived locally. While many East European migrants settled in London's East End, others dispersed across the capital in search of work opportunities and cheap housing. There was a sizable migrant community in and around Tottenham attracted by jobs at factories producing furniture and footwear; rubber was also increasingly in demand for car tyres. At this time, a cluster of streets near the Tottenham Hotspur football ground at White Hart Lane was colloquially known as Little Russia, and there was another locality where new migrants congregated around Ferry Lane in Tottenham Hale.

At about 10.30 a.m. on 23 January 1909, a chilly winter morning, a car driven by the Schnurmann family's chauffeur, James Wilson, returned from the normal Saturday run to the bank in Hackney. He was accompanied by a seventeen-year-old office boy, Albert Keyworth, who was carrying about £80 in cash in a canvas bag – that's £10,000 in today's money. It was all in coins – the Bank of England didn't issue £1 notes at this date – and weighed up to 10 kilograms (22 lb). In an era before getaway cars, this bulk must have impeded the robbers in making a speedy flight on foot. Hefeld and Lepidus had been loitering nearby for the best part of an hour. Lepidus tried to grab the cash bag and wrestled the office boy to the ground. The driver came to the boy's assistance. Hefeld fired several shots at the chauffeur, while Lepidus got to his feet and fired at the office boy and then started to run. A passer-by, a gas stoker, rugby-tackled him and the canvas bag containing the wages money fell to the pavement. In response, Hefeld fired several more times and the gas stoker released his grip, allowing Lepidus to grab the bag. Although all the shots were at close range, leaving bullet holes in coats and clothing, no one was seriously injured.

Lepidus attempted to conceal the money bag in his clothes and the two men dashed down Chesnut Road, heading east, away from the High Road and into a maze of backstreets, firing at those seeking to follow them. Both men had modern semi-automatic handguns – Hefeld's was a Browning while Lepidus had a Bergmann and also carried a stiletto-style dagger. They were carrying several hundred rounds of ammunition, and this at a time when police issued with revolvers were usually only given ten rounds. A woman standing at her front door on Chesnut Road, selecting vegetables from a costermonger's cart, witnessed the robbery. 'Murder! Stop those two men!' she shouted as the men ran past, and she picked up a potato and threw it at them. One of the men trained his gun on her but didn't pull the trigger.[1]

The sound of shots being fired and the alarmed shouts from the street caused a frenzy of activity in the police station. Within a few minutes, a stream of policemen – not all fully dressed – emerged from the building, some in their haste jumping through the ground-floor windows. They headed off down Chesnut Road in pursuit of the gunmen. Cycles were commandeered, and the Schnurmanns' driver, who must have been in a state of shock, was persuaded to get back in the car and join the chase with his boss in the passenger seat, the young office boy in the back and a police officer perched on the running board. Some of the crowd also climbed up on the back of the car, bending and damaging the rear wheels. Armed robberies of this sort were rare, and police stationed at Tottenham were not used to being issued with guns. They were sent out unarmed in pursuit of men who had already shown their willingness to use their guns – the key to the police station's gun cupboard couldn't be found and it eventually had to be forced open.

To describe the hue and cry as a chase is not strictly accurate. The two robbers occasionally ran, sometimes ambled, and at times paused to reload and to take aim at their pursuers, most of whom wisely kept their distance. The numbers following them mushroomed, among them quite a few men who – unlike the first wave of police – had guns and rifles, either trophies of army service or used to shoot wildfowl on the marshes nearby. It was quite a circus. The Schnurmanns' car quickly caught up with the gunmen and the driver sought to run them down. Hefeld and Lepidus opened fire, striking the windscreen and the bonnet and putting the vehicle out of action. One of the bullets hit and killed a ten-year-old boy, Ralph Joscelyne, who spent his Saturday mornings earning a few coppers helping a local baker on his delivery round. His parents only found out about Ralph's fate much later in the day.

It's not clear whether the two men knew the area and had a route in mind, but by chance or design they were heading for a bridge over a busy railway line which opened on to the marshes alongside the river Lee. In an attempt to head them off, Police Constable William Tyler, a 31-year-old army veteran, cut across ground adjoining what was known as the Dust Destructor, a domestic waste incinerator. He confronted the robbers face to face. According to witnesses, he shouted out, 'Come on; give in, the game's up.' That's not how Hefeld and Lepidus saw it. They came from a part of the world where giving yourself up in such circumstances would probably have led to torture as well as a death sentence. Hefeld took aim at Tyler and shot him in the head. The police constable was carried into a nearby house where basic first aid was administered, but he died a few minutes after arriving at a local hospital. William Tyler was the first British police officer to be killed on duty for eight years.

At this stage, the police operation moved up a gear. A phone call was made from the incinerator plant to Stoke Newington Police Station, which despatched all available men and horses to the scene. 'The chase which had now become most desperate was continued with a splendid determination,' according to the report later compiled by Stoke Newington police.[2] The marshland, then much more extensive than now and stretching for around 3 kilometres (almost 2 miles) from west to east, was criss-crossed by footpaths, bridges and fords, with a river and canal to cross and several large reservoirs to circumvent. It offered opportunities to shake off pursuers but also posed a risk as stepping off paths could mean quickly becoming waterlogged.

Postcard showing the spot where Police Constable Tyler was killed.

At one point, a police constable went ahead of the pursuing crowd, knelt down on the riverbank and took aim at the two men with a revolver. But it was a borrowed gun and proved to be faulty. The policeman, for his pains, suffered bullet wounds in his calf and thigh from the return of fire. The police kept up the pressure nonetheless, co-opting the support of footballers having a game on the marshes while a group of wildfowlers were encouraged to train their shotguns on the robbers. 'The two men were walking quite coolly,' one wildfowler told a local paper, 'and every few moments turned round to return the fire.'[3] Several of the robbers' bullets found their mark, and a number of pursuers required hospital treatment. The fowlers' lead shot also hit the target, but without disabling the two men.

As Hefeld and Lepidus approached farmland on the Walthamstow or eastern side of the Lee Valley, they discovered that both police and local workers were lying in wait. There was several minutes of heavy fire, the robbers hiding behind a haystack, and a man with a local reputation as a pugilist decided he would have a go at challenging the robbers. He suffered serious gunshot wounds to both legs. Increasingly hemmed in and no doubt desperate, the two Latvians staged an armed hijack of a No. 9 tram making its way along Chingford Road. Lepidus jumped over a ditch and onto the tram, waving his gun. He ordered the vehicle to slow down so that Hefeld, who was some 45 metres (50 yds) behind, could catch up and get on board, and then motioned for it to speed up. The driver fled to the upper deck and hid under the seats; the conductor was forced to operate the tram with a gun to his head. Of the three passengers, two managed to jump off; the third, an elderly man, was shot and wounded. A large group of police and public climbed on board a tram heading in the other direction, which then gave chase by travelling in reverse. Volleys of shots were fired between the two duelling trams. A commandeered car was also closing on the tram, as was a pony-drawn cart used for pasting advertisements – until a shot hit the pony and those in the cart spilled onto the road.

The tram conductor recalled afterwards that one of the gunmen 'held the revolver so close to my cheek that I could feel the glow of the hot barrel. At times he would fire at some passing object, which he thought was a pursuer, and immediately put the revolver to my head again.' As he shared the adventure with reporters, he added, 'Never have I had such an exciting time in my life before!'[4] With considerable presence of mind, the conductor tricked the hijackers into believing that the tram route was about to pass a police station. Hefeld and Lepidus abandoned the tram and jumped on board an unattended horse-drawn milk cart. When the milkman realized what was happening, he remonstrated with the two men – and was shot. The cart was not constructed for speed and when the robbers took a corner too fast, it overturned. They hijacked another horse and cart, a greengrocer's. Lepidus sat at the front while Hefeld, with both guns, was seated at the back of the cart facing his pursuers. But they didn't fully disengage the brake on one of the wheels, so their progress was slow. Both men had suffered pellet and bullet wounds and must have been desperately cold and exhausted, and aware that their chances of escape were slim. They jumped off and made their way on foot to a railway arch traversing a stream but found themselves hemmed in by a tall fence. Lepidus managed to get over it; Hefeld tried and failed, fired one last shot at those closing in on him, and then shot himself just above the right eye. It didn't do the job – he survived and was sent to the same hospital as his victims.

Lepidus must have known he was cornered. He took refuge in Oak Cottage, a tiny two-up two-down house at Hale End, close to a section of Epping Forest. It was the home of a coal carrier and his two young children were in the house. An excitable crowd bearing guns, poles and staves surrounded the building. Lepidus, still armed and with a little ammunition left, at first tried to hide in the chimney breast and then retreated to a small room on the first floor. A policeman climbed a ladder and sought to fire at Lepidus through the bedroom window using a gun from a bystander, but that got nowhere as he didn't know how to operate the safety catch. Three armed police officers then determined to end the stand-off. They advanced up the narrow staircase and fired three shots through the bedroom door, and shortly after – according to some accounts – heard a fourth shot. When they forced their way into the room, they found Lepidus on the bed with blood streaming from a wound to his head. Within a few minutes he was dead. A policeman gave the body a kick to check that the robber wasn't feigning. The police present assumed that their bullets had killed Lepidus. Indeed, Police Constable Charles Eagles gave evidence at the inquest suggesting that he had fired the fatal shots. But the inquest jury was presented with evidence that the bullet removed from the dead man's head had been fired from his own pistol and its verdict was that Lepidus had taken his own life.[5]

That brought to an end the most remarkable armed pursuit in London's history. The two gunmen had fled, mainly on foot, across a large swathe of North London; giving chase were, at one time or another, probably hundreds of members of the public and perhaps a hundred policemen. By the best estimate, up to a thousand rounds of ammunition were fired by and at the robbers – though it seems that the only bullets that caused loss of life were fired by the Latvians.

AS MANY AS seventy of the police who sought to apprehend the two robbers received gallantry awards, promotions, pay rises or financial or other recognition of their bravery. The King's Police Medal for Gallantry was established as a direct result of the incident, and the three policemen who confronted Lepidus at Oak Cottage, all newly promoted to sergeant, were the first recipients. Civilians were also honoured and rewarded with sums as large as £100 (£12,500 in today's value) and £50 for those most seriously wounded while in pursuit of the gunmen, down to a modest £1 for Mary Ann Cawley, the woman who chucked the potato. The authorities invited compensation claims from the public, which ranged from five guineas (£5.25) for depreciation in the value of the advertising company's wounded pony – they seem to have been trying it on but were granted three guineas – to 12*s* 6*d* for bullet damage to a pair of trousers and 3*s* 9*d* for repairs to a bicycle commandeered by a policeman.[6]

For the newspapers, the 'Tottenham Outrage', as the robbery became known, was a sensational story. It was 'the most dramatic and daring crime of recent years', according to the *Daily Chronicle*, and resulted in 'a long and thrilling chase'. *The Star*, one of London's main evening papers, got a full – if not fully accurate – account on the front page of Saturday's final edition, squeezing every drop of pathos and drama from the morning's events:

> London has been shocked from end to end by news of an astounding crime at Tottenham.
>
> Not the Australian Bush with its Kelly and Captain Starlight, nor the rude cities of the American backwoods can furnish a crime more sensational and unexpected than that which turned quiet suburban streets into something like a shambles and saw hundreds of furious citizens pursuing with fury two desperate murderers who had shot a score of innocent people, killing a policeman – who was only married 12 months ago – and a boy who had the misfortune to obstruct for a moment their sanguinary flight.[7]

'Twenty Shot' was the banner headline, the gunmen were described as 'highwaymen', and a rudimentary map indicated the route the two men had taken across North London. The first draft of history is not always the most authoritative, and *The Star*'s initial description of the robbers as 'desperate armed Italians' was off beam – except that it suggested that the perpetrators were not home-grown criminals. In the words of the Metropolitan Police, the robbers were 'two men of foreign type'.[8] By Monday's edition, the gunmen had become 'Russian Anarchists from Riga', which was much closer to the truth.

Alongside the expressions of horror and anger, the newspapers also praised the heroism of the police – particularly of the unarmed officer who challenged the robbers and lost his life, and those officers who risked their lives at Oak Cottage. The funerals of the gunmen's victims became expressions of national outrage and of support for London's police. Six days after the killings, PC William Tyler and Ralph Joscelyne were buried in adjoining plots in an imposing joint ceremony. More than 2,000 police officers lined the route of the procession to Abney Park cemetery in Stoke Newington or followed the coffins. At the head of the procession was a contingent of mounted police. Six black-plumed horses pulled Tyler's hearse, his coffin draped in the Union Jack, while four horses bearing white plumes drew young Ralph's coffin. The Metropolitan Police band played Handel's 'Dead March' and as well as family members, the procession included representatives of the fire brigade, the army and the local tram company. A delegation of the unemployed was given permission to take part as a 'demonstration of respect to a member of a Force which they said had always been tolerant to them'.[9]

The procession set off from PC Tyler's home and took almost half an hour to pass Tottenham Police Station, which was draped in black; flags along the route were flown at half mast; many shops closed as a sign of respect, while homes had their curtains drawn or blinds down. King Edward VII sent a message of sympathy conveying his 'high appreciation' of the 'gallant conduct' of the police.

Memorial card for the policeman and ten-year-old boy killed in the Tottenham Outrage.

His private secretary commented that it was 'almost inconceivable that such a thing could have occurred in these days on the very outskirts of London'.[10] The Commissioner of the Metropolitan Police was among the mourners; the government was represented by a Home Office minister, Herbert Samuel (paradoxically, given the anti-immigrant and antisemitic prejudice stirred by the shootings, Samuel later in the year became the first practising Jew to be appointed to the Cabinet). 'The conduct of the Police in this affair', the Home Secretary told the police commissioner, 'reflects the utmost credit on the Force, which has never stood higher in the public estimation.'[11]

In preceding days, the vivid reporting of the outrage had attracted large crowds to Tottenham and Walthamstow, and the residents of Oak Cottage offered guided tours of the bloodstained rooms for a donation. Postcards were rapidly printed and sold of groups of onlookers gathered round the locations where Tyler and others had suffered fatal injuries. At the funeral, the swell of the crowds lining the procession route was immense. The *Daily Mirror* estimated that half a million Londoners came onto the streets; *The Star* said it 'seemed to the onlooker as though half North London had turned out'.[12] Hawkers sold memorial cards, some bearing portraits of the two victims and pointedly proclaiming that Tyler and Joscelyne had been 'murdered by two aliens'.[13]

William Tyler's grave at Abney Park bears a striking memorial, now listed by Historic England. A canopy of white marble covers a sculpture in the same stone of a police helmet bearing the constable's number, N 403, resting on a folded uniform, which in turn lies on a miniature sarcophagus. It is both eye-catching and effective. The inscription states that Tyler was 'killed at Tottenham while bravely doing his duty'. Ralph Joscelyne's burial place a few feet away is nothing like as grand and records that the gravestone was 'erected by his fellow scholars at Earlsmead School'. His family are said to have been upset that their son's death was overshadowed by that of the police officer.

The mystery remains as to what happened to the bulk of the stolen money. About £5 was found in a paper bag on the body of

Lepidus, but the fact that most of the cash was unaccounted for has prompted suggestions that the two Latvians had an accomplice to whom the money was passed. This was certainly a line of inquiry, though the police pronounced themselves 'certain that [the two robbers] had no communication with any confederates during the whole of the chase'.[14] There must have been a getaway plan more likely of success than running off helter-skelter into the backstreets, but it seems unlikely that a bulky canvas bag could be handed over without attracting the notice of the rapidly swelling crowd. The bag could perhaps have been found by one of those giving chase, or by a passer-by, and the money kept, though again the number of those involved in the pursuit makes it implausible that such an act would remain secret. The *Daily Mirror* published a photograph of men searching for 'the money stolen by the Tottenham Anarchists', which they believed could have been thrown over a wall at the one point where the robbers were out of view of their pursuers.[15] But this wall surrounded the waste incinerator and was several hundred yards from the scene of the robbery, so probably too far away to be an organized drop to a waiting accomplice. *The Times* surmised that

The grave of PC William Tyler at Abney Park cemetery.

the money bag had been dropped into the river Lee and reported that the police were intending to drag the riverbed, but that also failed to retrieve the cash.[16]

Plenty of theories have circulated over the years about what happened to the wages money. One account suggests that Lepidus hid the loot up a chimney in the cottage where he died and that it was eventually found, and spent, by the family who lived there, but there's no evidence to support that and the police would surely have checked such an obvious hiding place. Another possible explanation emerged many decades later in response to an appeal by the local museum. An elderly woman related how, not that long after the robbery, her brother, then aged about ten, found a canvas bag containing sovereigns – gold £1 coins – amid reeds on the marshes. Unaware of the value of the coins, he and his friend used them for skimming across the surface of the water. He went home with the bag and just one sovereign. His father, realizing the potential significance of the find, handed the bag and coin in at Tottenham Police Station but heard no more about it.[17] While crossing the marshes, Hefeld and Lepidus certainly had the opportunity to stash away the money, and of course they were never in a position to reclaim it. This is at best not proven, but it is a plausible hypothesis.

While Police Constable William Tyler and Ralph Joscelyne were being interred as heroes, a very different burial was taking place just a few miles away. Jacob Lepidus, at that stage not identified beyond his first name, was quietly placed in a grave in an unconsecrated corner of a cemetery in Walthamstow, close to the spot where he died. 'The usual service was omitted, but a minister read a few prayers,' the *Daily Chronicle* reported. 'The secret had been well kept, and by having the burial while all attention was fixed on Tyler's funeral, the murderer was removed unnoticed.'[18]

His comrade, Paul Hefeld, was initially said to be recovering well in hospital. 'He is perfectly conscious,' the hospital governor told a reporter, speaking as if of a captured beast:

> He glares all round the ward with an expression of terrible ferocity, as if it maddens him to think of his impotence.

He is a big fellow of a magnificent physique, very heavily developed. As he lies in a bed, guarded on each side by a big policeman, he looks the dangerous ruffian he has shown himself to be.[19]

There was great excitement when a man claiming to be Hefeld's brother turned up at the hospital and managed to bluff his way to the patient's bedside. The visitor was detained as a possible accomplice – but it turned out he was a journalist in search of a scoop.

Paul Hefeld faced a charge of murder but he never appeared in court. The same edition of *The Star* that reported on the funerals of Tyler and Joscelyne also recorded that Hefeld had suffered a relapse in hospital. Two weeks after the shooting, he was operated upon to remove fragments of bone from his head wound. It was not a success. He died on 12 February 1909 from meningitis. His only reported words while in the hospital ward were 'My mother is in Riga,' the Latvian capital. He was placed in an unmarked grave in an unconsecrated part of Tottenham cemetery. No friend or relative attended either gunman's burial.

2
The 'Alien Invasion'

In the aftermath of the Tottenham Outrage, the Russian authorities were quick to repudiate the actions of their nationals. Imperial Russia had itself suffered from political violence – assassinations, uprisings and politically motivated crime. But the Russian establishment didn't simply denounce the acts carried out in North London; it insisted that the perpetrators were not really Russians. A few days after PC William Tyler's funeral, imperial Russia's consul general in London wrote to the Metropolitan Police asking for a wreath to be placed in his name on the grave of 'the fearless Police Officer, who fell a victim of the recent Tottenham outrage'. The Russian government wished to express repugnance at the act of its citizens and its support for the forces of law and order. 'The murderer who is said to be a Russian subject was not a Russian ethnographically,' the diplomat insisted in a form of words that, while apologetic in tone, was certainly not an apology.[1] In the customary imperial manner, tsarist Russia claimed the territories of the non-Russians it ruled but disowned the people.

The Tottenham gunmen were Latvians and they were also on occasions described as Jewish. That religious labelling was unreliable. The overwhelming majority of migrants from Eastern Europe were Jews, and the term 'alien', widely used for these newcomers, was often synonymous with 'Jewish'. But most Latvian émigrés living in Britain were not Jews. It's not straightforward to ascribe religious identity to individual Latvian revolutionaries. They made no distinction based on religion and, unless police asked directly whether they were Jewish, did not identify themselves in that way (and the answers to police questions, of course, might not always be candid). Other identifiers such as names are also none too reliable because of the multiple assumed names émigrés adopted. Yet the mass Jewish migration to Britain is part of the expropriators' story, for the East European Jewish diaspora was the sea in which the Latvians swam. Most lived in Jewish neighbourhoods, patronized Jewish shops and eating places, and were part of the same street culture. While Tottenham didn't at this time have a substantial Jewish population, Houndsditch was on the eastern fringes of the City of London in an area where there had for some decades been a substantial Jewish community, and Sidney Street in Stepney was at the heart of Jewish East London.

The Jewish presence in what became known as London's East End pre-dated the mass migration of Yiddish-speaking migrants, but the arrival of large numbers of impoverished and sometimes traumatized East Europeans transformed both this area of London and Anglo-Jewry. Prior to 1881, when the Russian emperor Alexander II was blown up in St Petersburg by revolutionary activists, there were perhaps 40,000 Jews living in London. Within twenty years, that number had increased to around 140,000 and it continued to grow until the First World War.[2] The supposed involvement of Jewish leftists in the assassination of the tsar provoked pogroms, vicious anti-Jewish riots, across the Jewish 'Pale of Settlement'. This was the region to which almost all Jews in the Russian Empire were restricted and which encompassed all of what is now Belarus and Lithuania, much of Ukraine and of east and central Poland, and a small part of Latvia. This antisemitic violence often had the implicit approval of the authorities. The following year, further repressive measures against Jews were introduced. Tens of thousands of Jewish families, mainly from small towns, fled west, finding refuge in cities across Western Europe as well as in the United States and Argentina. The violence and oppression continued, as did the exodus. Brutal pogroms in 1903 and 1905 in Chișinău (then Kishinev) in what is now Moldova again prompted many thousands of Jews to leave, as well as focusing global attention on the persecution of Jews in Russia. Economic migration was also a factor and some Jewish migrants lived beyond Russia's borders, in Austrian Galicia and Romania. In total, it has been estimated that 2.5 million Jews migrated from Eastern Europe between 1881 and the outbreak of the First World War in 1914. Most headed for America.

Of the Jewish migrants to Britain, while there were significant communities in cities such as Leeds, Manchester and Glasgow, by far the largest number gathered in London, and within London the East End was the main area of settlement. The proximity of the docks where some immigrant ships berthed was a factor in the rapid growth of East End Jewry, but not the decisive one. The area had an established Jewish community and a lot of cheap housing. Within a generation of the beginning of this influx, parts of the East End – and particularly the western section of the borough of Stepney – had become largely Jewish and Yiddish-speaking enclaves. These new Londoners stood out in language, religion, appearance and social custom – and, distasteful as it seems today, the word 'alien' was widely used, including by the authorities and in legislation, to describe impoverished foreign migrants. There was alarmed talk of an 'alien invasion', and the rapid social change in some parts of the capital, accompanied by increasing competition for low-cost housing, caused friction.

An East End tailoring workshop before the First World War.

Many Jewish migrants worked in the tailoring and garment trades, boot and shoe making, the cheaper end of the furniture trades and cigar and cigarette making. These were all artisan or semi-skilled trades in which only a little capital was needed to establish a small workshop, though most of the migrants were not proprietors but employees, or were paid by the piece. For some East European migrants, heading west was a moment of immiseration and proletarianization. Whatever their livelihood had been, the range of economic opportunities open to them in London was restricted. As so often with poor newcomers, the migrants crowded into rooms and houses in a manner that shocked and discomfited public opinion. In areas where Jewish immigrants were preponderant, they tended to re-create the lifestyle and social relations of the *shtetl*, the small towns from which they had come. A character in a novel by the Yiddish-language author Sholem Aleichem expressed pleasure that so much was familiar in the East End, not least the food and the shops, and it was 'even just as muddy as at home. And it smells as bad. Sometimes even worse. We were delighted with Whitechapel.'[3] The Anglo-Jewish establishment was conflicted, seeking to be supportive of the new migrants and offering practical help and relief while also being at times anxious that anti-alien sentiment might disturb the qualified acceptance that middle-class Jews had achieved in commerce, the professions and politics.

The wave of immigration fundamentally changed the urban landscape, as many of the jerry-built courts and alleyways and two-storey East End 'mean streets' described by the novelist Arthur Morrison gave way to bigger, sturdier red-brick terraces and mansion blocks in which Jewish households rented rooms and workshops. These included Martin's Mansions, the terrace block of which 100 Sidney Street was part, which had four storeys (if you include the attic) and was completed in 1900. The 1911 Census, taken just three months after the siege, revealed that all the heads of household in these eight properties had been born overseas; of the 56 residents, the only people who appear not to have had East European antecedents were two young live-in women servants. Those living on the other side of Sidney Street were also largely, but not exclusively, of East European origin. Charles Martin, the developer and owner, angrily rebuffed reports that he had a 'no English need apply' policy. 'The premises were let for the most part to Jews,' he conceded, 'although he had never refused any English applicant. The fact was that English people did not care about living in close neighbourly relationship with Jews.'[4] But the controversy persisted, and when Martin claimed compensation for the damage done to 100 Sidney Street during the siege and fire and other losses, the Home Office received an angry letter from a member of the public citing evidence that Martin was an 'English Jew' and describing him as 'one of the Jewish money grubbers who pulled down Englishmen's houses to erect shelters for Aliens'.[5]

The newcomers established a network of religious groups, self-help associations, schools and trade unions and a vibrant Yiddish theatre, music hall and press. These provided some of the social groups and meeting places among which émigrés from imperial Russia, whether Jewish or not, found a welcome. East End Jewry developed a distinctly left-wing political profile which persisted into the 1950s. By then, the Jewish East End was fading fast and Yiddish was no longer heard on the streets. The pattern of movement in ripples out of the East End is reflected in the family story of the writer Alexander Baron, who worked on the screenplay of a 1960 feature film, *The Siege of Sidney Street*. He was born in 1917. His grandparents, who, broadly, migrated as adults from Eastern Europe, lived in and around Spitalfields at the heart of the old East End; his father was born in Poland, was brought up speaking Yiddish and worked in the fur trade; when his parents married, they moved just a mile or two out of the East End to Dalston and then Stoke Newington, and Baron himself ended up in Temple Fortune near Golders Green in what was dubbed the 'northwest passage', the part of suburban North London in which middle-class Jewish families congregated.

Resentment of Jewish migration, fuelled by antisemitism and the argument that 'sweated' Jewish labour was pulling down wage rates, led to demands to restrict alien migration. This was supported by some established trade unions as well as by racist organizations

'In an East-End Russian Restaurant', from George R. Sims, ed., *Living London* (1902).

such as the British Brothers' League, formed in 1901 with the slogan 'England for the English'. The league became a substantial force in and around the East End and gained the support of several Conservative MPs. The league's biggest success came with the Conservative government's establishment of a Royal Commission on Alien Immigration and the subsequent introduction of the Aliens Act of 1905, which was designed to restrict the entry of criminal, destitute or seriously ill migrants from outside the British Empire. Under the terms of the Act, immigrants could only disembark at fourteen approved ports, and holders of the newly established post of immigration officer had the authority to refuse 'leave to land' to any would-be migrants deemed 'undesirable'. But the rigour of the Act was much diminished by the stipulation that the regulations only applied to immigrants travelling third class, and only to ships that were carrying at least twenty such steerage passengers. Political and religious refugees were also exempt from the Act's provisions, so abiding by the principle of offering asylum. Only a small proportion of those immigrants covered by the Act were turned back. In the words of one historian, 'Jews were still free to come in, and did.'[6] But the legislation had a much bigger impact in discouraging Jewish migrants from choosing Britain as their destination, especially when the United States beckoned. Although the word 'Jew' didn't appear in the Act, there was no mistaking the intended target of the legislation. And there was no going back. While the scope and fine print of immigration law has changed markedly since 1905, the Aliens Act 'set the precedent for the ever-tightening web of immigration control that is in place today'.[7]

By far the greater number of migrants to Britain from the Russian Empire were Jewish, but there was also a long tradition of Russian intellectuals and political activists, regardless of their religious identity, finding asylum in London. Sergius Stepniak, a writer and revolutionary who in 1878 stabbed to death the head of Russia's secret police, spent most of the rest of his life in exile in England, where he died in 1895. His collaborator, Feliks Volkhovsky, also settled in London after escaping from banishment to Siberia. Peter Kropotkin, an anarchist intellectual, political scientist and geographer from an aristocratic family, escaped from a Russian jail in 1876 and spent more than forty years in exile – most of that time in England. The Tolstoyan Vladimir Chertkov, also from a wealthy Russian family, came to England as an émigré in 1897 and lived for more than a decade here. Vladimir Ilyich Ulyanov, who in 1901 adopted the party name Lenin, first came to London in 1902 and attended party congresses of Russian social democrats here, paying at least five short visits to the city over the next decade. Revolutionaries from across the Russian Empire came and went more or less at will.

Latvia (which at the time broadly constituted the Russian-ruled Baltic provinces of Livonia and Courland) in 1905 had a population of 2.5 million, significantly higher than today, of which very approximately 5 per cent was Jewish. Its capital, Riga, was one of the biggest cities under Russian rule and one of the busiest ports. Latvia also had a legacy of German influence, with a powerful Baltic German and Lutheran landowning class that was broadly

A photograph of Latvian revolutionaries sent to London police by the British Consul in Riga in January 1911: in the middle with fair hair is Kristaps Salnins or 'Grishka', and, sitting in front of him, Otilija Lescinska or 'Tija'.

supportive of the status quo and loyal to the Russian tsar; German was the official language in Riga until the 1890s. It was more industrialized and urbanized than most of imperial Russia and enjoyed a considerably higher literacy rate. But the countryside was still in part feudal. The emancipation of the serfs was achieved forty years earlier in the Baltic provinces than in Russia, but they were liberated without land and by the end of the century two-thirds of Latvian rural households still owned no land.[8] Rapid economic development led to migration into Latvia from other parts of the Russian Empire, including Jewish migrants escaping pogroms. In 1913, only a third of Riga's residents were native-born and most adults spoke a language in addition to Latvian (also known at the time as Lettish), the Baltic language most widely spoken in Latvia. There was also a less pronounced pattern of Latvian migration to other areas of Russia and beyond, and by the end of the nineteenth century an estimated 35,000 Latvians (sometimes described at the time as

Letts) lived in the West. Following the 1905 Revolution, about 5,000 political refugees and 2,652 deportees left Latvia, among them several whose activities form the focus of this book.[9] While the numbers were not huge, neither was Latvia; among young Latvian men in particular, as many as one in a hundred became political exiles as a result of the revolution and the repression it triggered.

A Latvian national movement developed from the 1860s, initially cultural in focus and resentful of Baltic German dominance but increasingly adopting a political edge. In the 1890s, several social democratic (that is, broadly, Marxist) parties developed a presence in Latvia. Most were illegal; while some advocated pan-Russian political activity, others also had a focus on regional autonomy. As in Ireland, India and other countries under imperial rule, political forces developed in Latvia that combined leftism and nationalism; and in the absence of anything approaching a democratic system of governance, these new political forces were willing to consider acts of violence both as political symbolism and as a stepping stone towards insurrection.

The defining moment of Russia's 1905 Revolution was Bloody Sunday in St Petersburg in January, when the Imperial Guard fired on demonstrators led by a Russian Orthodox priest, Father Gapon, seeking to present a petition to the tsar. Hundreds were shot dead, triggering industrial unrest, which then escalated into a challenge to autocratic rule. The revolutionary movement spread rapidly to Latvia, where it was pursued more energetically than in most areas under Russian rule. As in the Russian-speaking heartlands, the protests began in the cities and were accompanied by waves of strikes, and then spread to rural areas, where they extended to incidents of arson and attacks on landlords. Lenin, in an endorsement of guerrilla warfare, said that Latvia was where organized armed struggle, including assassination, confiscation and expropriation, was most developed.[10]

The nature of the Latvian uprising of 1905 is reflected in the political activism of the man who became the anti-hero of the Siege of Sidney Street, known to the British police and public by the most evocative of his many pseudonyms, Peter the Painter.[11] He was born into a farming family that owned a little land in the province of Courland. He had just turned twenty when he came to the attention of the police in the summer of 1903 as a social democrat activist and propagandist. A comrade gave his name while subject to torture. Peter the Painter (we'll get to the subject of his real identity in a later chapter) managed to evade arrest until May the following year when, amid an upsurge in political militancy, he was charged with possession of illegal socialist literature. He spent several months behind bars before getting bail – and, for a while, turned to earning a livelihood from the work that gave him his nickname, as a signwriter and painter. Early in 1905, Peter the Painter moved to Riga, Latvia's principal city, and sought to go underground by abandoning the name he had been given at birth. Within days, the Latvian revolution erupted. A general strike called in Riga to sympathize with the victims of Bloody Sunday in St Petersburg led to a massacre almost as grievous. Russian troops opened fire on a protest demonstration, killing scores of activists; many more are said to have drowned as they tried to escape on the thin layer of ice on Riga's main river. This in turn provoked more strikes, demonstrations and turbulent funeral processions, which led to further confrontation between Latvian leftists and soldiers and police.

Peter the Painter became a figure of some importance in the newly established Latvian Social Democratic and Workers Party. He took the lead in coordinating military training and organizing the making of simple firearms and bombs as the progressive movement responded to police and military attack. He spoke Yiddish – his mother may have been Jewish – and this allowed him to collaborate closely with the members of the Jewish socialist movement, the Bund. He had, in effect, according to the historian Philip Ruff, 'become the military leader of the Latvian revolution'.[12] In September 1905, Peter the Painter was given responsibility for organizing a jailbreak from Riga Central Prison of two prominent revolutionaries who were facing execution. Fifty leftists staged an attack and managed to spring the two prisoners in an action which caught the imagination of the revolutionary movement. The two men who had been freed made their way to London.

When, in October 1905, the tsar granted concessions in the face of widespread political turbulence, in Latvia that prompted a further upsurge in strikes and demonstrations which gave the protestors the upper hand. This was a national and social revolution, which also prompted a vicious and antisemitic counter-movement. Some of the revolutionaries had semi-automatic pistols and at times the streets of Riga resembled a battlefield. The declaration of martial law across Latvia in December didn't prevent an escalation of rural unrest into what has been described as an insurrection. Peter the Painter was part of an armed contingent supporting the rural revolution and, amid widespread torture and executions, was involved in the killing of unpopular estate managers and others who represented the rural establishment. Several of his colleagues were captured and sentenced to execution by firing squad. By the close of the year, a huge Russian military force was deployed intent on the 'pacification' of Latvia, which involved reprisals including burning farms and homes as well as torture and executions. In all, thousands of Latvians lost their lives; among them were more than a hundred members of Riga's municipal police, amounting to a quarter of the police force.[13]

Peter the Painter led an armed contingent often operating on its own initiative, as when it staged a guerrilla-style attack on Russian troops garrisoned in a rubber factory. Alongside him in that operation was another Latvian social democrat, Fritz Svaars, who was subsequently arrested and badly beaten. A few weeks later, Svaars was one of a group of prisoners rescued when Peter the Painter and others staged what sympathizers portray, perhaps a touch heroically, as an astoundingly bold armed raid on the offices of Riga's secret police. Five years later they were sharing rooms in the East End of London. The Latvian émigrés who grouped together in London had been hardened and brutalized by the revolution and counterrevolution in their homeland, and knowing of friends who had been executed or succumbed to torture gave them a sense of mission as well as the avenging recklessness of the outlaw. The temper of Latvia's uprising helps to explain the tone of Latvian émigré activity in succeeding years. Peter the Painter's reputation as one of the leading, and most militant, figures in Latvia's armed movement accounts for his standing within the émigré community.

The custom of expropriation, armed robberies of banks and wage heists, was also established in the fever of revolution and persisted in exile. Peter the Painter was involved in the successful robbery – on this occasion authorized by the Russian Social Democrats – of the Russian State Bank in Helsinki, the capital of then Russian-ruled Finland. He was part of a group that then went to Germany to use some of the proceeds to buy weapons. By the time he returned to Latvia in the spring of 1906, he had moved away from the social democrats and had become an advocate of a movement new to the Russian Baltic, anarchism. The social democrats had decided to contest parliamentary elections, while anarchists placed emphasis on self-organization. The new, and small, anarchist groups in Latvia were seen as more committed to armed uprising and as more ardent revolutionaries. They won over a significant number of recruits and Peter the Painter came to be regarded as Latvia's 'anarchist chieftain'.[14] But with prominence came a heightened risk of being betrayed by informers and, after a narrow escape, Peter the Painter left Latvia towards the close of 1906 – with a woman described as his wife, Lidije (also known as Anna) Schwarze – and by September 1907 he was living in Philadelphia, where he once again teamed up with Fritz Svaars. Several of those who were involved in the Houndsditch affair had spent time in the United States, where there is evidence that some at least were involved in armed robberies. Towards the close of 1908, an anarchist journal, *Briviba*, which means 'freedom' in Latvian, began publication in New York, describing itself as the journal of the American Latvian Anarchist Communist Group. By then, Peter the Painter was back in Europe.[15]

The gains of the 1905 movement in Latvia were a long way short of the aims of the young revolutionaries, but they were nevertheless significant. Across the Russian Empire, the establishment of a Duma (or parliament) and the introduction of religious toleration and a measure of academic freedom, along with a relaxing of censorship regulations, were substantial achievements. But more important was a change in attitudes, a radicalization of many of the young, which was intensified by the post-revolution repression pursued by the Russian authorities. 'Violence in the Baltic Provinces begot the counter-violence of punitive expeditions, which were among the bloodiest in the Russian empire and made compromise between Baltic Germans on the one hand and Latvians and Estonians on the other even less likely than it had been,' in the judgement of a historian of the Baltic. 'For the Latvians and Estonians, however, it was changes in political and social consciousness and a greater level of self-confidence that were most significant.'[16] A generation had been tempered in the flames of one of Europe's most cruel political showdowns in which both sides displayed a ruthless streak.

Russia's political turbulence was watched closely in Britain, where the Russian Empire had long been regarded as a rival and where there was a great deal of disapproval about the persistence of autocracy and of internal repression. The profoundly illiberal response of the Russian authorities to the 1905 Revolution was highlighted by those on the radical and socialist wing of British politics. The anarchist Peter Kropotkin's booklet *The Terror in Russia: An Appeal to the British Nation* was published by the broad-based Parliamentary Russian Committee in July 1909 and within two months was in its seventh edition. It focused particularly on the appalling conditions in Russian jails and the profound hardships faced by those forced into internal exile in Siberia and Russia's far north. While Kropotkin's pamphlet only dealt in passing with the Russian Baltic, he noted that 'the system of torture practised regularly in the Riga and other Baltic provinces prisons became notorious all over Europe.'[17] His account, intended to be more humanitarian than political, helped shape informed opinion, as did the optimistic note he struck about the rising tide of opposition to autocracy:

> There is no question that the movement of the years 1905–1907 has produced a deep change in the whole aspect of thought and sentiment in Russia. The peasant, the workman, the clerk, the small tradesman are no longer so

submissive to every rural police officer as they formerly were. New ideas, new aspirations, new hopes, and, above all, a new interest in public life have been developed in them.[18]

He was right, and just as the Russo-Japanese War played a part in paving the way for the 1905 Revolution, Russia's involvement in the First World War led to the twin revolutions of 1917, the rise to power of Lenin's Bolsheviks and the end of tsarist rule.

Another account of the 1905 Revolution more focused on the Baltic – though not as widely read as Kropotkin's work – was written by an unnamed member of the Lettish Social Democratic and Workers' Party and published in London in 1907 by the Independent Labour Party. *The Revolution in the Baltic Provinces of Russia* was a somewhat heroic account of the armed uprising in Latvia and of the litany of hangings, floggings and acts of torture and threats of sexual violence meted out as part of the region's pacification by Cossacks and other Russian forces.[19] 'The book is published to enlist the sympathies of our people for the Russian Revolution which is no longer a thing that may happen but an episode which has begun,' said the Labour MP and future prime minister J. Ramsay MacDonald in a foreword. He also lambasted Scotland Yard for behaving as 'a department of the Russian police' in its surveillance of Russian opposition leaders in London. MacDonald concluded by 'wishing the Russian Revolutionists God speed'.[20] His comments demonstrate a reservoir of sympathy in Britain for those challenging Russian autocracy in Latvia and elsewhere, an awareness of the brutality of the Russian response particularly in its Baltic provinces, and support for émigrés finding refuge in Britain and being able to meet and organize to challenge the tsar's rule. At this time, of course, there was no reason to associate refugees from the Russian Empire with shoot-outs on the streets of London.

3

The Worker's Friend

'The local Anarchists met to-day at their clubroom near Ferry-lane,' *The Star* reported just two days after the Tottenham robbery. 'One half of them repudiate the two assailants, and the other half are extolling them to the skies.'[1] Perhaps. For both the newspapers and the police, the killings posed a peculiar range of challenges. The perpetrators were quickly identified as Latvian political refugees. But they were part of a world that was almost impermeable to both journalists and police officers. The revolutionaries operated in a closed community – secretive, inward-looking and conducted in Latvian, Yiddish or Russian rather than English. Yet both the press and the police were under pressure to explain and inform. The police had an advantage as there would have been some surveillance of émigré political groups, though without the files containing reports from agents and informers it's difficult to know how effective this was. The Russian authorities had a more extensive network of undercover informants among political refugees, some of whom were probably agents provocateurs – on occasion inciting revolutionaries to acts of violence to expose the refugees' ruthlessness, to emphasize the value of the informers themselves and also perhaps to encourage governments to be less accommodating in offering asylum.

The tone of the press coverage was reflected in the *Daily Mirror*, which reported 'the deepest antipathy felt at Tottenham to the foreign colony, composed for the most part of aliens of the most undesirable character. Their members, their violence, and their anarchistic tendencies unite to make them a distinct danger to the neighbourhood.'[2] It forecast that an 'anti-alien outbreak is not at all unlikely'. The paper quoted a 'well-known member of the Russian revolutionary movement' as saying that the two men were members of the Lettish League, which advocated 'political terrorism'. More than that, they were *Bol'sheviky* – Bolsheviks, members of the more hardline faction within the Russian social democratic movement – and 'were criminals before they joined the revolutionary party'. The report also gave voice to a tale that proved stubbornly persistent, that Jacob Lepidus's brother had been 'a member of one of the most active Terrorist societies in Paris' and had 'met with a fatal accident while carrying bombs with a comrade'. *The Times* carried a similar report, unattributed and, one imagines, based on a briefing by the police or the Home Office, which declared that Lepidus was 'a member of a notorious Russian revolutionary family'.[3] In subsequent retellings, the bombs that went off prematurely were intended to assassinate the French president. One of the less reliable police memoirs suggests that the two Tottenham robbers were on the scene in Paris when the explosives detonated. It's difficult to sieve fact from invention, but the story doesn't ring true.[4]

The inquests into the Tottenham armed robbers, Lepidus and Hefeld, offered only slivers of information about their personal history and political involvement. At Lepidus's inquest a witness with indifferent English and variously described as Russian or Polish said that the dead man had lodged with him in Tottenham for a few months a couple of years earlier. He knew the man simply as Jacob and believed he was from Riga. When the dead man lost his work and couldn't pay the rent, he'd been turfed out. The coroner chose to draw a political homily from the case. 'England had always opened its doors to all aliens, whether they had committed political crimes in their own country or not,' he declared.

> They had a safe refuge in England, and, so long as they behaved themselves, they were allowed to settle here. But if they descended to robbery and wholesale murder, the time must come, and must come very soon, when the doors of England might be shut against them, and they would find

themselves turned back to their own country and to the tender mercies of those who, perhaps, knew them best.

The jury concurred and sought to 'draw the special attention of the Home Secretary to the perils the country was subject to under the existing Aliens Act'.[5]

More details about the dead man, albeit of dubious authenticity, were published by the evening newspaper *The Star* in the form of a letter from a friend of 'Lapidus', signed but with no address and 'in a foreign handwriting'. The paper gave this letter prominence on its front page. The letter writer said they had lived with the dead man 'for a considerable time', and stated that Lepidus had been born near Riga, had spent much time in the city and had been a seaman whose ship was blown up in the course of Russia's disastrous war with Japan in 1904–5. Lepidus survived, made his way back to Riga and then travelled on to England:

> I met him four years ago. He explained to me that he was a member of the Anarchist society, the headquarters [of] which were in Battersea, and where they are still, having been shifted from Soho.
>
> He was a regular attendant at all the secret meetings, but after a time he was expelled.
>
> I met him some months back, and he was then at the Communist Club in Soho.
>
> I asked for him one evening at the latter club, but was informed that he had proceeded to Tottenham, and had joined the Lettish Socialistic Society. It was impossible to rank him as an 'Anarchist,' as that body consists of clever men.[6]

Whatever the exact truth, this account points to the confusion about whether the perpetrators of the Tottenham Outrage were social democrats or anarchists. The demarcation line between the two camps was imprecise, and quite a few Latvian anarchists had earlier been social democrats. It was reported that much revolutionary literature was found in the men's rooms in Tottenham, presumably in languages other than English, but without more detail that offers no indication to any precise political allegiance.

The later inquest into Paul Hefeld heard evidence from the proprietor of a cigar store on Ferry Lane in Tottenham where Hefeld had lodged for a couple of weeks shortly before the robbery. The shopkeeper had nothing to say about his lodger's politics but said that Hefeld was aged about 21 and from Riga, and had come to Britain about a year previously.[7] There was little in the way of hard information about either gunman, as the *Jewish Chronicle* acknowledged while exploring their background and motivation. 'It is not ... at all certain that the malefactors in the present case were political refugees. The truth probably is that they hailed from the Baltic Provinces and were driven to a career of crime by the demoralising effects of Russian rule.'[8]

Armed crime was, at this time, not unknown but exceptionally unusual. In London in the 1880s, a spate of armed burglaries led to permission being granted for policemen in outlying districts of the capital to carry revolvers – but that scare faded. The gangs that ran protection rackets and organized crime had access to guns, and on occasion used them. The *Daily Telegraph* complained in January 1911 in the aftermath of the Sidney Street shoot-out that 'pistols and revolvers' were 'easier to come by in London than in the mining-camps of Nevada and the Yukon'[9] – but London was seen as much safer than the big American cities and the East End wasn't at all akin to the Wild West. As a consequence, while the police had some access to firearms, the guns were usually old and sometimes obsolete, and few police officers knew how to use them to best effect.[10]

Gun companies seized on the series of shootings as an opportunity to press the claims of their products on the London police. The Dedles Pistol Company was particularly quick off the mark, getting in touch just a couple of days after the Houndsditch shootings to advance the claims of its revolver, which had 'recently been adopted by the Russian Police'. It sold for a very reasonable 7s 6d (37½ pence), though the literature promoting its use for 'anyone wanting protection from Tramps, Burglars, or vicious Dogs' was clearly not devised with police forces in mind. The London agents for Mauser, a German-based company which made one of the more formidable semi-automatic weapons, also seized the moment. The agents warned that 'if our Police Authorities adopt any other form of pistol & have to again meet desperate men armed with the Mauser Long Range Pistol, they will be placed at almost the same disadvantage as they were at the Houndsditch & Sidney Street affrays'. They also enclosed a full-page article from *The Graphic* extolling the virtues of the Mauser, which could, depending on model, be loaded with six, ten or twenty cartridges and in the hands of an experienced gunman could fire eighty shots a minute, even allowing for reloading.[11]

The police weren't the only potential customers for these powerful weapons. Documents found in the wallet of George Gardstein, the gunman who suffered fatal injuries at Houndsditch, included a note of comparative specifications for five different makes of 'repeating pistols', including Browning and Mauser. And among the photographs seized by the police as they searched the rooms of those suspected of involvement in the Houndsditch shootings were two startling images – one looking down the barrel of a pistol in the hands of a capped and moustachioed gunman, and the other a profile of a gunman taking aim and ready to fire. These appear to have been promotional photographs for the Mauser c96, colloquially known as the 'Broomhandle' and exactly the type of semi-automatic weapon that was found in the burnt-out ruins of 100 Sidney Street. Some among the Latvian émigrés and their associates developed quite an expertise in these guns, and don't seem to have encountered too much trouble in acquiring them, through the black market in Antwerp or otherwise.[12] This model of Mauser was used by Irish republicans in the Easter Rising of 1916 and described by them colloquially as the 'Peter the Painter'.[13]

There are just glimpses of a pattern of armed crime in Britain involving Latvian and Russian migrants in addition to the Tottenham wages robbery and the subsequent shootings at Houndsditch and Sidney Street. On 10 April 1908 – nine months before the Tottenham shootings – the *Evening Times* in Glasgow reported a 'sensational affair' in Motherwell earlier in the day, in which three men attempted to rob a bank in the town centre. When one of the robbers produced a revolver, he was tackled by a bank employee who suffered cuts to his hand and cheek. In the struggle, a shot was fired but without causing injury. Two of the men immediately bolted, leaving the third, the man with the gun, to fight his way out unaided. More shots were fired when the two men were confronted by a police officer in woods near a railway track. They were arrested but the third robber was not found. The two men who stood trial, Ludwig Bruno and Carl Smith, were sentenced to ten and seven years in jail, respectively – and Bruno died in jail the following year. They had been living in the mining village of Craigneuk. There was a pattern of migration to this part of Scotland from Russia's Baltic provinces and from Poland to work in ironworks and mining and on the land. Bruno was a Latvian and as a London member of the Lettish (that is, Latvian) Social Democrats would very probably have been known to some of those involved in the London shootings; while little is known for certain of his two colleagues, they appear to have been recent migrants and were described at the time as either Russian or Polish.[14]

In the aftermath of the Siege of Sidney Street, the *Daily Chronicle* displayed some enterprise in sending a reporter to Craigneuk, 'a forlorn enough little place in spite of the pretty name'. The journalist was seeking to establish a link with 'the dangerous gang of Lettish criminals who have found a refuge in East London'. He alleged that the Motherwell robber who had escaped arrest was one of the Latvians who died in the attempted wages robbery in Tottenham the following year – while no name was given in the report, it was clearly referring to Jacob Lepidus. There were certainly similarities in the manner in which the two robberies were conducted – not least the reckless conduct of the gunmen. The reporter based his news story on a letter apparently written by this man, which only came to light after his death, 'to a member of the Lettish colony at Craigneuk'. There's no firm indication as to how the *Daily Chronicle* journalist came across this letter, but he seems to have been briefed by the police and certainly met and interviewed a local police superintendent. He also reported that after the Motherwell bank robbery, the police paid the Latvian community in the village 'so many polite attentions that they gradually disappeared from the district, and went to London'.[15] Although the assertion that Lepidus was involved in the Motherwell robbery attempt is, to use the Scottish legal term, not proven, neither is it outlandish. In the aftermath of the Tottenham Outrage, the local paper reported that both gunmen had moved to North London from Scotland some months earlier.[16]

There is another telling indication of émigré involvement in serious crime. Among the mounds of City of London Police files relating to the Houndsditch murders of December 1910 is a police statement that pre-dates that incident. In October 1909, William Sokolow (or Sokoloff) – who told police he was Jewish and from Moscow and had moved to England eleven years earlier – was working as a watchmaker and shop manager at a business on Old Street, less than half a mile from Houndsditch. He had keys to the safe. The shop was robbed and jewellery worth about £150 (about £18,000 in today's value) was taken. Sokoloff told police that on the evening of the robbery he had been at his club on Jubilee Street – the anarchists' club.[17] Whatever suspicions the police may have harboured, Sokoloff was not charged. He was fortunate. He was better known as Joseph, was later involved in the Houndsditch robbery and was one of the two gunmen who died at 100 Sidney Street. The supposition must be that Harris's shop in Houndsditch was not the first jewellery business in the area to have been targeted by revolutionary émigrés and their allies.

Sokoloff stood out from the rest of the group that gathered around Gardstein, Svaars and Peter the Painter. He was not Latvian. Nor was he, as far as we can tell, an anarchist, in spite of his association with the Jubilee Street Club. It's possible that he was enlisted because he had special skills and it's easy to imagine that a watchmaker might have a head start when it comes to cracking a safe. There was talk of a marriage of convenience between revolutionary expropriators and experienced criminals, and not all those participating in a robbery needed to have the same motivation. Yet almost all of those involved in the three acts of violence in London that are the focus of this book were veterans of the revolutionary movement in Latvia and saw themselves as working for a cause, even if at times that cause was sustaining themselves more than it was their movement. Their ideology has been described as 'a confusing mix of revolutionary socialism, ethnic populism and gangsterism. To British authorities it was anarchism by virtue of its extremeness.'[18] There was certainly a tendency to label émigré activists as anarchists whatever their precise political affiliations, and to outsiders – and sometimes to insiders as well – the differences between the various left-wing political currents were hazy. But the labelling wasn't simply a lazy stereotype. Several of the group clearly regarded (or perhaps had once regarded) themselves as anarchists or had links to Latvian anarchist groups. The shrill headlines of the tabloid press complaining of 'alien' anarchist murderers were sensationalist, but not entirely misleading.

There was a small and shadowy Latvian anarchist group that included most of those involved in the Houndsditch robbery attempt and their associates. It took as its name Liesma, the Latvian word for 'flame'. In 1906, Peter the Painter had published a 95-page pamphlet under this title which constituted a translation into Latvian of a collection of anarchist writings by Kropotkin and others. This was the first of three similar volumes, the last published in London in 1908.[19] The Liesma group seems to have taken shape the following year among a small number of Latvians who lodged together in Whitechapel and their visitors. By the autumn of 1910, Peter the Painter was in London and sharing rooms with his old comrade Fritz Svaars at Grove Street in Whitechapel, another important rallying point for this small band of comrades. In November, he was mentioned under a pseudonym as the treasurer of the Liesma group in London in the columns of a Latvian anarchist journal. There was an informal network linking émigrés in London, Paris and several American cities, with a handful of contacts in the Baltic and other areas under the tsar's rule. At least one of the letters seized by the police after the Houndsditch killings referred to Liesma. After George Gardstein's death, the police found in his wallet a membership card for 'the Lettish Anarchist Communist Group called "Leesma"', complete with the organization's stamp.[20] The Liesma group in London and the Houndsditch gang were almost coterminous.

In the late nineteenth century and the early twentieth, anarchism was tainted by an association with terror, with bombs and assassinations, intrigue and conspiracies. This was the world conjured up in Joseph Conrad's novel *The Secret Agent*, published in 1907 and set in large part in Soho, as well as in Henry James's *The Princess Casamassima* (1886), G. K. Chesterton's *The Man Who Was Thursday* (1908) and a stream of more ephemeral titles.[21] Many in the anarchist movement resented the implication that they were all bomb-throwing hotheads, mad and bad, but it can hardly be denied that there was a reason for anarchism's bad press. At its heart, anarchism advocates self-organization, mutual aid, the dismantling of the state and a repudiation of organized religion. It is anti-authoritarian and suspicious of hierarchies and orthodoxies. It has always been a very broad church, extending from 'do as thou will' individualism to revolutionary syndicalism, from Christian anarchism to insurrectionism, from communitarianism to terrorism. Anarchism is by its nature not a centralized political movement, and while London was home to one of the earliest and longest-lasting anarchist journals, *Freedom*, established in 1886, its influence in Britain has been modest. Elsewhere it attracted much more interest and support. At times in France, Spain and Italy, and among immigrant communities in the United States and Argentina, anarchism has been a mass movement – often noted more for what it opposed than for what it advocated.

From the inception of an organized anarchist movement in the 1860s, there were currents within it that had an ambivalent attitude towards violence. The charismatic Russian Mikhail Bakunin – Karl Marx's great rival in the International Working Men's Association or First International – famously declared that 'the urge to destroy is a creative urge.' The development of dynamite in the 1860s and gelignite in the 1870s made individual acts of destruction more feasible and terrible. The assassination of Russia's tsar, Alexander II, in

1881 by the People's Will group, although they were not themselves anarchists, had a marked influence on anarchist thinking. 'When the Russian revolutionaries had killed the Czar ... the European anarchists imagined that, from then on, a handful of fervent revolutionaries, armed with a few bombs, would be enough to bring about the social revolution,' commented the most influential anarchist of the era, Peter Kropotkin.[22] An international anarchist congress held in London in July 1881 endorsed 'propaganda by the deed', the phrase associated with anarchist assassination and terror, though for most that meant justification of tyrannicide and acts of violence at a moment of revolution rather than more random waging of war against establishment targets.

Very few anarchists practised propaganda by the deed, but the assassinations and bomb attacks carried out determined how anarchism was perceived, and the ferocity of the repression it often faced. In the early 1890s in particular, bomb attacks in France by the likes of Ravachol, Vaillant and Henry on up-market restaurants, cafés and the National Assembly caused – and were intended to cause – panic among the Parisian elite. The symbolism and the fear aroused was enormous, though the casualties were, by current standards, modest. Throughout the 1890s, the actions of anarchists – purported and real – across Europe, the United States and Australia probably accounted for a few dozen deaths at most.[23] From the mid-1890s, propaganda by the deed turned more to high-profile assassinations of monarchs, prime ministers and presidents. In the course of eight years, five heads of state and government were killed by anarchists – four of them by Italians or Italian-Americans: President Carnot of France was stabbed in June 1894; Antonio Cánovas del Castillo, the Spanish prime minister, was shot in August 1897; Empress Elisabeth of Austria was stabbed in September 1898; King Umberto of Italy was shot in July 1900; and U.S. President William McKinley was shot in September 1901. Unlike Russian nihilism or Irish nationalism, anarchist violence crossed borders; it was an international movement and while nothing like as powerful and well organized as the police and the popular press sometimes suggested, it was a formidable adversary.

The threat posed by anarchist violence prompted a more rigorous approach to protecting potential targets of assassination, the development of the political police and steps towards formal cooperation between governments to tackle the anarchist threat alongside largely informal cooperation between police forces. By and large, the early years of the twentieth century saw a downturn in anarchist violence (except in Spain, which lurched towards a spiral of acts of violence, cruel reprisals by the state and revenge attacks). But this was a brief respite. In France, a spate of robberies – what sympathizers might call expropriations – were carried out by *illégalistes* who believed that violating the law was itself a challenge to the state and the establishment. The motive in many cases was more criminal than political, and there's no doubt that there was a liminal zone in which some anarchists and criminals made common cause.

In Russia, the chronology was rather different. The Russian Revolution of 1905 and the vicious repression meted out in its suppression was a spur to the growth of the revolutionary left. Anarchism, which had very limited popular support in Russia until that date, gained adherents – though other left revolutionary movements also organized armed attacks, robberies and assassinations. The dispersal of Russian revolutionaries in the face of mass arrests, torture and executions led to some spread of their more violent and abrasive style of political activity into the countries where they took refuge. It's difficult to delineate which acts were anarchist violence and which were simply criminal or carried out in the name of another political cause, but one of the most authoritative studies of the subject suggests that, excluding Russia, in the forty years from 1878 about 220 people died around the world in anarchist violence. If Russia is included, then the death toll is a less precise estimate but may well be over a thousand.[24]

Although Britain was home to hundreds, perhaps thousands, of anarchist émigrés, as well as having a small home-grown movement, it escaped very lightly from the phenomenon of propaganda by the deed. The most notorious incident was the death of a French anarchist Martial Bourdin in February 1894 when the explosive device he was carrying went off near the Greenwich Observatory in

London.[25] This was the only death anywhere in England in the 1890s attributable to anarchism. Two years earlier, four men were convicted and imprisoned after the uncovering of a bomb-making workshop in Walsall in the English Midlands. In both incidents, there have been suggestions that either agents provocateurs or Russian agents were involved. The British police – which had a better reputation for efficiency than most of its European counterparts – managed to frustrate several other planned bomb attacks. The more pressing threat of political violence in Britain came from other quarters. Hard-line Irish nationalists commonly known as Fenians had, in 1867, tried to free two of their leaders by blowing up the outside wall of a jail in central London. The 'Clerkenwell Outrage' failed to enable the escape of the jailed Fenians but caused the death of up to twelve local residents and passers-by. In the first half of the 1880s, a Fenian bombing campaign targeted the London Underground, Scotland Yard, *The Times* newspaper, the Tower of London and the Houses of Parliament, as well as stations and clubs, creating huge alarm but causing few casualties. The most spectacular political assassination of the era on what was then British soil was the stabbing to death of Lord Frederick Cavendish, Chief Secretary for Ireland, in Phoenix Park in Dublin in 1882. Special Branch was set up as a unit of the Metropolitan Police in 1883 in response to the threat of Irish nationalist violence, and its remit slowly expanded. By the time of Sidney Street, a new threat came from another quarter. On 1 July 1909, William Hutt Curzon Wyllie, political aide-de-camp to the Secretary of State for India, was shot dead at a public meeting in London by Madan Lal Dhingra, a student and Indian nationalist. The sporadic revolutionary violence evident in parts of India had reached the imperial capital.

Why was London home to so many anarchists but the venue of so little anarchist violence? The calibre of the policing may have been part of the answer, but probably a small part. The tolerance of the British authorities was a more important factor. By and large, political émigrés in London were allowed to meet, organize and publish papers and propaganda. A Spanish official, visiting London in 1906 to discuss how to deal with anarchist violence, took notes of a conversation with Edward Henry, the Commissioner of the Metropolitan Police: 'he believes that the atmosphere of English society is a sedative; that in any case one does not encounter in this atmosphere passions, on the contrary they evaporate in the clubs and in the special press in which advanced ideas are ventilated.'[26] While there was a touch of complacency in this argument, the venom of anarchist exiles was directed at the governments in their homelands rather than against the British authorities. Britain was one of the few countries that was not stampeded into restrictive legislation by the anarchist bombings and killings across Europe and beyond in the 1890s. There's no doubt that many émigrés living in Britain appreciated that they could find asylum in Britain and did not wish to act in a manner that might disturb this arrangement – just as there is reason to believe that the Russian authorities in particular had an interest in fomenting incidents of violence on British soil to turn public opinion against allowing the right of political asylum. The German-born anarchist Rudolf Rocker was deeply, and rightly, concerned that the press coverage of the Houndsditch and Sidney Street shootings

> would be used to work up an agitation for withdrawing the right of asylum in Great Britain. It was the only country where political refugees really enjoyed the right of asylum, where they did not live with the constant dread of expulsion hanging over their heads, as in France, Belgium or Switzerland.[27]

Several European governments believed there was an unspoken pact between the British authorities and the foreign anarchists they hosted: the police didn't monitor too closely what these anarchists got up to on the understanding that any acts of subversion or violence they initiated would not take place on British soil. That was more perception than fact. The historian Richard Bach Jensen has argued that the view of London as 'the world's prime incubator of anarchist plots was largely a myth', with Paris having a better claim to that title.[28] But the sentiment persisted that a blind eye was turned to foreign anarchists hatching conspiracies abroad as long as they didn't disturb the peace in their adopted country.

The shootings at Houndsditch and Sidney Street prompted a retired senior police officer, Robert Anderson, to reflect on official attitudes to anarchist exiles. He was distinctly vinegary in attitude after the close of a career that had some troughs as well as peaks, but he had been an assistant commissioner in the Metropolitan Police and worked with the intelligence service. He had over the years been involved in guarding against both Irish republican and anarchist violence. So he had a close familiarity with what he called 'a peril which has hitherto seldom been noticed by the public' – foreign anarchists who were 'world outlaws, the enemies of mankind'.

> For a considerable period they used this country merely as an asylum. Well-known leaders indeed, whom I might name if libel actions were abolished, used to make inflammatory speeches at their secret meetings in Soho, but they always ended up by warning their fellow-conspirators that nothing was to be done in England to endanger their enjoyment of 'the hospitality of our shores.'[29]

However, he adamantly insisted that 'there is not a shadow of foundation for the insinuation lately made by certain foreign newspapers that the attitude of the authorities here was due to some sort of implied understanding with the criminals.'

If there was any unspoken pact that anarchist émigrés shouldn't soil their British backyard, the violence at Tottenham, Houndsditch and Sidney Street blew it apart. Robert Anderson stated that 'in view of the Houndsditch and Stepney crimes', it was absurd to argue that 'to declare war upon [foreign anarchists] will serve, by exasperating them, to increase the danger we wish to guard against'. He believed that the violence visited upon London's streets created an opportunity to cleanse the country of foreign advocates of anarchism. Indeed, Anderson – a devout Christian – urged that 'were it not for our belief in a future life we should do well to exterminate them like plague-infected vermin.' As he also recognized, such fiercely intemperate views were not in tune with liberal opinion and would be vigorously resisted by radicals and socialists. He would not have been altogether surprised that his appeal to act against exiled anarchists was not heeded.

THE THREE MOST renowned anarchists in Britain at the time of the shootings at Tottenham, Houndsditch and Sidney Street were all émigrés. All three would have described themselves as anarchist communists, accepting a class analysis of society and arguing that resources should be held communally and distributed according to need. They rejected what would later become known as the Leninist style of communism, with the notion of the vanguard leading and directing the working class in the form of a centralized and disciplined revolutionary party and arguing for the capture of state power rather than the dismantling of the state.

Peter Kropotkin was a Russian geographer, writer and political theorist from an aristocratic family who lived variously in the London suburbs and in Brighton and was the most revered anarchist intellectual of the era. His humility and evident integrity won him affection and respect from well beyond those attracted to anarchist ideas. 'Kropotkin had royal blood, a romantic aura, charisma, social status, and academic fame. All those characteristics created an image which was likely to be admired and respected regardless of his anarchist connection.'[30] He was the nearest the anarchist movement had to a polymath, combining the ability to write in a scholarly manner with the gift of being a very effective propagandist. Errico Malatesta was an Italian from a modest landowning family in the south of the country. He had lived in England for more than a decade and not only ran a small engineering workshop in Islington but was an industrious propagandist and activist. He too had an engaging manner and a political backstory, both of which won him esteem among many on the left who were otherwise wary of anarchism, though the police regarded him as almost diabolical.

The third figure in this revolutionary trinity, Rudolf Rocker, was born in Germany, came across Yiddish-speaking anarchists in Paris and (although not himself Jewish) learnt the language, became a rousing platform orator, and edited well-regarded anarchist papers and journals. Rocker has been described as an 'anarchist rabbi', a guide and mentor to his largely Jewish followers, and was unquestionably the key figure in the thriving anarchist movement in the East End of London. His partner, Milly Witcop (or Witkop), had been born to a Jewish family in a small town in Ukraine and was the most prominent woman in the movement. 'Physically, Milly and Rocker were two opposites,' according to Rocker's biographer:

> While he was tall, heavily built with fair hair and blue eyes, she possessed an emaciated dark figure accentuated by deep dark eyes and hair ... Their personalities were different too. Rudolf Rocker was friendly, lively, self-confident, and easy going. Milly Witkop, on the other hand, was earnest, pessimistic, introverted and driven by a mercurial temperament, quick to rise and quick to abate.[31]

They lived together for almost sixty years.

None of these three anarchist intellectuals advocated or sympathized with the sort of violence perpetrated by the Latvian expropriators. Two of them were, however, caught up in the maelstrom. Malatesta unwittingly helped the robbers as they prepared to break into the jewellery business in Houndsditch. He was, as we shall see, questioned by police and gave evidence during the trial. Rocker's role was more tangential, but he had certainly met some of the Latvians and welcomed into his home for a while, after she was cleared on appeal, the only person to be convicted on charges arising out of these three fatal shooting incidents. Kropotkin's association was indirect: several of his titles were among those retrieved by the police as they investigated those suspected of involvement in the violence.[32]

In February 1906, Rudolf Rocker opened the proceedings at what was a red-letter day for the mainly Jewish anarchist movement in the East End of London – the opening of a new club at Jubilee Street in Stepney. Kropotkin was the main guest and there was 'a great burst of enthusiasm' when he arrived and 'cheer after cheer' as he made his way to the platform. He congratulated those assembled on 'securing this fine hall for their new home, and also that it had been done out of their own hard-earned pence without any middle-class assistance'. And he made reference to those under Russian rule who faced the prospect of following him into exile:

> 'The hearts of our brothers,' he said, 'will be gladdened to know that here in London you have a home where they will be sure of finding a welcome awaiting them if circumstances should force them to leave the land where they are now fighting so nobly in the cause of Liberty.'[33]

Malatesta was among those who sent a message of congratulations on the opening of the club and also among the speakers were John Turner and Ted Leggatt, big figures in the small British anarchist movement. The evening concluded with songs, music and dancing.

The property at 165 Jubilee Street had been both a Methodist church and a Salvation Army depot. It was a two-storey building with an imposing frontage, including large Palladian-style windows. Inside, it was down at heel, and before the anarchists moved in, attempts to turn the building into a venue for music and dancing had been blocked because the building was hemmed in on three sides and had a 'badly constructed' staircase.[34] When a London County Council architect visited the site early in 1906, he was told by the caretaker that the building had been let to 'a Jewish Friendly Society who intended using the hall for lectures and educational purposes only'. The main hall, known as the Alexandra Hall, presumably after King Edward VII's consort, had a seated capacity of 340, including the gallery on the first floor – though on occasions that capacity was exceeded and a police informer estimated that five hundred people crowded in to hear Kropotkin speak in the autumn of 1909. On the ground floor there was also a kitchen and ample dining area; the first floor had a smaller hall which also served as a library and reading room as well as an office and a ladies'

Masthead of the Yiddish anarchist paper *Der Arbayter Fraynd*.

cloakroom.[35] This was much more spacious than the mean and cramped rooms that had previously served as political clubs for émigrés and the revolutionary left in London.

The club took the name of London's long-established Yiddish anarchist weekly, the *Arbayter Fraynd*, the 'worker's friend', which had been under Rudolf Rocker's editorship since 1898. The paper was produced and printed in an adjoining building; its circulation was buoyant, with a print run exceeding 4,000. 'There was no other movement at that time in the East End of London', Rocker boasted, 'which could compare with ours in numbers or activity.'[36] The club organized English lessons for new migrants and the lectures in Yiddish included Rocker's classes in history and sociology as well as talks on technical subjects. On Sunday evenings, the club hosted readings 'from famous thinkers'. Naomi Ploschansky, a teenager when she started to attend meetings at Jubilee Street, later remembered it fondly as 'quite a club':

> I mean, it was a beautiful place – not in the sense of art, for everybody was poor, very poor; but it was a place where we had fun. It was such a peaceful place, it was a place that was so friendly and peaceful and quiet. It was a place where we just came in and met people and talked and played chess, those of us who knew how, and had discussions; and of course we would have our big meetings there.[37]

Ploschansky recalled it as the venue where she would come across anarchist luminaries, and she helped set up an Anarchist–Communist Sunday School. 'There was a library, there was lectures. And that's where I met Kropotkin. We organised a little group of children, and William Wess – he was an anarchist and very important – and his wife, they would come and teach us songs,' she reminisced many decades later. She also met Malatesta at the club:

> I came in one day and I saw him – saw a little man sitting up by the bar. We didn't sell any liquor, just coffee and tea, a sandwich, something like that. I went over and looked at him – it looked to me like he was Jewish, I didn't know he was Italian. With a beard and eyes – you would have thought the eyes would go right through you.[38]

The decision not to serve alcohol, a distinct break from earlier clubs of this sort, was carefully considered. 'The Jubilee Street Club played such a great part in East End Jewish life because it was open to everyone,' Rocker recalled:

> Anyone could use our library and reading room, or join our educational classes, without being asked for a club membership card. This made it impossible for us to sell drinks in the club, from which most other clubs got the greater part of their revenue. For the law restricted the sale of intoxicants in clubs to club members. We sold only coffee and food. So we had to find other ways of meeting our running costs.[39]

The policy to allow open access also meant there wasn't much inducement to become a club member – it's likely that only a small proportion of those who patronized the club held membership cards. To sustain the club, meeting space was hired out to – among others – local trade unions, the Workers' Circle friendly society, a local branch of the Russian Social Revolutionaries and groups of English comrades (though *Freedom* announced that Sunday morning lectures in English at the club were being discontinued after just a few weeks 'as they were not responded to as hoped by the English workers in the district').[40] Women were actively involved in the club, though not perhaps on a fully equal basis. 'They were regarded as equal but there is always a difference,' Ploschansky commented; 'you can't say that they're equal because they're not.' Women members were certainly more conspicuous as volunteers in the kitchen – Millie Sabel recalled preparing gefilte fish, chopped liver and pickled herring for club customers – than on the speakers' platform.

Among those from outside the East End who used to visit Jubilee Street was Guy Aldred, a precocious and maverick anarchist from the Clerkenwell district of London. He was twenty when he first came along to the club. 'It was an entirely different world from that in which I moved at that time in ... North London', he recalled. In February 1907, he spoke at a benefit there for the *Voice of Labour* journal, and afterwards was sitting by himself drinking a cup of tea and feeling a little awkward when the anarchist trade unionist John Turner introduced him to sixteen-year-old Rose Witcop, the younger sister of Rudolf Rocker's partner. 'There was some music and a little

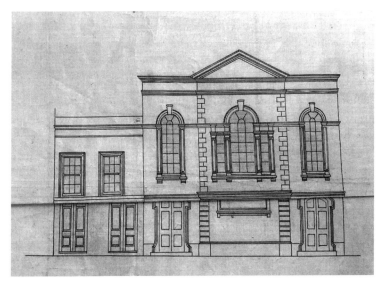

Architect's drawing from 1904 of the building that became the anarchist club on Jubilee Street.

dancing,' he recalled of the evening. 'The gathering was very much alive and somewhat erratic. In the main, it was happy, gay, and full of animation.' Within a few months, Guy Aldred and Rose Witcop had become lovers, in the face of opposition from both their families; their son was born in May 1909. Aldred was a regular at Jubilee Street and set down an affectionate account of the club:

> There was a small cafeteria at the foot of the large room which served for the hall. Here one had Russian tea, coffee, cakes, tinned fish, ices (sometimes), and soft drinks. The atmosphere was bohemian and mostly friendly and warm. Russian, German, and Yiddish and even French was spoken. Just a small amount of English. Of course, some of the discussion was vigorous, and even violent; but a heated argument would conclude in perfect friendship prevailing between the contestants.[41]

Aldred was something of a specialist in heated arguments, and he didn't get on too well with Rudolf Rocker or the general style of the East End movement. But he admired the energy with which they published and propagandized, estimating that the printing press next door to the club may, over the years, have produced half a million copies of various papers, pamphlets and books.

The anarchists based in Jubilee Street made a point of maintaining contact with and offering support to the movement in Russia and Poland. 'We received and printed a great many reports from our secret groups in Warsaw, Vilna, Grodno, Bialystock and other places about events in the lands of the Czar,' Rocker wrote. 'Sometimes emissaries from the Russian groups arrived in London, and consulted us about smuggling our literature into Russia.' There was a long-lasting and successful operation involving a bookshop in Spitalfields and a publishing house in Russian-ruled Lithuania to send left-wing Yiddish publications into the Russian Empire. Rocker's paper would have had a readership in the Baltic states and beyond.

As a young activist in Paris, Rocker had expressed some sympathy with 'propaganda by the deed' but he had come to believe strongly that terror and violence damaged the anarchist movement much more than they did its targets. But some of the young activists newly arrived from the Russian Empire, Rocker believed, 'couldn't possibly fit in with our activity in England':

> It wasn't their fault. They had been brought up with the idea that revolutionary activity meant secrecy, conspiracy, and terrorism ... They treated us as though we were playing at being Anarchists. There were often unpleasant scenes between them and our older comrades, who had lived for years in England.
>
> We were haunted by the fear that some of them might do something desperate that would put our whole movement in danger.[42]

Rocker recalled that in November 1909 a Russian comrade in London told him of a plan to throw a bomb during the Lord Mayor's Show. He went along to talk to the group behind the intended attack – five youngsters, one of them a woman, meeting at a house in Stepney. 'I told them we knew of their plan. I explained what a terrible blow it would be to all the people who had been able to find refuge in London.' The plan was abandoned and soon after all but one of the would-be bombers went back to Russia. It's a strange tale but illustrates both the attraction of terror to a few of the revolutionary émigrés in London and Rocker's courage as a leader and his determination not to jeopardize the right of asylum that he and many others enjoyed.

The Jubilee Street Club came to serve as an informal reception centre for new migrants to London, particularly those who saw themselves as political dissidents. 'When a refugee would come and had no place to go, they'd bring him to the Jubilee Street club,' Naomi Ploschansky recalled:

> The police would say: that's a place for you to go, they'll find a place for you ... One time we had four big husky fellows, came from – I don't know – some from Russia, some of

them from Latvia. But they'd been in trouble with the law. They got out. And they came to London. And sure enough they were sent to the club.

She had good reason to remember the men, as they were billeted in her home:

> We had no place for them to sleep. So we had a very big bed where all the kids used to sleep. So these kids got out of bed and these four fellows slept across the bed. I slept in the kitchen, tiny place, on a folding bed. And my mother put three chairs facing each other and made a bed for the little ones to sleep in the living room. That's how we managed . . . They stayed with us for quite a long while. They were very friendly. We got them jobs. We got them introduced to some people in Soho, some comrades, and got them jobs in restaurants.[43]

Through one of these men, Naomi Ploschansky was introduced to some of those who were later involved in the Houndsditch robbery attempt. They also came to the Jubilee Street Club and wanted Naomi to teach them English. Her mother put her foot down; she was forbidden from visiting the men in their lodgings and the English lessons never happened.

The witness statements the police compiled in the aftermath of the Houndsditch murders demonstrate how central the Jubilee Street Club was to the lives of the Latvian émigrés and their circle. It was where they met, ate, socialized and made new contacts. Not every piece of evidence recited to the police might be accurate, but the frequency with which the Jubilee Street Club crops up is striking. George Gardstein met Malatesta at the club, which led to him using Malatesta's workshop to adapt equipment for the Houndsditch robbery; Yourka Dubof attended lectures in astronomy there; Karl Hoffman went to a concert at Jubilee Street; Nikolai Tocmacoff played mandolin at the club, and went there for the entertainments and theatrical performances; Fritz Svaars frequently patronized the place; Osip Federoff and John Rosen were occasional visitors; Jacob Peters went to a Latvian concert at the club; Charles Perelman's daughter first met her boyfriend there; Fanny Gordon went along when her lodger, Nina Vassileva, persuaded her to 'come to see our club'; Luba Milstein went to the club most Friday and Saturday evenings because she knew there would be 'cheerful company' and a chance to speak in Russian. 'Every one of the gang', insisted the head of the City of London Police, 'was a constant and well-known frequenter of the Anarchist Club in Jubilee Street.' Rocker himself accepted that the gunmen may have come 'to our meetings or used our reading room without our knowing anything about them', but insisted that they were not club members.[44]

It's perhaps surprising that the principal figures associated with the Jubilee Street Club were not more actively investigated in the aftermath of the Houndsditch and Sidney Street shootings. A history of the Metropolitan Police described the club as the 'headquarters' of the gang responsible for the Houndsditch robbery attempt. There was certainly gossip and innuendo suggesting that Rocker was in some manner complicit. A police officer picked up word from a newsagent in Stepney Green about 'a man named "Rocco" . . . known as a dangerous anarchist', who was 'the head of anarchist's party concerned in the Houndsditch murders'.[45] Yet neither Rudolf Rocker nor his partner Milly Witcop seem to have been questioned, even informally. A slip of paper in the police files records the address of Morris Brodie, 'principal' of the Jubilee Street Club, but there's no witness statement in his name. The main reason why the police didn't inquire more actively into the club's operations was because it had shut down a short time before the Houndsditch shootings. If Peter the Painter wasn't a regular visitor to the club, that was – Luba Milstein explained at the Old Bailey – because the club closed just a few weeks after he arrived in London from Paris.

In the days after the Houndsditch shootings, the *Evening News* did a bit of investigating into the Jubilee Street Club, which it reported had closed five weeks earlier. The paper said that the club still had announcements in Yiddish and Russian pasted on its noticeboard. It had just concluded a series of lectures on 'The Romantic

Revival in Literature' and before that there had been talks on Wagner and Ibsen. The reading room had been well stocked with Russian newspapers and open to all, whether members or not. While the club was described as 'the haunt of anarchists and revolutionaries', its proceedings seemed to be entirely unthreatening. 'It's difficult to make out what Peter the Painter could want in such a place.' The paper reported that the police gave the club 'a good name for orderliness and sobriety, and the neighbours say that the dances and socials held there were quite as dull as such affairs usually are'. The paper reported that the club closed 'because it did not pay'.[46]

The *Arbayter Fraynd* sought to convince its readers that the decision to shut the Jubilee Street Club towards the end of 1910 was as much political as financial. 'When we acquired the space for the club five years ago', the paper declared, 'the Jewish workers' movement here in London had a completely different character than it does now.'

> The unions were blossoming and had thousands of members and the spirit of the Russian revolution [of 1905] exerted a strong influence on all sectors of the movement. At that time, we believed that the club was going to develop as a true centre of the Jewish workers' movement and that the movement itself would be in a good position to finance it. But unfortunately, these hopes were not fulfilled. The large organizations were diminished and the victory of the forces of reaction in Russia also had a strong effect on the entire movement.[47]

The article explained that the club cost £8 a week to keep going (about £1,000 in today's money), and to cover that cost they had been obliged to rent out space to 'strangers', so diluting its original purpose:

> The comrades came to a decision that it would be better to take a smaller place which would belong to us in its entirety rather than set aside time and work in order to maintain

a space that wouldn't be able to be put to the moral and intellectual uses that we had worked for.

In the aftermath of the Sidney Street siege, the landlord gave a very different account of the closure of the club. Charles Martin – who in a remarkable coincidence was also the owner of 100 Sidney Street, the site of the siege – declared, unconvincingly, that he had no idea of the 'nature or character' of the people who had taken a 21-year lease on the Jubilee Street property:

> They described themselves as 'friends of the workers,' and he thought they were a body of Christians. When, however, he found that they advocated very advanced views . . . he gave instruction for the lease to be terminated. He paid the occupiers £100 to clear out, which they did about two months ago.[48]

That version in turn was challenged by Rudolf Rocker. He concurred that the anarchists had been given £100 to vacate the Jubilee Street premises but insisted that they had initiated the conversation about the terms for relinquishing the lease some months earlier. 'The suggestion that we were asked to leave the premises is quite wrong,' Rocker declared.[49] But the consequence was the same. Without the Jubilee Street Club, the local anarchist movement turned to a range of pubs, hired halls and small hotels as venues for meetings.

The movement had been too ambitious in renting such a large building, and simply couldn't maintain the personal and financial effort. There's also a suggestion that the venue was being used as a rallying point by some who were bringing the movement into disrepute. But the closure was a blow to the anarchist movement in the East End. The club had put the Yiddish-speaking movement on the map, literally and figuratively. The weekly paper continued and its office and printing press remained in the building adjoining the club at 163 Jubilee Street, but the anarchist movement never regained such a spacious London base. The *Arbayter Fraynd* called on 'all active comrades to work with deliberation and energy for the establishment of the sort of club that will actually be a true home for the anarchist movement here in London' – but no new club was set up. After the anarchists' departure from 165 Jubilee Street, the main hall was converted into a cinema and a few years later became the Jubilee Street Great Synagogue.

4
Comrades and Lovers

The Latvian exiles in London were constantly coming and going, and rarely stayed at the same place for more than a few months or a year or two at most, but amid the perpetual churn, two addresses stand out. A house in Great Garden Street in Whitechapel – it's now Greatorex Street – was where the group coalesced. And Grove Street, less than half a mile away, is where they gathered for the final time, hours before the Houndsditch robbery attempt which left three police officers and one of the robbers dead. The social and political network can be retrieved to a degree from the interrogations of police investigating those murders, and the statements and witness depositions they gathered. These documents are by their nature not always reliable but they still offer a remarkable window into the coming together of a group of friends and comrades, and in some cases lovers – though as is almost universal with friendship networks, there can be no precise delineation of where the group's boundaries lie and of course being good friends cannot be taken to imply joint complicity in armed crime.

Charles Perelman moved into 29 Great Garden Street at some time in the second half of 1908, along with his wife and six children. He told the police that he migrated from Saratov, a city port on the river Volga, in July 1906; he was Jewish. He worked as a photographic enlarger and was in his late fifties. In the family's first couple of years in London, they lived at several different locations in the East End. Renting the house in Great Garden Street was a sign of starting to settle in. It was more spacious than their earlier places, and large enough to enable him to take in lodgers to supplement his income. His eldest child, Fanny – then aged fifteen or sixteen – was already 'courting'. She had met her boyfriend at the Jubilee Street Club, the anarchists' meeting place. His name was Evan Vanoveitch and, shortly before the family moved to Great Garden Street, she brought him home to meet her father. 'He told me that he was a sailor and was employed on a cargo ship that went to America,' Charles Perelman recalled. 'During a period of about six months he used to visit my home about once a months [sic] when his ship was in Dock.'[1]

When the Perelman family moved to Great Garden Street, Fanny's boyfriend moved in with them as a lodger, taking the front room on the ground floor. He told his landlord that 'he had got a holiday from the ship.' After a couple of weeks, the lodger introduced a friend and it was agreed that the two men should share a room. 'They remained with me about two months, when I gave them notice to leave,' Perelman said – though he also suggested that Vanoveitch left Great Garden Street because he was going to America by sea, presumably working his passage. The two lodgers in the Perelmans' front room were among the most battle-hardened Latvian émigrés in London. Vanoveitch's real name was Janis Palamieks, though he was widely known by his nickname, Bifsteks (Russian for steak). His friend, generally known as Grishka, was Kristaps Salnins, who also used a bewildering array of assumed names, including Jacob Fogel.[2] A pencilled note in Perelman's witness statement, presumably made by a police officer, noted that Grishka was 'wanted for murder in Russia'. He certainly seems to have fought alongside Peter the Painter during the 1905 Revolution in Latvia before heading into exile.[3] The two revolutionaries, Bifsteks and Grishka, were lodging with the Perelmans at about the time of the Tottenham Outrage, and the police suspected that Grishka in particular may have been involved in some manner in that armed robbery, though they had no hard evidence.[4] There is nothing to link either man to the Houndsditch robbery attempt, but they were part of the same social and political circle as those responsible.

The manner in which Perelman recounted to the police how he came across his lodgers offers no indication that he was aware of the sort of people he was hosting. It's difficult to believe that he was quite that innocent. And he quickly became more immersed with Latvian political exiles. Before Bifsteks and Grishka left Great Garden Street, they introduced a third Latvian, Fritz. He said that he had just arrived from America and was working as a locksmith in London's West End. He dossed down for the night in his friends' room and then, the following day, arranged to rent the front room on the first floor. This was Fritz Svaars, another comrade of Peter the Painter from the days of the Latvian revolution, who a couple of years later died at Sidney Street. After another two or three weeks, Svaars in turn brought in an additional lodger, George Gardstein, the gunman who was to suffer fatal injuries at Houndsditch. 'They remained with me about three months,' Perelman said, 'and during that time a number of men used to visit them' – including two of those charged in the aftermath of the Houndsditch killings, John Rosen and Yourka Dubof. Also among Perelman's lodgers was Nina Vassileva, who had been introduced to Perelman's wife by a mutual friend. At some stage, she and Gardstein became lovers. She was also among the Houndsditch defendants. One of his longer-lasting lodgers was a watchmaker called Sokolow, probably Willam Sokoloff, who was more widely known as Joseph – 'sometimes he used to go into the other men's room.' He was not a Latvian but became one of their associates and died alongside Fritz Svaars in Sidney Street. When the Perelman family eventually moved on to a house on Wellesley Street in Stepney Green, Vassileva moved with them – and Dubof became one of their new lodgers.

Charles Perelman's teenage son, Isaac, who was apprenticed as a woodcarver, told the police that others among the Houndsditch suspects – Jacob Peters and Karl Hoffman – used to call. They were among a group of nine or ten friends. 'They used to mee[t] in Fritz's room at Great Garden Street & Nina's room at Wellesley Street. They used to speak in a language which I did not understand. I believe it was Lettish.'[5] So among the Perelmans' lodgers were all three of the gunmen killed at Houndsditch and Sidney Street and two of those charged with complicity arising from the Houndsditch killings. And among their visitors were three others who faced charges. Several of those who gathered at Great Garden Street already knew each other and the lodgers brought in like-minded friends to share the rooms, but this was also where ties were forged and reforged and new comrades introduced to the movement or brought in from the margins to the core. This was for a while the nerve centre of Latvian anarchist and revolutionary expropriators in London.

WHEN CHARLES PERELMAN was questioned by police seven weeks after the Siege of Sidney Street, he and his family had moved to rooms in a block of flats off Brick Lane. They either had no room or no need for lodgers. We can pick up the trail of one of the key figures in the Houndsditch shootings, Fritz Svaars, in the summer of 1910, about five months before the tragedy. He started renting a first-floor room at 35 Newcastle Place, a tiny, insalubrious backstreet in Spitalfields. His teenage Jewish girlfriend, Luba Milstein – a Russian-speaker from Ukraine – came to live with him there. A few weeks later, Svaars's old friend and comrade from Latvia and America, Peter the Painter, arrived in London from Paris. The old comradeship was resumed. He spent his days at Newcastle Place but, for want of space there, he bedded down in the room of another of the group, Karl Hoffman, in Stepney. Svaars and Peter the Painter – in the testimony of Svaars's partner, Luba Milstein – 'wanted to be together'. In early November, Svaars rented two first-floor rooms at 59 Grove Street, and Peter the Painter moved in there with the couple. He took the larger of the two rooms overlooking the street.[6] Fellow Latvian exiles gathered both at Newcastle Place and at Grove Street, much as they had earlier at Great Garden Street, and helped each other out. George Gardstein papered Svaars's room at Newcastle Place. Karl Hoffman and Peter the Painter helped to push the handbarrow taking Svaars's and Milstein's possessions to their new rooms. Those at the heart of the group were close friends as well as political comrades.[7]

From the accounts the police assembled of the manner in which these men met and spent their time, a picture emerges of a group who were outsiders to England and unfamiliar with the language and culture and who stuck together to find work and rooms and some sort of solace and pleasure. They called on each other, occasionally went out to the club or the café or the cinema, played board games and music, and sometimes drank and feasted and bedded down in each other's rooms. Yourka Dubof's account of meeting Peter the Painter in the Jubilee Street Club – rendered tersely and awkwardly, though we can't know whether that reflects how the account was narrated or interpreted or transcribed – gives a glimpse of this hidden world:

> I go to East end to bu[y] cigarettes – Russian Cigarettes – in shop I see bill of Balalaika. I go to Club in Jubilee Street. I sit in one chair, Peter sit in other. He say nice, I say all right. He ask me what I work. I say, painter. He say I am a painter also ... He gave me his address Grove Street, No. 59. I got sack last Monday week. I go to Grove Street No. 59, last Friday 3 o'clock to 4 o'clock to see Peter for work. I give Peter a picture. Yes that my picture I painted.[8]

The painting was intended to cement a friendship and to demonstrate ability – both men had an interest in art as well as commercial painting. It was given to Peter the Painter just hours before the Houndsditch robbery attempt. The police found the landscape at 59 Grove Street, impounded it and stashed it away in their archives, where it still languishes. It's a small and rather gloomy watercolour and, while frayed, faded and generally battered by the years, it has to be said that it shows little sign of artistic distinction.

On the afternoon of 16 December 1910, just hours before the attempt to break into the jewellers on Houndsditch, those planning and executing the robbery, along with friends who may not have been fully aware of what was coming, gathered at 59 Grove Street. Several weeks after her initial arrest, Luba Milstein – the most candid of those interrogated by the police and among the least political – gave a fairly full account of the day. She had been out of work for a week and didn't get up until after midday, and then went to see her brother about a piece of cloth. She returned within the hour and heard men's voices from the front room, Peter the Painter's room. She went into the back room she shared with Fritz Svaars 'as I was not accustomed to go into the front room when the men were meeting there.' Fritz gave her some money to buy meat, though it was Milstein's close friend, Rosa Trassjonsky, who went to the shops. The two women then prepared the meal and the men came through in two sittings to eat in the back room. Milstein went in the front room at some stage in the afternoon to take down the curtains, which she wanted to take to the laundry; one of the men helped her carry them. She gave the police a list of the men she recalled being present. As well as the two men who lived in the house, Fritz Svaars and Peter the Painter, there was Tocmacoff, Federoff, Sokoloff, Rosen, Dubof, Smoller, Gardstein and Hoffman.[9]

This was an assembly of the inner circle – all close friends and comrades. Of the men Milstein named, three were dead within three weeks (Gardstein in the aftermath of Houndsditch and Svaars and Sokoloff at Sidney Street), two were wanted by the police but never found, and four were charged in relation to the Houndsditch shootings. The other man, Tocmacoff, may well have informed on his friends to avoid arrest. Only two people were charged who were not present at Grove Street on that Friday afternoon: Fritz Svaars's cousin, Jacob Peters, and Nina Vassileva, who wasn't on good terms with Svaars and Milstein.

Nicholas Tocmacoff was detained the day after the shootings and he promptly gave the police his own account of the gathering at Grove Street. He wasn't a core member of the group but a musician. He played the mandolin and the balalaika; for the previous few weeks he had been giving mandolin lessons to Fritz Svaars and they would meet several times a week. Tocmacoff told the police that he was Russian and had been in England for six months; he insisted he was not a political refugee. He was 21 years old and worked as a seam presser. Long before Luba Milstein opened up about the gathering, he provided the police with a cast list of who was present at Grove Street just a few hours before the shooting:

> The man [Gardstein], who is now dead, was talking to Fritz all the time I was there, which was about twenty minutes.

Yourka [Dubof] was lying on the bed, the tall slim man was standing up, with his arm leaning on the rail of the bed, listening to my playing the mandoline [*sic*]; Peter [the Painter] and a man ... were playing chess; Rosa was cutting up the meat for dinner; Louba [*sic*] went out while I was there. A man, whom I know as 'Ocip [Osip] Federoff' came in and also layed [*sic*] on the bed.[10]

He was doing his best to be helpful. He also gave the police incriminating evidence about Fritz Svaars's ownership of firearms:

Fritz had revolvers – one a Browning – which he always carried in his pistol pocket, the other – a Mauser – which he kept at home. Peter did not carry a revolver. I have seen about five or six hundred cartridges in the back room [at 59 Grove Street]. Fritz told me he always carried a revolver and that he wanted to buy another one ...

This statement put Svaars at the top of the wanted list. It placed him at the centre of the web and offered damning testimony about his ownership of powerful semi-automatic weapons.

WE SHOULD PAUSE for a moment in the run-up to the tragedy about to be played out at Exchange Buildings in Houndsditch to look at the cast list of those implicated, whether by involvement or by association. Most were of much the same age, born in the mid-1880s.

George Gardstein was said to have been described by one of his collaborators as 'the ablest of the lot and the leader of the gang'.[11] The gun, chemicals and manuals later found in his room in Gold Street, and his use over several months of Malatesta's engineering workshop, point to his leading role in planning the Houndsditch robbery. He also appears to have gathered information about the store and to have pawned items of jewellery, probably stolen, to raise money for the equipment needed for the break-in. Gardstein had two lengthy absences from Gold Street in the months running up

Photograph found in George Gardstein's room apparently showing him and an unidentified woman.

to the robbery attempt. He seems to have visited Paris, where he called on the anarchist Max Nomad (whose real name was Maximilian Nacht) with an introduction from Nomad's brother, whom he had met at the Jubilee Street Club. Nomad recalled Gardstein as 'a man of herculean build' who habitually carried an automatic pistol, which at night he kept under the pillow in his hotel room – but he inadvertently left it there one morning and when he returned to the room it had gone.[12]

Gardstein was Latvian and his original name seems to have been Hartmanis, but more than most of his associates, he was a man of many names. In the East End, he was widely known as Muronzeff or a variant of that name; to his landlord, he was P. Morin; to his friends, he was known by the nickname Poolka or Puika (or 'boy'); his travel documents were in still other names.

The post-mortem examination conducted after Gardstein's body was found at Grove Street on the morning following the Houndsditch shootings recorded that he had a 'slight dark moustache, slightly turned up at [the] ends' and a 'good physique'.[13] He was well over 6 feet tall, and handsome too – 'a good-looking young man', as Detective Inspector Fred Wensley put it while giving evidence at the Old Bailey. 'That shows good looks don't always produce good deeds,' the judge commented. This in turn drew a riposte from the lawyer representing Nina Vassileva, Gardstein's lover (or more probably one of his lovers), that good looks 'are calculated to influence the feminine mind. A good-looking young man is sometimes a favourite with the fair sex, I am told.'[14]

Fritz Svaars, in whose rooms the gang met before the robbery attempt and where Gardstein died hours later, was another of the key organizers. Like Gardstein, he not only owned powerful guns but knew how to use them and he had a special pocket to hold a concealed gun in his trousers; and he too was handsome and considered attractive to women. He was a Latvian and, as we've seen, fought alongside Peter the Painter in the 1905 Revolution and its aftermath and teamed up with him again in the United States – one informer told the police that there was a reward for his arrest in Pennsylvania. His cousin, Jacob Peters, told the police indiscreetly that he was wanted in Russia for robbing a government wine shop. That was only part of the story – according to the Russian authorities, in the course of the robbery Svaars had killed the shopkeeper and a policeman and subsequently twice escaped from detention. The prosecution in the Houndsditch murder trial alleged that Svaars entered Britain as a fugitive carrying a Mauser automatic pistol, which he had acquired in Antwerp.[15]

Svaars was his real name though he also used a number of other names, notably Trohimtchik. He at various times worked as a merchant seaman and a locksmith. His friends saw him as well connected and the sort of person who could help find them work. The police tried to suggest that his brief absence in the autumn of 1910

– which his partner Luba Milstein said was the fallout of a domestic row – was a period when he travelled abroad to prepare for the Houndsditch robbery and perhaps to conduct similar crimes. The prosecution presented pawnbrokers' slips for gold pocket watches to suggest that he had a track record of involvement in theft. Svaars told his friend and fellow musician Tocmacoff that he was waiting for money from his mother which he would use to go to Australia. He never made it.

Yourka Dubof was another Latvian and veteran of the revolutionary movement there. He told the Old Bailey that he had been arrested and beaten with *nagaikas*, the fearsome traditional Cossack whip made out of braided leather which sometimes had a metal tip. His real name was Juris Laivins. He came to London in June 1907 but only stayed a few days before travelling on to the United States and later also worked in Switzerland. He moved back to London in September 1910. He was a painter and lodged (sharing a room and a bed with another lodger) at the home of a workmate and his wife in Shepherds Bush – the only member of the group to live at a distance from the East End. Not long before the Houndsditch shootings, he got drunk and stayed the night at 59 Grove Street. While he spent time with his fellow Latvians and probably had sympathy with their aims and activities, there's no evidence linking him to firearms.

John Rosen – whose real name was Janis Zelin or Celins – was universally known as 'the Barber', because of his job. He was from the Latvian capital, Riga, and had been involved in left-wing politics there. He moved to London at the beginning of 1909 and got to know Bifsteks, a sailor who was prominent among Latvian political exiles in London who introduced him to his girlfriend's family in Great Garden Street. At the time of the Houndsditch shooting, Rosen was working for another Latvian who had a hairdresser's shop in Hackney. He lived in the back room. He had an English girlfriend, Rose Campbell, who was 21 and a shop assistant. She said they met in March 1910 when Rosen was living and working in Bermondsey. According to Campbell's brother-in-law, Rosen had taken his girlfriend to his room one evening in October 1910, 'where

John Rosen, the 'Barber'.

he assaulted and seduced her'. The police were involved 'but no criminal proceedings could be taken as Rose Campbell accompanied Rosen to his room of her own free will'. The brother-in-law also alleged, based on what he had been told by Rose's mother, that – a few days after the Houndsditch shootings – Rosen had introduced his girlfriend to Peter the Painter. 'Rosen has also informed Rose Campbell that he is also a member of the gang and that if any of them had been sick on the night of the murders he was the next one to be called upon to assist.'[16] This testimony may well be unreliable and wasn't introduced in the trial, but at the least it raises questions. The couple married in Hackney Register Office on

Photograph of Karl Hoffman taken on his arrest.

31 January 1911, six weeks after the Houndsditch killings and two days before Rosen's arrest. The new Mrs Rosen visited her husband in jail and was a defence witness at the Old Bailey – *The Star* described her as a 'pretty and well-dressed young Englishwoman'.[17] It must have been a deeply alarming introduction to married life.

Rosen is one of the more mysterious figures in the Houndsditch tragedy. He was certainly well in with the key figures in the planned robbery but his role, if any, is unclear. He did, however, give a statement after his arrest that his colleagues regarded as a betrayal. And among the City of London Police files is a scrap of paper suggesting, 'from information received', that Rosen was also known as Strosch. 'Strosch is an anarchist + police spy + is flying from Russia for suppose[d] murder. Supposed to arrange robberies + then inform police. Was a Carpenter in Riga + learnt Hairdressing here.'[18] Again, this is unsubstantiated and was not information introduced at Rosen's trial – and Rosen told police that he had once shared rooms in Poplar with a carpenter and hairdresser called Stroch, which adds another layer of complexity to the narrative.

A few months after his acquittal, Rosen sailed for Australia. His wife and their son joined him there a few years later. They settled in the town of Beechworth in Victoria, where Rosen worked as a hairdresser and tobacconist. He died in 1956; Rose outlived him.[19]

Karl Hoffman was a central figure in the group, though he wasn't present when the shots were fired at Exchange Buildings. He was born Alfreds Dzirkalis (later anglicized to Driscoll) in Latvia, also used the name Trautman and was known by various nicknames, including Masais (or 'shorty'), Chochol (perhaps 'chuckles') and Fred. He left Latvia in or around 1906. 'I used to go to sea in the summer time and work on land in winter as a House Decorator,' he told the police. 'I have sometimes stayed the winter in London, sometimes in France, in Holland and elsewhere.'[20] There were suggestions that he used his maritime work as a cover to smuggle weapons. At the time of the Houndsditch killings, he had been in London for several months working as a paper hanger and living on Lindley Street, just off Sidney Street, in Stepney. His landlord said he spoke Russian imperfectly and didn't speak English.

Max Smoller was a Russian Jew who got to know some of the Latvian émigrés when they were living at Great Garden Street. One of those staying there, Nina Vassileva – who didn't have a lot of time for Smoller – apparently told her lawyer that he and Sokoloff were wanted for jewel and fur thefts in Crimea.[21] He lived with his family in Stepney Green. Among the names he used was Joe Levi – for several months the police thought that Joe Levi and Max Smoller were different people; he was also known as Marks. A Metropolitan Police document from March 1911 cited 'reliable

Scotland Yard 'wanted' memo for Max Smoller.

information' that Smoller had initiated the planning of the Houndsditch burglary and stated that he was 'an exceedingly dangerous and desperate criminal'.[22] A 'wanted' alert was issued including arrest photographs taken in 1907 apparently supplied by a police force on the Continent. When the robbery attempt went wrong, others in the group held Smoller to blame and suggested that he had fired the shots that killed George Gardstein. Perhaps because of that, he was the first to flee.

William Sokoloff was better known as Joseph or Yoska. He was from Moscow and – like Smoller – a Russian Jew rather than a

Latvian. He described himself as a watchmaker. He was a little older than the others, about thirty, had been in Britain for more than a decade and had worked for a while in Scotland and in the north of England. When he was interviewed by police investigating a robbery in October 1909, he was living at 29 Great Garden Street. He was noted for having an awkward walk, the result of an old leg injury. In the course of 1910 he lived for several weeks in George Gardstein's room in Gold Street, while Gardstein himself was away, but was asked to move out because he didn't pay the rent.

Sokoloff appears to have had a criminal background. Nina Vassileva supposedly confided to her lawyer that Sokoloff had 'boasted of being a pupil' of Smoller in conducting robberies. This supports the supposition that these two non-Latvians were recruited into the Houndsditch team because of their criminal skills and experience. Little more is known about him beyond his friendship with Betsy Gershon, in whose room in Sidney Street he and Fritz Svaars took refuge.

Last is Osip Federoff, who was also Russian, though the Russian authorities believed he had spent a fairly inconspicuous ten years living and working in the Latvian port of Liepaja (then Libau). He was described at various times as a locksmith and a tailor's presser, lived in Romford Street in the East End and had been in London (his second stay in the city) for a little over three months. While Federoff may have had some political sympathies with the Latvians, he seems to have been a friend more than a collaborator. Writing from jail, in a letter intended for the police as much as anyone else, he lamented his fate in being charged with conspiracy: 'What conspiracy? Simply because I knew him, that Fritz. And this is conspiracy. I don't understand. I will perhaps be charged for having known my father and mother. Awful, simply awful. The devil knows who he was: he did not carry a label on his nut.'[23]

Of the other key figures, Peter the Painter deserves a fuller account, and we'll also look more closely in later chapters at the remarkable story of Jacob Peters and at the lives and loyalties of three women charged in the aftermath of the Houndsditch murders. We now need to explore how those police killings happened.

5

Houndsditch

In late November 1910, a man who gave his name as Joe Levi arranged to rent a property at 11 Exchange Buildings in the City of London. This was a narrow yard opening off Cutler Street. The houses were, even by the standards of working-class homes at the time, desperately cramped. There was just one small room on each of the three floors and at the back a tiny yard, around 1 metre by 4 metres (3 ft × 14 ft), with an outside toilet at one end and a sink at the other. Joe Levi was better known as Max Smoller (or Smellor) and also used the name Marx or Marks. He was part of a group of revolutionary expropriators, staging robberies with the aim (in some measure) of funding revolutionary activity in Latvia and supporting the families of jailed activists. The attraction of the property on Exchange Buildings was not the accommodation it offered, but its location – backing onto H. S. Harris's jewellery business on Houndsditch, a busy street leading from Bishopsgate to Aldgate and the East End. Or rather, it almost backed onto the jewellers. Some of the gang's preparatory work was poor, for it transpired that the rear of No. 11 didn't directly overlap with 119 Houndsditch. A better prospect was 10 Exchange Buildings but it was already let to a Romanian businessman and inventor who was on a quixotic and unsuccessful mission to market a game he had devised.

The tenancy started at the end of the month. The property had, in addition to a conventional front door, a ground-floor frontage of three folding doors, as was the style with some commercial premises. These had been painted an unattractive dark green. Furniture was brought over from Grove Street on a costermonger's barrow and Smoller – who already had a room with his family in Stepney

– sought to give every indication of a normal household. He arranged to have a gas supply installed with a penny-in-the-slot meter. One of the gas installers said the new tenant 'appeared to me a Jew and spoke good English'.[1] Nina Vassileva and at least one other man moved in along with Smoller. Vassileva was seen by neighbours opening and closing the window shutters and sweeping the house. She slept on a couch on the ground floor; the two men shared the room on the floor above; the top floor was bare. When Detective Superintendent John Ottaway entered the house within an hour of the shooting, he found 'the gas alight, and fire burning in the grate and the room contained a table covered with a white quilt, on which was a cup of freshly made tea, tin of sardines, jar of jam, small piece of bread, and a jar of paste'.[2] A small book entitled *Simple Cookery for the People* was among the items listed in a nine-page police inventory of the contents of the building. This veneer of domesticity was designed to provide cover for what a prosecuting lawyer later alleged was a 'skilful and daring' theft.

The target of the planned robbery was carefully chosen. The jewellery business had only been established at 119 Houndsditch six

The target of the Houndsditch robbery attempt.

months earlier. The proprietor's son, Harry Harris – who ran the shop – told the police that the whole of the stock was put in the safe each night and the value of these items at the time of the robbery attempt was about £7,000, almost a hundred times the amount involved in the Tottenham escapade and the equivalent in today's prices of £850,000. Even allowing for some exaggeration and the deep discount involved in getting cash for the goods using a fence who dealt in stolen jewellery, this offered the prospect of a huge haul. 'The safe is double locked and I take the keys home with me each night,' Harris explained. 'The safe is in an office at the rear of the shop. The door of the office is always left open at night and a light is left burning over the front of the safe so that it can be seen by any person passing the shop front in Houndsditch.'[3]

There was an additional problem for anyone trying to break in from the back. The rear part of the ground floor of the Houndsditch property was let to a lace importer and that would have to be accessed before getting to the room with Harris's safe. But the expropriators were well prepared. In sharp contrast to the crudeness of the Tottenham wages grab, the robbers were equipped not simply with guns, but with rubber tubing, a large cylinder of oxygen, chemicals, tools and cutting equipment, and – to judge from some of the literature later seized by police – research had been done on how best to use these items. In the words of the prosecution, 'men of skill, experience and practical knowledge' were behind the planned robbery.[4] George Gardstein had acquired acid and other chemicals and for some months was an occasional visitor to an engineering workshop in Islington, where he fashioned and adapted equipment and arranged for the supply of the cylinder. The workshop was run by the renowned Italian anarchist and political émigré Errico Malatesta, and while police eventually accepted Malatesta's insistence that he had no idea Gardstein was preparing for a robbery, it came close to leading to his deportation.

Both the jewellery business and the lace dealer at 119 Houndsditch observed the Jewish sabbath. Harry Harris told the police that he closed the shop by seven o'clock on Friday evening and didn't open again until ten o'clock on Sunday morning. This gave the would-be robbers two nights and a day to break in, open the safe and make good their escape. They began work on the evening of Friday, 16 December 1910.

THE MEN WHO had gathered at 59 Grove Street earlier that day left singly towards the close of the afternoon, by which time it would have been dark. Fritz Svaars told Luba Milstein that he was going to meet a friend in the West End and collect some money and probably wouldn't be back that night. She asked for some cash to go to 'a Picture Palace' and Fritz gave her a shilling. When she went out at about 5.30 p.m., Peter the Painter was the only person left in the first-floor rooms. Some of the men regrouped in the evening at 11 Exchange Buildings, where they were joined by Nina Vassileva. And that's when they started trying to burrow their way into Harris's jewellery shop. They did so not from 11 Exchange Buildings but from No. 9. One of the group had arranged to take this second property on a short lease, keeping it unfurnished and saying it would be used to store Christmas goods. The agent recognized Gardstein as the man who paid the rent. The houses in Exchange Buildings didn't directly align with the business premises on Houndsditch, but part of the wall of No. 9's outside toilet overlapped with the rear of 119 Houndsditch. It was a nuisance to have to clamber over the backyard of No. 10 – which was now empty – to move between the two buildings, but access to the rear of No. 9 offered the most practical option of breaking into the jewellers and then cracking the safe.

There was a fatal flaw in the design of the robbery. Setting to work on a Friday evening gave the gang a sizable window when the Houndsditch shop was closed, but in the absence of daytime traffic and hubbub, the sound of the drilling and chipping away at bricks to get access to the property stood out, particularly as – in a mainly Jewish locality – it interrupted the Jewish sabbath. In mid-evening, the robbers set to work trying to break through from the outside toilet at 9 Exchange Buildings. When Superintendent Ottaway turned up, he found evidence of a sophisticated operation: 18 metres (60 ft) of rubber piping attached to a gas pipe, four sheets of

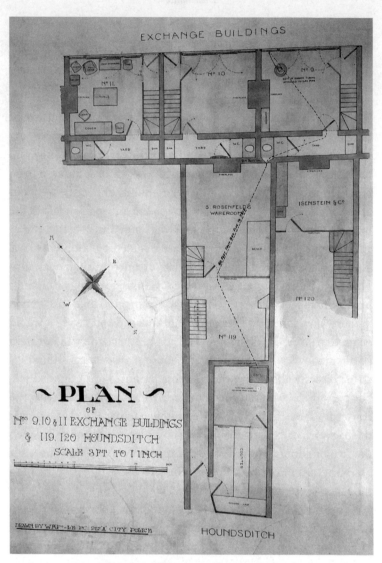

Plan of Exchange Buildings and Harris's jewellery shop
made by the City of London Police.

asbestos, two wooden boxes, a carpenter's brace bit, a bag of sand, some mortar and two candles. In the backyard was the oxygen cylinder and other bits and pieces.

> The seat of the water closet was covered with brown paper on which I found a carpenter's brace, three diamond pointed drills, one ¼ inch chisel, three crow bars or jemmies, and one special wrench ... with jagged jaws, one end made for ripping metal.
> There was a considerable amount of broken bricks in the pan, on the seat and on the floor of the water closet, and a hole 24 inches by 20 inches across, and 9 inches through ... reaching to the matchwood [on] the other side of the wall.[5]

They were almost through. But the din had alarmed a neighbour, Max Weil, who lived above his fancy-goods business at 120 Houndsditch. Alerted by his sister and the maid, he 'listened for about a ¼ of an hour & heard noises that resembled the drilling, sawing & breaking away of brick work' coming from the jewellery shop next door. He set out to find a policeman.

Police Constable Walter Piper stated that he was on duty along Bishopsgate at about 10.45 in the evening when Weil came up to him and said there was an unusual noise coming from the back of a silversmiths on Houndsditch. Piper went into Weil's premises and listened to the banging and drilling and then tracked down the noise as coming from somewhere at the rear in Exchange Buildings. He recalled that 'the neighbourhood was very quiet, owing to the Jewish Sabbath. There were not more than two or three persons in Cutler Street – Exchange Buildings being completely deserted.' There was a light on at No. 11. PC Piper knocked and 'a man ... opened the door in a suspicious manner' – he later identified the man as Gardstein. The policeman's line of inquiry was almost comically asinine. 'I said "is the missis in?" He replied "she has gone out". I said "right I will call back".'[6] The appearance of a uniformed policeman must have deeply alarmed Gardstein and his colleagues, though curiously they appear to have made no attempt to get away when they had the chance. PC Piper was probably not much less alarmed to have interrupted what he must have realized was a robbery in progress. He arranged for a police constable to keep lookout in Exchange Buildings and another to stay in Houndsditch and returned to Bishopsgate to alert his sergeant.

There was already some awareness among the local police of the new occupants of Exchange Buildings. When a plain-clothes police officer, PC Arthur Strongman, set off from Bishopsgate Police Station in response to the incident, his chief inspector told him to inform the senior officer on the spot 'that some foreigners occupied

Exchange Buildings: no. 11 is on the left just the near side of the gas light.

a house on the right hand side of Exchange Buildings of whom he was suspicious'. Half an hour or so after the alarm was first raised, a police sergeant came into Weil's premises and heard the drilling for himself, peered out of the back windows and called in at the dairy on the other side of the jewellers. 'You can leave it in our hands, we will see to it,' he declared.[7] Within a few minutes, there were at least nine police officers in the vicinity, all unarmed, in response to the apparent robbery attempt. When Sergeant Robert Bentley knocked at 11 Exchange Buildings, Gardstein again opened the door but appears not to have answered any questions and retreated inside. Bentley then advanced into the empty ground-floor room – standing for a while just inside the door.

Sergeant William Bryant offered his own dramatic testimony of the shooting. He said he was one of six police officers in Exchange Buildings:

> I saw Sergeant Bentley knock at the door of No. 11 – After Bentley knocked at the door he turned round and said something to me – Then I went towards him – As I approached Bentley stepped inside the passage – I saw the lower part of a man who was standing on the staircase – I also saw inside the ground floor room which was lighted. I stood on the footway on the left of the street door. I heard Bentley say to the man on the stairs:
>
> 'Is anyone working at the back?'
>
> The man said 'no'. Bentley then said:
>
> 'Is any one making noise down there?' The man said 'no'. Bentley then said:
>
> 'Can we look out at the back'. The man replied 'yes'. Bentley said 'well show us the way'. The man on the stairs put his hand towards the top of the ground floor doorway and said 'In there'.
>
> Bentley took a step to the right into the doorway of the room and I stepped into the passage –
>
> Immediately I saw a man come from the back door into the room between Bentley and the table... As he appeared

I noticed he had a pistol in his hand. He at once commenced to fire towards the right shoulder of Bentley who was just in the room – The shots were fired very rapidly. I distinctly heard three or four – I put my hands up as he commenced to fire – I felt my left hand fall – I was shot – I fell out on to the footway – When the man commenced to fire, Bentley staggered back against the post of the doorway of the room … I next recollect getting up – I staggered along the wall for a few yards towards the blind end of Exchange Buildings … When I recovered, I was standing by the wall of No. 10 – I saw Bentley's body on the doorway of No. 11. Two other uniform men – Woodhams and Choate [sic] – were lying on the carriage way in Exchange Buildings - PC Martin was standing in the carriage way just outside No. 10 – I saw no one else.[8]

Bryant said that on visiting the morgue, he recognized Gardstein as the man who had opened fire; he didn't see the face of the man on the stairs and couldn't say whether he had fired any shots. He added that he was dazed and had only a 'very faint recollection' of what had happened after he was shot. That wasn't surprising. At the hospital, it was found he had been shot in the chest as well as the arm.

James Martin, a police constable in plain clothes, was also an eyewitness to what happened when Sergeant Bentley entered 11 Exchange Buildings:

> the back door opened very quickly and I saw a hand and forearm of a person holding a revolver and instantly I saw a flash from the revolver which was pointed at Sergeant Bentley. Almost simultaneously I saw a flash on the stairs and heard the report of another revolver, and at that moment Sergeant Bentley fell backwards towards me and the street door. Sergeant Bryant and I rushed up to the door and at the same time I saw a hand holding a revolver first pointing towards Cutler Street and then down Exchange Buildings continuously firing.[9]

Martin said he ducked and then stumbled and fell – though it would be more accurate to say that he went to ground and a judge later castigated him for cowardice.

One of the gang stepped out of the house shooting incessantly, or so it seemed to onlookers. PC Arthur Strongman said this man 'pointed the revolver in the direction of Sergeant Tucker and myself, firing rapidly. P.S. Tucker and I stepped back a few yards when the Sergeant staggered and turned round. I caught him by the right arm and we walked towards Cutler Street. I looked over my left shoulder and saw the man fire two more shots in our direction.'[10] Sergeant Charles Tucker had been hit twice; one of the bullets entered his heart. Strongman later identified Gardstein as the gunman. Amid the dark and confusion, Constable Walter Choat ran to the door in Exchange Buildings, trying – it seems – to wrest the gun from Gardstein. He was repeatedly shot at close range; the hospital found eight gunshot wounds on his body caused by at least five bullets. One of the bullets fired at Choat unintentionally hit Gardstein in the back. PC Strongman, who escaped injury, estimated that from first shot to last spanned about ten seconds. In all, at least 22 shots were fired by the robbers.[11]

Some of those living in Exchange Buildings gave dramatic testimony of the events that unfolded just by their front doors. Solomon Abrahams was fourteen years old and had lived all his life in 12 Exchange Buildings, immediately next door to the house taken by the would-be robbers. His father was a hawker, selling door to door. He made a total of seven witness statements, some of which were at times fanciful, but his fullest account feels unvarnished. Solly Abrahams worked at a barber's shop. On 16 December, he reached home in the evening having had a dinner of fried fish:

> I was undoing my boots when PC Piper came to our house, and asked if we had complained about a noise. My mother said to him, 'I have got no one doing anything for me'. He then said to my mother, 'Don't let the boy come out' (referring to me) ... I was standing by the door to see what was going on. PC Piper came to our house a second time, and

enquired as to the noise, and my mother told him to come and look for himself. He said, 'How far is Harris's from here?' Mother told him.

The teenager then ran to a pub in Houndsditch to summon his father home and noticed some police officers in the area:

> As I was going inside my house, I saw Sergeant Bentley standing at the door of No. 11. He was going to touch it with his hand. I went inside the front room, as I thought I would hear better in there. I heard Bentley say, 'Is anybody working here?' The answer given was, 'No'. He then asked, 'Anyone in the back?' Reply, 'No'. He then said, 'Can I have a look in the back?' Reply, 'Yes'. Suddenly I heard a noise, which I thought was that of windows being broken. I went to mother and said to her, 'All the windows have gone and smashed'. She told me to be quiet. The sounds that I heard was that of shots ... I went towards the door, but father dragged me inside ... I went to the door, and saw four Policemen lying in Exchange Buildings, and another (Tucker) lying at the corner of Cutler Street by Houndsditch.[12]

Ada Parker, in her mid-twenties, was that evening sitting with her parents in a ground-floor room directly opposite 11 Exchange Buildings:

> I heard something go 'bang' 'bang'. I did not know what was the cause of the noise. I said 'this is a fine house to live in, I believe the chimney has fallen off'. Then there were several more bangs and father and myself rushed to the street door. I prevented father from opening the door as I thought the noises were caused by a revolver and he might get shot. Shortly afterwards I opened the street door and saw several police officers lying on the ground. I said 'oh mother some of the policemen have been murdered', and rushed out of the house.[13]

Three policemen – Sergeants Bentley and Tucker and Constable Choat – were dead or dying; two others, Sergeant Bryant and Constable Woodhams, had serious bullet wounds and neither was able to return to active police duties.

The most urgent task was getting the wounded police officers to hospital. A passing cab was waved down and its occupants evicted; that vehicle took Tucker to the London Hospital. He was dead by the time he was seen by a hospital doctor. Choat was also treated at the London Hospital, where he died at about 5 a.m.; Bentley was rushed to St Bartholomew's Hospital at Smithfield, where he died the following evening. The police files include post-mortem photographs, with helmets carefully put back in place, of all three men. This was the worst loss of life the police force in London had ever suffered and only once since, in 1966, have three London police officers died in a single incident.

George Gardstein, who had played such a central role in planning and preparing for the robbery, was badly hurt. Two of the gang held him up by his arms and started to help him away from the scene. Isaac Levy, the manager of a tobacco shop, was making his way home at a little after 11.30. He heard a shot and then a volley of shots – between fifteen and twenty, he reckoned – as he walked along an alley towards Cutler Street:

> The first thing that attracted my attention was three men coming along towards me . . . Behind the three men was a woman. I first saw them in the middle of the road, about four steps away from me, coming from the direction of Exchange Buildings. The man in the centre of three men was being supported by the other two; he seemed dazed, or exhausted, and was holding his head down . . . When I was facing them, about four feet away, both the outside men pointed revolvers at me. The revolvers were pointed direct at my face . . . While pointing the revolvers at me, both the men spoke; one of them said 'Don't follow us', and the other said [']Don't follow'.[14]

He didn't follow. At Exchange Buildings, Levy recounted that he saw four policemen lying on the ground. A woman who lived in the Buildings was shrieking 'murder'; another, also screaming, tripped over the body of one of the policemen. He helped them to the relative safety of a pub on the corner and then ran to the police station on Bishopsgate to summon help.

To the passer-by, the sight of a man being helped home by friends late on a Friday night – a night when the pubs were at their busiest – was unexceptional. Once away from Cutler Street, the group were able to make their way through the East End without attracting much attention. They headed up Harrow Alley and across Middlesex Street, and were spotted along Wentworth Street heading towards Spitalfields, apparently avoiding the main roads. Gardstein's room on Gold Street in Stepney was around 3 kilometres (2 mi.) from Houndsditch. He was too weak and had lost too much blood to be taken that far, and the burden on the two men supporting him must have been exhausting. So they made instead for 59 Grove Street, the rooms occupied by Fritz Svaars, Luba Milstein and Peter the Painter, which had served as the nerve centre of the enterprise. In normal circumstances, that would have been at most a twenty-minute walk from the scene of the shooting, but encumbered by a badly injured comrade it must have taken them longer than that.

At Grove Street, Luba Milstein and her friend Rosa Trassjonsky had returned from the cinema and had their dinner and were preparing for bed. Milstein had arranged that Trassjonsky, who lived close by, would spend the night with her 'as I wanted company'. Whether or not the two women knew of the planned robbery, they must have sensed that the men who regularly gathered at Grove Street were up to something. Milstein's testimony is both more detailed and more credible than most, and even in the cautious wording of a police statement her sense of terror seeps through:

> when we were undressing we heard someone coming upstairs, as if they were carrying something heavy, and they went straight to the front room. As we heard the people

going into the front room we wanted to see who it was there. We went to the front room, but the door was held from the inside, and someone called out, 'Don't come in.' (I recognized Fritz's voice). Peter the Painter was in the room – he had not been out ...

Fritz came into the back room, and asked me to give him a sovereign (He had given me £2 in the early part of the week to buy a costume). I gave him a sovereign, and he told me I had better get away from the place at once. I asked him what had happened, but he was in such a state of excitement that he did not speak, and made me more frightened than I was. He then turned to Rosa and said, 'Mouremitz [Gardstein] is in the other room. Go and bathe him with cold water; he has been wounded.' He told me to get out at once. I recognized Josef [Sokoloff] standing outside the other room, by the light, as Fritz went out of the door. They both rushed out down the stairs.

All this happened, she reckoned, in a couple of minutes. Trassjonsky estimated the time as a quarter past midnight.

Rosa Trassjonsky later told the police that when she went in the front room, there was a man lying on the bed: 'he was fully dressed, and there was blood on his shirt. I displaced his shirt and placed a wet towel [*sic*] on the wound and took off his boots ... I stayed with the man alone as he was so ill I could not leave him.' Milstein, at nineteen some years younger than Trassjonsky, was both panic-stricken and nauseous. She headed to the room of one of Svaars's friends, Karl Hoffman, nearby on Lindley Street – this may have been the agreed rendezvous after the robbery. According to Milstein's version, when she got to the room, she found that Svaars, Sokoloff and Peter the Painter were already there: 'Fritz caught hold of me and screamed at me, "What are you doing here? Get out of it at once." I asked why he had brought Mouremitz [Gardstein] to our room. He replied, "I carried him like a child; I couldn't leave him["].'[15]

Luba Milstein was ordered to go back to Grove Street, gather up her photographs there 'for [her] own safety' – because they could be used in 'wanted' posters as well as to establish links between activists – and then leave and tell Trassjonsky also to get away. She was told that the men would arrange to get a doctor. That wasn't true. Once they had got Gardstein to Grove Street, his comrades left him to die.

Karl Hoffman also set down an account of the late-night visitors to his room in a witness deposition for the defence at the Old Bailey – so inevitably pointing to the guilt of those who were not on trial. He said he was in bed and asleep when Josef (that is, Sokoloff) woke him up. 'He said Max had wounded Gardstein. He did not say how it happened.' Sokoloff was carrying a Mauser pistol. Two or three minutes later, Fritz Svaars came in, bearing two pistols, a Mauser and a Browning. He was followed shortly after by Peter the Painter and then by Luba Milstein. According to Hoffman, Svaars explained how he and Max Smoller had carried the injured Gardstein, initially intending to leave him on the street somewhere near Commercial Road, but when Gardstein started to scream they decided to take him back to Grove Street. Max then handed over the Browning and left. The men said they intended to stay the night in Hoffman's room. He insisted they couldn't.[16] There is, no doubt, some special pleading in this version of events, but it is broadly plausible.

Once she left Hoffman's room on Lindley Street, Luba Milstein went back to Grove Street, got some photographs and told Trassjonsky that they should leave. But Gardstein, who was still conscious, appealed to Trassjonsky not to abandon him. She stayed but Milstein was 'too frightened to remain'. Trassjonsky's room was just two minutes' walk away on Settle Street. She gave her friend the key. At about 3.30 a.m., Trassjonsky came round to the room saying that Gardstein's condition was grave. They went together to summon Dr Bernstein, who had a practice in Commercial Road and a nameplate in Yiddish – his assistant, Dr Scanlan, accompanied them back. Milstein was not willing to return to Grove Street, so she went once again to Trassjonsky's room and stayed there.

Dr Scanlan saw that a bullet had struck the wounded man in his back and lodged in his body. Gardstein was still sufficiently alert to tell the doctor his name and that he had been shot accidentally by a friend and to tell Rosa that there was money in his pockets to meet the doctor's charges. Scanlan told the inquest that the bullet that struck Gardstein had perforated his stomach and his lung: 'The man was very weak – blood came from his mouth while I was examining him ... He was in great pain.'[17] He recalled that the gaslight, already dim, sputtered and went out during the examination, prompting Trassjonsky to put a penny in the meter. The only language he could speak to her in was French. Gardstein refused to go to hospital. Trassjonsky went back to the doctor's surgery in the middle of the night to pick up a painkiller for Gardstein. At about 7 a.m., the injured man told Trassjonsky to leave 'as I could not do him any good'. When she arrived at Settle Street she told her friend that Gardstein was 'very bad'. An hour later Trassjonsky returned to Grove Street and offered Gardstein more medicine, which he refused. The two women were at a loss as to what to do. They called on a shopkeeper in Old Montague Street who was on good terms with some of the men and gave them credit. They explained the situation – the shopkeeper's wife told them to go away.

Luba Milstein recalled that the two women rather reluctantly returned to the first-floor rooms on Grove Street. 'We then found that Mouremitz [Gardstein] was dead, and I rushed out of the house and Rosa followed.' By her own testimony, Milstein went round to a series of friends' and associates' rooms, uncertain what to do and deeply alarmed at the peril she was in: 'I thought that I might be accused of murdering Mouremitz [Gardstein].' She wouldn't venture back to Grove Street herself, but persuaded Trassjonsky and a friend, Pavel Molchanoff, to go there and retrieve more of the photographs. At this stage, she may well have been wanting to recover anything that might incriminate her partner, Fritz Svaars. She stopped for a while at a house on Havering Street, where she again came across Peter the Painter and broke the news to him of Gardstein's death. By Saturday afternoon she was at her mother's house, which is where (she said) she first heard mention of the murders in Houndsditch and realized 'that the people with whom I lived had shot the Policemen'. We'll pick up Luba Milstein's trail in due course.

Although Dr Scanlan had come across a patient with a serious bullet wound that could not have been self-inflicted, he made no attempt to alert the police either straight away or first thing in the morning. The police later castigated his conduct as 'most extraordinary'.[18] When, late in the morning, Scanlan and his colleague became aware of news reports of the Houndsditch shooting, they belatedly contacted the City of London Police. This was the breakthrough the police had been seeking – the first firm indication of who was responsible for the murder of the three police officers. But the doctors were reluctant informants, explaining that 'they were most anxious that nothing should be said or done to cause anyone to believe that they had given any information, as it would be ruinous to their practice in consequence of the peculiar views held by foreign Jews on the subject.'[19]

The police asked Scanlan to call again at 59 Grove Street, as he had undertaken to do during his overnight visit, but 'without creating suspicion'. Police officers then arranged to go round to the surgery at 12.30:

> Dr Scanlan informed us that the man was lying dead on the bed, and to our astonishment added that he had communicated with the Coroner's Officer: this made it imperative that we should go [to Grove Street] at once which we did and had only been there a few minutes when a large number of Newspaper Reporters assembled in the street, undoubtedly due to information supplied them either by the Doctors or the Coroner's Officer.[20]

There is a touch of special pleading in the police complaint. You might have thought that they would have arranged to meet the doctor at or near 59 Grove Street or at least put the property under immediate surveillance, but it seems they didn't.

Detective Inspector Ernest Thompson of the City Police, along with his Metropolitan Police counterpart Fred Wensley, reached the house in Grove Street at a little after 1 p.m. 'We were let in by the landlady, a fat old Jewess, who couldn't, or wouldn't understand

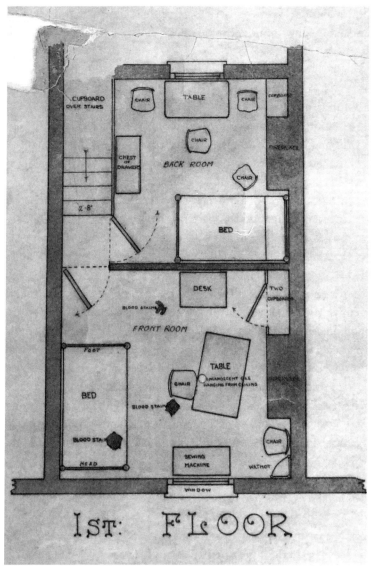

Plan of 59 Grove Street, first floor, made by the City of London Police.

our questions,' Wensley later recalled, reflecting the undertow of antisemitism within the London police:

> There was no time to waste. If one of the murderers had died in the house others, for aught we knew, might be still lurking there.
>
> Cutting short a confused babble I applied a rough test. I signed to her to lead the way up the narrow stairs. I guessed that if armed men were awaiting us no power on earth would have got her up. With some reluctance – due, as I afterwards discovered, to a distaste to go near the dead man – she preceded me. Her bulk amply protected me from any possible bullet, although I might have been crushed to death if she had fallen backwards.[21]

Gardstein's body was still on the bed, and in his pockets they found a clip of cartridges, several loose cartridges and various other items, including a pocket map and guide to London. The trousers he was wearing had what the police described as a 'revolver pocket' designed for concealing a gun. Pushed down the side of the mattress was a loaded revolver. A search of the room uncovered a box of fifty cartridges, some loose cartridges, a cartridge belt and a dagger, along with what was described as 'a quantity of printed matter relating to Anarchism, also a quantity of correspondence in the Lettish and Russian languages'.[22]

In the back room next door, Detective Inspector Ernest Thompson came across Rosa Trassjonsky burning photographs and papers. 'She had evidently been doing this for some time as there was a quantity of black ash in the grate and on the hearth.'[23] The police also found more anarchist literature, some of it charred, in Russian and in Latvian. Trassjonsky was taken to Bishopsgate Police Station. The following day, Luba Milstein turned up at another police station at Leman Street, brought there by her brothers. Both women were charged with being accessories to murder, assisting in the escape of a wanted man and conspiring to commit burglary. The police must have felt that their murder inquiry was starting to make progress.

The big question for the City of London Police – and one for historians to grapple with too – was: who was at 11 Exchange Buildings when the shots were fired that killed the three police officers? The ballistics expert that the police turned to concluded that at least three revolvers were used at Houndsditch. The Dreyse pistol found stuffed down the side of the mattress on which Gardstein's body lay was the main murder weapon. Two bullets from this gun hit each of the three dead policemen and a seventh bullet was found nearby. It's unlikely that Gardstein had the strength to conceal the weapon once brought to Grove Street – whether one of his comrades left it to incriminate Gardstein or to allow him to defend himself is an open question. Another revolver, a Mauser or a Borchardt, sprayed bullets around quite liberally – one of these was retrieved from Constable Choat's leg, and of the five others, one was embedded under the floorboards of the first floor of 11 Exchange Buildings while another was in the first-floor ceiling. The bullet retrieved from Gardstein's body was fired from a Belgian Browning – just such a gun was discovered in Gardstein's room in Gold Street, but it wasn't the weapon used at Houndsditch. The ballistics evidence fits with the eyewitness accounts that three men were seen with guns at Exchange Buildings.[24]

The only man that police officers who survived the shootings firmly identified as among the robbers in Exchange Buildings was George Gardstein. PC Piper testified that Gardstein was the man who opened the door to him at 11 Exchange Buildings when the banging and drilling noises were first reported. PC Martin said it was Gardstein who opened the door on the second occasion the police came to the property. Sergeant Bryant and PC Strongman identified Gardstein as the man who entered 11 Exchange Buildings from the rear yard and opened fire on Sergeant Bentley. All four police officers attended line-ups which included Osip Federoff, Jacob Peters and Yourka Dubof, and some also inspected later identity parades including Hoffman and Rosen. They failed conclusively to identify any other suspect.

Of those involved in some way in the shooting, the evidence most worth dwelling on is that of Nina Vassileva. This was obtained in an underhand manner and wasn't presented in court but it remains in the police files. On 2 March 1911, Vassileva met her lawyer at Holloway jail. The interpreter passed on a partial – and seemingly jumbled – account of this privileged conversation to the police. Vassileva insisted to her lawyer that she was not present at Exchange Buildings on the night of the shootings but at the movies with her friend Masha. With a trial looming, she was hardly likely to admit that she was present when the policemen were shot. But she also made clear that she knew exactly what had happened. 'Marks' (that is, Max Smoller) was 'the organiser' of the attempted robbery and was the first to open fire, and Gardstein, Svaars and Sokoloff 'also took part in the shooting'.[25] While this was a convenient narrative – because none of the four were among those in the dock alongside her – that doesn't mean it was untrue. In a later meeting with her lawyer, with the same interpreter feeding information to the police, she went further and said Sokoloff had told her that 'Marks' or Max had organized the robbery for the express purpose of shooting Gardstein. This points to the venom among the group directed at the man they seem to have held responsible for the robbery going wrong, and so for their comrade's death and their own desperate predicament. But it's not the only account that states that Max Smoller fired the shot that fatally wounded Gardstein. Karl Hoffman, when called as a defence witness after the charges against him were dropped, told the court that Fritz Svaars had said 'it was Max' who shot Gardstein.[26]

Much of Nina Vassileva's account is in line with the testimony of another key witness. Luba Milstein's statements to the police were inconsistent but by the time of her most detailed accounts, given on 23 January and then at Holloway jail on 17 February, her partner, Fritz Svaars, was dead. She was not an active accomplice nor an activist and she had no particular motive at this stage beyond seeking her own acquittal. She insisted she had never been to Exchange Buildings and didn't know its location. But she was clear about who brought the wounded Gardstein up the stairs to the rooms she shared at Grove Street, even if the wording of the statement suggests a certain amount of police prompting: 'I am prepared to go into the witness box and swear that the men who brought in Mourmeitz [Gardstein] were Fritz [Svaars] and Yosef [Sokoloff].'

She said that Max Smoller arrived separately 'immediately after Fritz' – which suggests that he might have been keeping an eye out behind Gardstein and his accomplices so that he could fend off anyone in pursuit. Peter the Painter was also in the room to which Gardstein was brought – indeed it was his room – but Milstein was clear that he had not been in Exchange Buildings that evening as she had heard him playing the violin when she and Rosa got back from the cinema.[27] If Nina Vassileva was part of the group that initially accompanied Gardstein, which in all likelihood she was, then she had peeled off before they reached Grove Street.

The police gathered evidence that challenged this account. In his initial statement to the police, Isaac Levy – the tobacconist who was warned at gunpoint not to follow the wounded Gardstein and those accompanying him – said he was unable to give any description of the men and woman he came across. A few days later, in a follow-up statement, he had changed his mind, saying that in spite of the time of day 'there was a fair light shining on the faces of the men.' After attending identity parades he identified the two men as Jacob Peters and Yourka Dubof, an assertion which the judge declared to be 'so unsatisfactory that he could not allow any jury to find the prisoners guilty on such evidence'.[28] Levy later identified the woman, with a bit of prompting, as Nina Vassileva. One of the policemen at the scene, PC Piper, thought he spotted Yourka Dubof loitering nearby – the robbers are likely to have positioned a lookout – but he added, 'I am not definitely sure,' and he failed to pick out Dubof at an identity parade. The evidence placing several of those who were later charged at Exchange Buildings at the time of the shooting was slim and it's hardly surprising that several suspects were discharged before trial and those whose case was heard at the Old Bailey were acquitted, with the sole exception of Vassileva, who was later cleared on appeal. As Justice Grantham told the jury at the Old Bailey, those most clearly responsible for the murder of Sergeant Bentley, Sergeant Tucker and Constable Choat were already dead (or in Max Smoller's case had fled). 'I am strongly of the opinion that the three men who were really the chief murderers', he declared, 'have each of them met their doom.'[29]

6

100 Sidney Street

St Paul's, the cathedral which had staged the funerals of such national heroes as Nelson and Wellington, was the venue of the service for the three murdered policemen. It was held on 22 December 1910, the Thursday after the shootings. On its eve, all five of the officers who had been shot at Houndsditch were awarded the King's Police Medal, instituted in the wake of the Tottenham Outrage two years earlier. Three horse-drawn carriages carried the coffins, all bedecked with flowers, to the steps of St Paul's: 'no great prince of our people has had a funeral more wonderful in its solemnity and grandeur,' declared the *Daily Chronicle*.[1] The Home Secretary, Winston Churchill, attended along with his 25-year-old wife, Clementine. King George V was represented. The order of service pointedly noted that the three police officers had been 'murdered in the discharge of their duty'. Among the wreaths was one from the Jewish residents of Houndsditch, and another bearing the single word 'Duty' from Samuel Harris, whose jewellery business was the target of the robbery attempt.

After the service, a funeral procession headed by the City Police band and a contingent of mounted police slowly made its way round the City of London. The streets were thronged with silent and respectful onlookers. Around Mansion House and the Bank, there were, said one newspaper, 'great crowds of well-dressed men belonging to the Stock Exchange and the great banks, and the rich business houses. Reverently they bared their heads before the bodies of the men who had died for duty's sake.' As the cortège headed east, the character of the crowds lining the streets changed. 'The poor of London had come out. The factory hands and warehousemen were here. The people of the underworld, the people who struggle for a living wage, the people of mean streets and squalid lodging-houses.'[2]

From Spitalfields, the hearse containing the coffin of Constable Choat headed to Waterloo station and a further service and interment at Byfleet in Surrey; the remains of Sergeants Bentley and Tucker continued through the East End to the City of London cemetery near Ilford. The two sergeants are buried there in adjoining plots. A red granite column topped with a cross records that they, along with Choat, were 'killed in the execution of their duty while endeavouring to apprehend a number of armed burglars'. Robert Bentley's wife, Louisa Bentley, was heavily pregnant at the time of his death. Five days later, she gave birth to a boy, who took his father's name. Robert junior died of diphtheria when he was three and is buried in the same grave as his father.

The government was under pressure to respond to the killings. In the hours after the funerals, Winston Churchill announced that the London police would have available to them 'more modern, efficient and handy' revolvers, and tests would be held to work out which would best suit the purpose. It was acknowledged that the guns in the police's arsenal were 'heavy, clumsy and out of date' and no match for the more modern and efficient firearms used by criminals.[3] This would have been of no help to the police on duty at Houndsditch, who were all unarmed and did not know they were dealing with armed adversaries. And it was not implemented in time to be of service when there was another shoot-out at Sidney Street eighteen days later.

The more urgent need was to identify and arrest the killers. The police had mortuary photographs of George Gardstein, some with

Memorial card for the three policemen shot dead at Houndsditch.

his eyes open, which were widely distributed to solicit information about what he had been up to and who his accomplices were. Rosa Trassjonsky and Luba Milstein were in detention and Luba in particular was providing some information about the circle believed to have been behind the robbery attempt. The police also had a piece of luck. One of the men present at Grove Street on the afternoon of the robbery, Nicholas Tocmacoff, called back round the next afternoon when the police were there – he was intending to collect a mandolin that he needed for a performance. He was promptly taken in for questioning and, as we've seen, gave the police a full list of those present on the Friday afternoon as well as evidence of Svaars's ownership of two semi-automatic weapons. He also told police that immediately before his detention he had been at 36 Havering Street along with Luba Milstein. And he mentioned another associate: Jacob Peters. The police now at least had a few leads, and they appear to have made a priority of finding and arresting the men Tocmacoff had named. By the evening of the following day, Sunday, he was out and about and meeting up again with his old friends.[4] The decision to release Tocmacoff while continuing to hold the two women suggests that the police thought he might, unwittingly or otherwise, serve as an informer. The information he provided was certainly of value, and the police brought him along to identity parades and he gave evidence for the prosecution both at the initial committal hearings and at the Old Bailey trial.

In the days after the shootings, the press reported that arrests were 'hourly expected'. The East End was 'swarming with detectives', according to the *Daily Chronicle*, 'for it is believed that the assassins are still lurking in that quarter.'[5] Three days after the murders, the police told reporters the names of those they were seeking: 'Peter the Painter', the first time this alliterative *nom de guerre* made a public appearance, along with Fritz and Yourka (no surnames given), and a woman who was still unnamed. A day later the police were able to add that 'the "wanted" men belong to an Anarchist group'.[6] The Home Office was assured by the police that they were 'taking all possible steps to trace these men + watching all stations + ports to prevent their escape. They have persons helping the Police

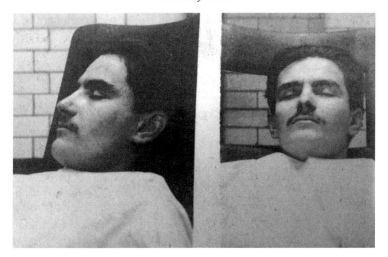

Post-mortem photographs of George Gardstein.

who can identify them as the men who occupied the rooms at 59 Grove Street'. The Home Office note concluded with an observation suggesting sensitivity to an upsurge in antisemitic sentiment: 'The men are certainly anarchists and are almost certainly not Jews. The dead man was not a Jew.'[7]

The arrests came on the day of the funerals: Yourka Dubof was picked up in the afternoon at his home in Shepherds Bush; Jacob Peters was arrested at a little after 8 p.m. at his room on Turner Street in the East End; and, towards the end of the day, Osip Federoff was detained at his room nearby on Romford Street.[8] The following evening, they were part of an identity parade at Bishopsgate Police Station, where more than thirty potential witnesses inspected the line-up, with inconclusive results. All three men were charged as accessories to murder and appeared in court on Christmas Eve. Federoff declared on behalf of them all, 'We deny all knowledge and we are not guilty.' They joined the two women on remand. A few days later, they were obliged to take part in another identity parade close to the police cells at Guildhall, where another twelve people walked up and down the line. On this occasion, Jacob Peters made a complaint through the interpreter: 'I do not think it fair, as the photos have appeared in the newspapers.'

As those arrested were Russian subjects, the Russian consulate was represented at the parade and had instructed a lawyer who was also present 'on behalf of all the prisoners' – which can hardly have been much comfort to those in detention. Unsurprisingly, both the Russian consular official and the lawyer 'expressed their satisfaction at the fair manner in which the identification was conducted'.[9] No further arrests leading to charges were made until February, when John Rosen was picked up, and then Nina Vassileva and, a few hours later, Karl Hoffman.

The evidence against Dubof, Peters and Federoff was not strong. They were certainly companions of Gardstein and part of the same social and political circle, and they may have spent time at Exchange Buildings in the days before the robbery. There is some evidence that Yourka Dubof was in the vicinity of Exchange Buildings on the evening of 16 December.[10] But the identification evidence that suggested Dubof and Peters were the men wielding guns and helping the injured Gardstein away from the scene was flimsy and unreliable. The only positive identification of any of the men who opened fire was of Gardstein, and he was dead.

A week after the shootings, the police issued posters in English, Yiddish and Russian with the macabre post-mortem photograph of George Gardstein. A few days later, they located Gardstein's room – at 44 Gold Street, one of a row of very ordinary two-storey terraced houses near Stepney Green. The inventory of items found there included small bottles of acid, mercury, phosphorus and several other chemicals; scales and glass tubes; a Browning pistol; a cartridge belt containing 150 Mauser cartridges and other ammunition; a dagger; publications in English, including specifications for guns, torpedoes and explosives; Russian-language publications, including a price list of guns and ammunition; and a manufacturer's catalogue that included blowpipes of the sort used to cut metal. The literature found and sent for translation turned out to include a guide to making explosives, a book about using oxygen and acid to cut metal, and a publication containing 'advice to Anarchists and Revolutionaries to fight against the Government, Soldiers and Police', which included details of how to make bombs. There were also letters from Latvian revolutionaries in New York and a pamphlet issued by a left-wing group, the Russian Social Revolutionaries. The family Gardstein lodged with said that he described himself as a chemist, but the bottles of chemicals had only started arriving in the previous four or five weeks.[11]

The police inventory demonstrated that Gardstein had assembled an armoury of weapons, ammunition and chemicals and had sought to gain the know-how to use these to best effect. Some newspapers, relying no doubt on information from the police, splashed news of the discovery of a 'bomb factory'. *The Star* described the haul as 'a perfect arsenal of daggers, magazine pistols and "soft-nosed" cartridges; and, what is more significant, the materials for the manufacture of deadly bombs'. Not to be outdone, the *Daily Chronicle* posed the question: 'Was there a plot to mar the Coronation?' – the new king, George v, was due to be crowned in the summer.[12] The police quickly backtracked, perhaps worried about the public alarm such sensationalist headlines might cause. They conceded that there was no evidence that explosives had been manufactured at Gold Street and that the quantities of chemicals found were too small for this to be a bomb-making workshop.[13] A note hurriedly sent on to the Home Office confirmed that the police had 'no information, either from examinations of the premises or from other sources, to show that anything of an actively anarchist character was being carried on in the house or that any preparations for an outrage were being made.' The literature in Russian appeared to be less ominous than first reports had indicated. The Latvian émigrés were quite ready to use violence in carrying out robberies or defending themselves, but they never deliberately targeted members of the public. The chemicals were more likely to have been intended for what the police inelegantly termed 'burglarious purposes', and particularly breaking into safes. Nevertheless, none of the other premises searched had such a formidable assembly of material and munitions. It must have confirmed the police's impression of the relative sophistication of the gang and Gardstein's leading role within it. But it had taken the police ten days from finding George Gardstein's body at 59 Grove Street to searching his room and interviewing his landlord less than a mile away on Gold Street.

The police were well aware that the key players in the Houndsditch shootings were still at large. Their posters bearing Gardstein's photograph solicited information that would lead to the arrest of Fritz Svaars and Peter the Painter and their still unnamed woman accomplice. And to try to break through the reluctance of East Enders to assist the police, a substantial reward was offered of £500 (that's more than £60,000 in today's money). The sentiment *don't snitch* was deeply embedded in the culture of the East End, and it was particularly strong among those in left-wing groups who were always on the lookout for informers in their ranks and sometimes staged informal hearings when members were accused of spying. Naomi Ploschansky, the teenage anarchist activist, strongly disapproved of armed robbery, even if notionally for a cause, but she had met some of those involved. During the hue and cry in the East End, she came across one of those being sought in the street. 'I tried not to look at him. I tried to make believe that I didn't see him. Because I thought: if he sees me and then he gets arrested, he'll think I was the one. And if I hated anybody, I hated an informer, couldn't stand them.'[14]

Those most culpable in the deaths of the three policemen didn't hang around at home waiting to be arrested. They hid – and if they could, they fled. That was certainly the case with the four people (other than Gardstein) who can be placed with some confidence at Exchange Buildings at the time of the shootings – Fritz Svaars, 'Joseph' Sokoloff, Max Smoller and Nina Vassileva – and with two key associates who were not present but were clearly implicated, Peter the Painter and Karl Hoffman. If you didn't go to ground, then almost by definition you weren't part of the inner circle. The experience of these revolutionaries in Latvia had taught them that if they were at risk of arrest for a serious offence, they needed to get moving. Indeed, of this group only Vassileva and Hoffman ever saw the inside of a London prison cell.

Max Smoller performed the most complete disappearing act. He was at Grove Street on Friday afternoon and came back late that evening immediately after the wounded Gardstein and his colleagues, but then got clean away. 'I have not seen or heard of him since that night,' Luba Milstein told the police. The description she gave of him was hardly flattering: 'grey eyes; thick lips; an ugly nose; thick at the nostrils; he was not a nice looking man'. He was viewed by his comrades with resentment and suspicion. Smoller was unusual among the group in having a wife and children. He may have returned that night to the family home in Stepney, but if so it was simply to say farewell. He seems fairly promptly to have managed to get out of the country – perhaps on the same night as the shootings. Many decades later, Charles Perelman's son suggested that Perelman had helped Max Smoller get to Paris immediately after the incident.[15] A few months later, his family were able to follow him. They had moved to a room in Brick Lane. A detective constable was keeping watch on the place one evening towards the end of April when Mrs Smoller, with her daughters Rachel and Cecilia, aged five and three, walked to St Katharine Docks and boarded a ship heading across the North Sea. What luggage they had was pushed by a friend in a costermonger's barrow. Reuben Frankel, the shopkeeper on Old Montague Street who was such a constant friend and aid to the group, 'was following her about forty yards behind apparently watching to see if Mrs Smoller was being followed. At the corner of Leman Street they all met + shook hands with her, then parted.'[16]

Within the group, Peter the Painter clearly had a position of authority. He wasn't so much liked as respected; he was, in the words of one of his associates, 'very reserved in manner'. Peter had a long and prominent involvement in the Latvian revolutionary movement. He had a natural elegance. And he seems to have had at least some money. Although he was a painter by profession, he didn't take a job while living at Grove Street. 'Fritz told me that Peter's parents had sent him money from Russia, and that he lived on this money,' Luba Milstein told the police. 'He did not do any work.'[17] Although he was not one of those who fired at the police, he shared rooms with one of the gunmen, Gardstein's body had been found on his bed and he was deeply implicated in the plan to rob Harris's jewellery business. He didn't intend to hang around and see how much evidence the police could accumulate against him.

Peter the Painter, along with Svaars and Sokoloff, headed to Karl Hoffman's room on Lindley Street, perhaps a fifteen-minute walk away, as soon as Gardstein had been brought to Grove Street. A panic-stricken Milstein saw him there in the early hours of Saturday morning. Peter quickly moved on and spent the night and much of the next day in the room of a friend, Pavel Molchanoff, on Havering Street in Stepney. Pavel and Peter had been comrades together in Marseilles the previous year. Molchanoff told police he hadn't at first recognized Peter when he came across him in London three months earlier; in Marseilles Peter sported a pointed beard, as displayed so prominently on the photographs that the London police later distributed, but had since become clean-shaven, apart from a moustache. On Saturday morning, when after Gardstein's death Milstein once again came to Hoffman's room, she found Molchanoff there. He agreed to go back to Grove Street to try to retrieve any incriminating papers and told Milstein to head for his place at 36 Havering Street. When she arrived there, she found a group of five or so men talking excitedly, one of whom she knew. Nicholas Tocmacoff warmly shook her hand. '[A]s I didn't like to be in the room with all the men, I went into a back room to wait for Pavall [sic],' she told police several weeks later. 'When I got into the room I saw that Peter the Painter was in there. I told him that Mouremitz [Gardstein] was dead at Grove Street. He seemed very excited . . . and started to walk up and down the room.'[18]

Peter the Painter wanted money. When Molchanoff came, he said he had found half a sovereign (50 pence) in Gardstein's pocket. He changed it for smaller coins and from that money, Milstein gave Peter the Painter half a crown (12½ pence). According to her testimony, Peter the Painter asked how much it would cost to get to Poplar and put on his coat and prepared to leave. Molchanoff said he didn't hear what Luba and Peter said, but he did pick out the word 'Paris'.

From here, the trail went cold – and by the time the police worked out Peter's apparent next steps, there was no trail to pursue.

That took more than twenty years. In August 1932, the security service MI5 heard from an informant who in turn had been told the story by his friend, Victor Veldie (or Weldie), who had emigrated to Canada, rose to the rank of captain in the Canadian armed forces during the First World War and later worked for the Royal Canadian Mounted Police. Veldie was, in 1910, a Latvian revolutionary lodging in a house in Dock Road, North Woolwich, half a mile or so from Poplar. According to this account, Peter the Painter came round seeking refuge – exactly when isn't clear, but quite possibly the evening after the shootings. With the reluctant cooperation of his landlord, Peter was concealed in a small box room, and was there – apparently with a gun – when the police called to talk to Veldie. Peter spent four days in Dock Road. After that, with the help of the landlord's wife, he travelled to Liverpool Street Station and took a train for Harwich connecting with a boat service to Holland. This would be just another of those tales about Peter the Painter and his near mythical escape but for the trust MI5 clearly placed in its informant.[19] If this account is reliable then by the time of the funerals of the three policemen, Peter the Painter had managed to slip through the net and get across the North Sea.

There were people in the East End able to help revolutionaries get out of the country in a hurry, not so much because they sympathized with expropriation but more out of common feeling. Among them, Naomi Ploschansky recalled many years later, was the family's lodger at their home on Stepney Green. Solomon Mars 'was a good guy, he was not one of the group – he had made out things for them, some sort of passes for them ... He forged it.' These false documents helped some of the wanted men to get away. Ploschansky's memory was that the police came round looking for Mars and she was inveigled into hiding some of his documents. 'So I put those papers inside the small pillow that the baby slept on in the crib – I put the things inside that cover of the pillow and baby would sleep on them.'[20]

Nina Vassileva made an attempt to flee but left it too late and perhaps didn't have access to the support network that the men in the group could tap into. She appeared back at her lodgings at about eight o'clock on the evening after the shootings. Her hair had been dyed black, she was burning clothes and documents and she was clearly alarmed. As we'll see in a later chapter, her landlord alerted the police, and the following evening officers came round to the house to question her. She wasn't arrested but was placed under surveillance. When, a few days later, she declared her intention of getting to Paris, she gave up after a few hours and returned to her lodgings complaining that she was being followed by detectives. She was eventually arrested and ended up on trial at the Old Bailey.

Another of those implicated in Houndsditch was more successful in getting out of the country. Karl Hoffman, a Latvian whose room on Lindley Street was briefly the assembly point for the group once they had fled from 59 Grove Street, left about two days after the Siege of Sidney Street for (by his own account) Antwerp. He said he returned from Antwerp at the end of January. If he thought the coast was clear, he was wrong. A little over a week later, he was arrested in the early hours of the morning while bedding down with Latvian friends, Theodor and Lonnie Janson and their child, at Cannon Street Road in the East End. Theodor Janson had already given a statement to police and told them of what might have been a chance encounter with a man he called Masais, a name used by Hoffman, nine days after the Houndsditch shootings:

> I said to him 'Three of the men [Dubof, Peters and Federoff] are arrested, are they the men'. He laughed and said 'No, there were nine men in the plot, none of them are yet arrested. Its a pity the man is dead (meaning Gardstein), he was the ablest of the lot and the leader of the gang. He so managed it that some members of the gang did not know the others'.
>
> He also said he thought one of the murderers had left the country. I asked him how he could get away and he said aboard ship.[21]

When Hoffman was arrested at Janson's home and subsequently charged, Janson insisted that Hoffman wasn't the man about whom he had given the police information. While some aliases were used by more than one activist, that doesn't seem credible.

The two men most deeply implicated in the Houndsditch shootings, Fritz Svaars and 'Joseph' Sokaloff – the men Luba Milstein insisted had supported the dying Gardstein when he was brought into 59 Grove Street – went to ground. It's not possible to say with certainty when they took refuge in 100 Sidney Street but it is probable that they went there directly from Hoffman's room on Lindley Street, a distance of around 100 metres (little more than 100 yards). It is certain that the testimony of the woman in whose room they hid, Betsy Gershon (or Gershaw), was at best evasive. She was a dressmaker and had the front room on the second floor, which she sublet from the Fleishman family, who lived on the ground floor and ran a tailoring workshop on the premises. Gershon told the coroner holding the inquest into the deaths of Svaars and Sokaloff that she was from Crimea and had been in England for five and a half years. Her husband had returned to Russia some eighteen months previously. He wrote to her every week or two and she occasionally sent him money. She had several Russian friends in London. According to her landlady, she had a child she visited at weekends – he was a two-year-old boy who presumably lived out so as not to impede his mother's twelve-hour shifts at a local workshop. 'I have only had one man who visited me,' Gershon said. 'His name was (Yosaf) Joseph. I don't know his surname. He used to come once a week or once a fortnight.'[22] This was Sokaloff – she mentioned a distinctive aspect of his walk: 'he seemed to have the right foot more behind than the left one . . . [and] used to twist his body as he walked.' He and Gershon may well have been lovers. He was the occasional caller that Rebecca Fleishman, who lived downstairs, mentioned to the police: 'a tall dark man, with a big moustache and dark curly hair, who came two or three times to see her. I heard her let this man out at 12 midnight.'[23]

Betsy Gershon said she had not seen 'Joseph' for several weeks before he turned up with a friend (but no longer with a moustache) on Sunday evening, 1 January 1911. They spent a couple of hours with her. 'I know nothing about the other man,' she insisted. 'He spoke

Russian, but it was a different kind of Russian to mine. Joseph [Sokaloff] spoke good Russian, but the other man spoke Lettish.' The following night – uninvited, according to Gershon – the two men returned, arriving late in the evening after she had come back from work. She gave them a cup of tea, they talked and Sokaloff said he had arranged a sea passage the next day back to Russia. At midnight, she suggested that the men should leave. Her account is that they refused to go and warned her to stay silent about their presence: 'They showed me their fists if I didn't keep quiet,' she told the inquest. The two men ordered her to take off her skirt and shoes (seemingly to stop her raising the alarm because she would be embarrassed to be seen partly clothed), gave her a pillow and told her to bed down in the room next door to hers. The Fleishmans used this as a stock room but Gershon had access to it as the gas meter there also served her room. During the night, Rebecca Fleishman knocked on the door of her room. If Svaars and Sokoloff had got any sleep, then the knock would certainly have woken them. Gershon emerged from the adjoining room, making an excuse that she was just putting a penny in the gas meter. Fleishman said to her, 'My husband is taken ill, will you come down?' The police had already surrounded the house and this was a ruse devised to get Gershon out. She came downstairs still without skirt or shoes, then was seized by the police and 'carried bodily next door ... in a state of evident consternation'.[24] She told police officers that there were indeed two men in her room. She was then taken to Bishopsgate Police Station.

The narrative that Betsy Gershon rehearsed to the police and then to the coroner was designed to avoid any imputation that she was an accessory to murder or had willingly provided sanctuary to wanted men. She was on the fringes of the social circle that met at Grove Street and at the Jubilee Street Club. Nina Vassileva told her lawyer that she knew Gershon, though as Gershunova. Among that circle was an informer. In the police archives, there are scribbled pencil notes based on what seems to have been a conversation with a source that is not specified. This gives a very different version. The informant said Gershon had come round at six o'clock on Sunday evening – New Year's Day – and confided that 'Yoska and Fish' were hiding in her room and had been there since 17 December, the day after the Houndsditch shootings. She was seeking the address of two men, 'Abraham and Pavell [Molchanoff]', whom the men she was sheltering believed would help them.

The informer pledged to assist the wanted men and arranged to call at 100 Sidney Street the next day. According to their testimony, on the following day,

> I went to the front room on the 2nd floor with Gershaw [*sic*] who was waiting in the stairs were [*sic*] I saw Fritz + Yoska standing with their hands in overcoat pockets. I told them I would find them rooms if they had money. Fritz said I have £20 + would like to find me [*sic*] a room in Dalston.[25]

The informant arranged accommodation at 83 Nelson Street, which was not in Dalston but adjoining Sidney Street. It would have been another small hop. The two men intended to move there on the day they died.

While it's difficult to imagine two men living for a couple of weeks in a small, second-floor room that had no kitchen of its own and a shared toilet without other tenants being aware of their presence, it's not that improbable. Fear of arrest and the death penalty would have been a huge inducement to Svaars and Sokoloff to avoid detection. East End households would have routinely brought in cooked food rather than preparing their own meals, and chamber pots were part of daily life. A glimmer of supporting evidence can be found in the Fleishman family's statements to the police. Rebecca Fleishman had detected a smell of tobacco on the Jewish sabbath, when the men in the house normally refrained from smoking. Then, on 30 December, she noticed while cleaning the stairs that a key appeared to be in the lock on the inside of the door to Betsy Gershon's room even though she was out at work. That evening she sent her fourteen-year-old son, Jacob, up to the room on the pretext of seeking to borrow a shilling (five pence). It was in darkness. Gershon only opened the door a sliver and told Jacob to wait. She brought the shilling to him on the landing. There seemed to be something in the room that she didn't want the boy to see.[26]

When their ally-turned-informer called at Sidney Street as arranged on Monday afternoon, Fritz Svaars entrusted him with a letter to post. It was addressed to Svaars's father at Liepaja (then Libau) in Latvia – the envelope in Russian gave one address, an envelope inside in Latvian recorded another. It ended up with the police. That letter offers a remarkable insight into the mindset of the Latvian émigrés involved in the Houndsditch shootings. Svaars told his family of the search under way for him – 'they are looking for us anywhere,' he said, adding that the 'whole of London is buried in police' – while insisting (how could he do otherwise) that he was innocent and had no connection with the attempted robbery. He spoke of how well advanced his plans were to meet up with his wife and head for Australia. And he gave a convoluted account of financial dealings with Gardstein. Then he recounted how,

> At 12 at night, two acquaintances came to my flat bringing Puika [Gardstein] who'd been shot and could no longer walk. I could no longer stay in my flat for another minute because I wasn't sure that their bringing in the wounded man hadn't been seen and I, who was clean, would be arrested for nothing and certainly hanged. Those who brought in the wounded man themselves fled immediately and I grabbed the most necessary things, a weapon and ammunition and also went to some known members, from there I sent two girls to go and bandage Puika, to get hold of a doctor, clean out the flat, burn the letters and other papers . . . I told them to try and bring out my new clothes, photographs and the ship's tickets; if Puika should die, to pour paraffin over him and the bed and start a fire so that he is burnt together with the flat, then the police wouldn't even know that he'd been wounded and also all the things would get burnt.[27]

He said one of the women had managed to retrieve the tickets for the sea passage, but the arrival of the police prevented any attempt to set fire to the building. He recounted how another man living at his place – he didn't mention a name but this is clearly Peter the Painter – had also fled and so far had not been arrested. 'He like me, if arrested, will without doubt be hung because the guilty ones are unknown.' Svaars had clearly been in contact with associates, or perhaps Betsy Gershon had picked up on gossip in the street, and he wrote that 'Jekabs', his cousin Jacob Peters, had been arrested, as had two other men 'because they'd come to my flat and were my friends'.

While this account is clearly not the unvarnished truth, in everything but the insistence of innocence it rings true. Svaars's increasing desperation is also apparent – indeed he seems to be bidding farewell to his family:

> Two weeks I've been on the run, how much longer I can manage, I don't know. To leave soon doesn't bear thinking about because they're guarding all the roads intensely. I'm not at all depressed because everyone knows that one has to die at some time and the good a person such as I can bring to humanity is not worth talking about . . . So be peaceful. If I'm lucky then I'll still live and I'll share joy and sadness with you, and if not, you also know that at some time that same hour will come to you and you'll be ashes the same as everyone.

Fritz Svaars wasn't lucky and within a couple of days, he was – quite literally – ashes.

So who was the informer? The evidence is inconclusive but points towards Charles Perelman (or Pearlman), who had at various times let rooms to Gardstein and his associates and was regarded by the Latvians as politically sympathetic. He was an older man, about sixty years old, and from Minsk. Perelman's motive may well have been the £500 reward being offered, though there's no hard evidence that he ever received any of it.[28] He seems to have got in touch with the police early on Monday, 2 January, or perhaps very late on New Year's Day, within hours of being approached by Betsy Gershon.

Police drawing of 100 Sidney Street.

The police opted to keep the Sidney Street house under surveillance and planned to surround the building the following night. They didn't want to stage an operation that could lead to a shoot-out during the day because of the fear of civilian casualties. There was a huge risk in delaying the operation. If Svaars and Sokoloff had chosen to move, they would have done so during the day, when the customary to-ing and fro-ing would have provided an element of cover, rather than at night when they could more easily be spotted and picked off. But Perelman's promise to arrange a new stopover for the two men would have encouraged them to stay put in Sidney Street for a little longer.

Rebecca Fleishman was at hand on Monday afternoon when the informer had arranged to call at Sidney Street. 'The man had in his hand a long parcel, it looked like a broom handle wrapped in American Cloth. While I was talking to the man Mrs Gershon spoke from the stairs. She said, it is all right Mrs Fleishman, he is going to

Plan of 100 Sidney Street, second floor.

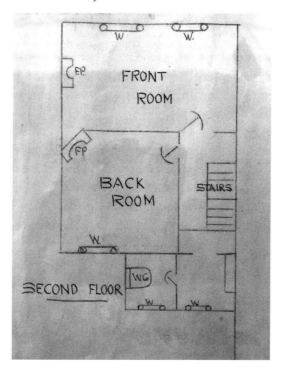

take my photograph.' Charles Perelman was a photographic enlarger. Fleishman was suspicious and made a point of being around when the visitor left. He'd spent half an hour upstairs and was still carrying his parcel, which could have been a photographer's tripod. Her description of the man, however, is not such a good fit for Perelman: she said the visitor was aged about thirty – but he was wearing a hat and it's not at all clear how good a look she got.[29]

A rough pencil sketch in the City of London Police files, attached to the details provided by the informer, showed the location of 100 Sidney Street, and which police officers would be stationed where as the cordon was put in place.[30] The building was part of a recently built four-storey block known as Martin's Mansions. After the siege, the police commissioned architect-style drawings of the house and of the plan of each floor, to prepare for the committal hearings and trial.[31] It was part of a terrace and the front door opened directly onto the pavement. There were two cramped rooms to each floor (including the attic floor), all of which had windows, and kitchens on the ground and first floor; the second floor had the only inside toilet, but there was also an outside toilet in the tiny yard, at the back of which was the flank wall of an adjoining property. The property was very hemmed in – easy to defend, and difficult to breach.

WELL BEFORE FIRST light on Tuesday, 3 January 1911, armed police were in position. The most delicate task was extracting all the residents from the building. At 3.30 a.m., Rebecca Fleishman was woken by a tap on the ground-floor window. She explained to a journalist that she thought at first it was the milkman:

> My husband got up and went to the window, and [the detectives] told him in Yiddish not to be afraid as they were come to save his life.
> My husband asked how he was to know that this was not a ruse, and that they were really detectives.
> They showed him their revolvers and truncheons, and that satisfied him ...[32]

Mrs Fleishman bundled her children out of the building to the house next door, which had been commandeered by the police, and then helped to get everyone else out. Davis Schieman, who had two rooms on the first floor, recounted that he was woken up in the middle of the night by Mrs Fleishman, 'who said they must all get up and leave the house, as there were "two murderers upstairs"'.[33] She had more difficulty with an elderly man who lodged in the back room on the ground floor and who made a fuss at being told to move out into the street in the early hours of a winter morning. But within a short time, Svaars and Sokoloff were the only people remaining in the building and they must by now have known that they were under siege.

7
'A Devilish Kind of Courage'

At 7.30 on the morning of Tuesday, 3 January 1911, just as dawn was breaking, a policeman threw gravel at a window of 100 Sidney Street. Several of the officers positioned nearby, both uniformed and plain-clothes detectives, were armed – though not with weapons that were a match for the guns the robbers had used at Houndsditch two weeks earlier. The police carried whatever firearms 'they could lay their hands on – old-fashioned bulldog revolvers, shot-guns, and Morris-tube rifles'.[1] A small group of senior police officers had been planning the operation the previous day. 'With my City colleagues and some of my own staff I went to have a quiet look at the house,' recalled Detective Inspector Fred Wensley of the Metropolitan Police in one of the more reliable of the police memoirs of the siege.

> To have made any inquiries among the teeming population of the quarter at that time would have probably led to the suspects becoming aware that we had traced them, without any advantage from our point of view. For we had decided that, if the men were there and it was their intention to leave that night, our most effective course would be to intercept them when they got into the street. So men were left to keep observation and we waited on events.[2]

Late that night, the police drew a cordon around the house, using all available detectives from the two forces, supplemented by uniformed men. This was in place by two o'clock in the morning. 'It was a miserably cold night, with gusts of sleet and rain,' Wensley

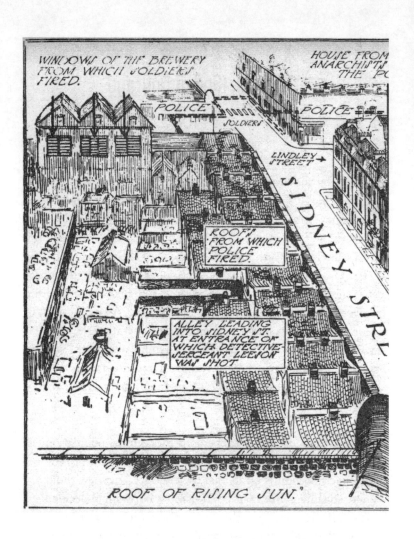

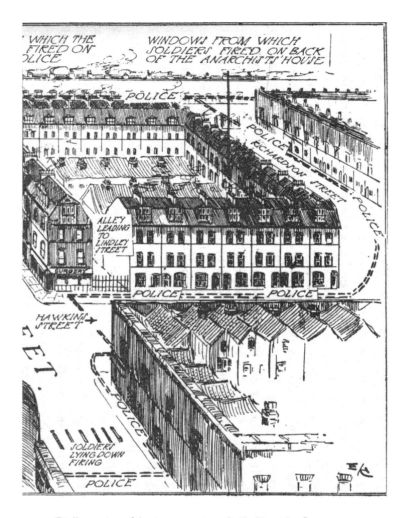

Bird's-eye view of the siege operations, *Daily Chronicle*, 4 January 1911.

recalled. He was sheltering opposite 100 Sidney Street at a spot where a small archway gave access to a yard in which vans and carts were kept. The police were confident that the wanted men were in the building and aware that the Latvians were likely to have semi-automatic weapons. 'It was known that they were desperate men and would not be taken alive,' recorded Superintendent John Mulvany of the Metropolitan Police in a report drawn up four days after the siege. Armed police were concealed in doorways, in the front room of the house immediately opposite 100 Sidney Street, and 'along every avenue of escape from front or rear'.[3] The police seem to have been so convinced that the two men would not give themselves up that no appeal appears to have been made in Russian or Latvian (or indeed English) urging them to surrender. But the police were constrained by the protocol that force could only be used to repel force; they couldn't open fire unless they were demonstrably in peril. Some consideration had been given to storming the building, but the staircase and landings were narrow and there was a real risk that officers could be picked off one by one as they made their way upstairs. The London police had just suffered the gravest loss in their history and they were determined not to endure further police casualties.

The gravel rattled against the second-floor window. 'Nothing happened for an instant,' Inspector Wensley recalled. 'I was stooping to gather more pebbles when suddenly shot after shot rang out in swift succession.'[4] The firing came from the first floor. The curtains of the room remained closed – the gunmen couldn't be seen. Sergeant Ben Leeson – who, according to press reports, had just thrown a larger stone which shattered a window – was caught in the volley of gunfire. 'The first shot passed through my right boot injuring my foot,' Leeson recounted. 'The second struck me just below the heart passing through my lungs and out through the back. My condition was very precarious for both lungs were affected, and it was thought my injuries would prove fatal.'[5] Leeson was convinced he was was not going to survive, exclaiming, 'Mr. Wensley, I am dying; they have shot me through the heart. Good-bye. Give my love to the children. Bury me at Putney.'[6]

The immediate difficulty was getting the stricken police sergeant to safety. He was carried into the back room of a house opposite. A man volunteered to climb over walls and roofs to summon a doctor, who similarly had to scramble over outhouses to reach the patient. He said the sergeant needed to get to hospital as soon as possible. Once Leeson was on a stretcher, provided by the adjoining Mann, Crossman & Paulin brewery, he had to be carried on a ladder. When a policeman's helmet appeared above a wall, it attracted another hail of bullets. 'You are taking me into the line of fire again,' the sergeant cried out. The gunmen continued firing for at least ten minutes, trapping those trying to get the policeman to safety. Leeson eventually rolled painfully off the stretcher on to a shed roof and was helped to the ground. He was sent to the London Hospital nearby. Scotland Yard initially reported that Leeson had died. It was a close call, but Leeson survived. His injuries kept him in hospital for three months and brought an end to his police career.

This opening fusillade demonstrated that the gunmen were well armed and were determined to go down fighting. The armed police had initially held their fire but there was soon an intense exchange. 'The firing from the house was more or less continuously throughout the morning, more particularly in the front, but in the back as well,' Chief Superintendent John Stark of the City of London Police told the subsequent inquest. 'It would have been death for anyone to have approached that house.' A quick conversation between senior officers at the scene led to a momentous decision – to bring in the army. This was the first time since the Metropolitan Police was established in 1829 that it summoned soldiers to open fire on London's streets – and it has hardly ever happened since, the SAS's role in ending the 1980 Iranian embassy siege being a rare instance. Consideration was given to asking for army rifles that the police could use, but in the words of one senior police officer, 'there are none of the Police that I could put my hand on as having sufficient skill in the use of them.'[7]

Superintendent Mulvany of the Metropolitan Police, who was on the spot, explained the rationale for the decision:

The firing from the house continued, and Supt. Stark, City Police and myself discussed the situation from all points of view. It was palpable that these men dominated the situation, there was no approach to the house but by the front door, the roofs were of the kind known as gable and unapproachable. It was equally plain that any attack by the front door would have resulted in a great sacrifice of life. Their weapons were far superior to our revolvers, of which at this time we only had a few. It was therefore decided that Military aid be sought as more effective weapons were required.

Having obtained authority of Major Wodehouse, Assistant Commissioner [of the Metropolitan Police], to do so, I proceeded to the Tower of London and requested Military aid, which was granted. Lieutenant Ross, 2 Non-commissioned Officers and 17 men being furnished, they were placed in positions of vantage and replied to the fire of the men in the house.[8]

These soldiers were uniformed Scots Guards armed with service rifles. They arrived at about 10.15 and took up position lying prone on Sidney Street on both flanks of the besieged building. Three of the soldiers were deployed on the top floor of the brewery's bottling plant, from where they had a vantage point over the second floor and attic of 100 Sidney Street. Others were based in requisitioned two-storey houses immediately opposite the besieged building.

The War Office got in touch with the Home Office to let them know that the City Police 'had asked that an armed guard of 20 soldiers should be sent down to assist the Police'. Senior civil servants at the Home Office seemed rather incurious about the role the Scots Guards were expected to play. 'I suppose the soldiers are wanted to escort the prisoners (if taken alive) to the Police Station,' one noted. 'The crowd would probably lynch them if they got the chance.'[9] In fact the troops, who had been issued with ball cartridges, were soon opening fire on the two men inside 100 Sidney Street. Far from trying to protect the Latvians, they were trying to kill them.

The *Daily Mail* commented that this was 'the first time in the last hundred years' that soldiers had been called into action on the streets of London. The *Daily Telegraph* quoted a police constable as saying that 'it for all the world reminded him of his experiences of some of the brushes which he had during the war in South Africa.'[10] Word of soldiers in uniform marching through the East End and then taking position in public view spread rapidly. 'The sight of the Guardsmen hastening to take their part increased the tremendous excitement in the neighbourhood,' the *Evening News* reported. 'The crowds cheered them wildly.' The breathless coverage in the early editions of the evening papers prompted more people to leave their offices and businesses and make their way to the scene. 'Excitement in the City was so great that business was practically suspended,' according to the papers.[11] There was a touch of carnival about the morning, combining spectacle, a break in the daily routine and an excuse to drop what you were doing and join the throng. Most of the police deployed in and around Sidney Street were on crowd control duties.

On occasions the gunmen were glimpsed at windows on different floors, and at the front and back of the house. A hand gripping a gun would on occasion protrude for an instant. The gunmen were usually concealed by blinds and billowing lace curtains. A police sergeant told the inquest that at one point he spotted both men at a back window on the third or attic floor. One of them bore a pistol in each hand. The two men seemed to be roaming around the house to give them an edge of surprise when firing at their besiegers. Within minutes, every pane of glass in the windows had been shattered by gunfire. Police piled up bedding and furniture in the house immediately opposite in an attempt to give themselves cover. A dummy in police uniform was put on display to draw fire. 'There was a great deal of confusion and it would have been utterly impossible for any one man to have exercised effective control of proceedings,' Inspector Wensley said. 'For those at the front of the house to communicate with those at the back, for instance, meant a long and intricate detour through houses, back-yards and over walls, and to find any particular person was a long job.'[12]

Much of the gunmen's fire was directed at the soldiers in the houses immediately opposite. Given the huge number of shots fired by both sides, and the press of spectators well within reach of the powerful weapons in use, it's surprising there were no fatalities among police, soldiers and onlookers. Inevitably, some injuries were sustained. 'At 12.15 or thereabouts I attended the first casualty at my end of the street, a young man who had had his scalp ploughed by a ricochet,' recalled a police surgeon who was at the scene. 'He was greatly excited, and would not keep his head still for me to examine the wound. I therefore seized him by the ears, and in this somewhat unprofessional attitude we were photographed and duly reproduced in the pictorial papers.'[13] That was a good after-dinner yarn for the doctor to retell and a more painful ordeal for the youthful bystander. The *Daily Mail* reported that, in total, ten people were admitted to the nearby London Hospital: five suffered bullet wounds of various sorts – Sergeant Leeson, a Scots Guard and three onlookers – and the other five were firemen injured after the shoot-out ended.

Winston Churchill was working at home at Eccleston Square in Pimlico when an urgent call came from the Home Office. With perhaps just a touch of melodrama, he later recalled that he was in the bath at the time and came 'dripping wet and shrouded in a towel' to the phone.[14] The Home Secretary was told of the shoot-out under way in Stepney and wrongly informed that a policeman had been shot dead. When Churchill took the post the previous February he was, at 35, the youngest Home Secretary since Robert Peel. Like Peel, he saw himself as a reforming Home Secretary; unlike Peel, at this stage in his political career Churchill was a Liberal. The message stated that the police had requested army support, and that Scots Guards were being sent from the Tower of London. A Home Office memo recorded that at eleven o'clock, Churchill gave retrospective approval over the phone to the deployment of troops 'on the requisition of the City Police'.[15] He had attracted controversy a few weeks earlier when the army was sent to South Wales to help maintain public order during a miners' strike, but an armed encounter in which the police were being outgunned was quite a different matter. Churchill insisted that his approval was not legally necessary, though the coroner's comment in endorsing this approach, that the Scots Guards 'came as armed citizens and not as soldiers', suggests a touch of legal sophistry.[16]

On reaching the Home Office, Churchill was frustrated that he couldn't get anything more than a cursory account of what was happening at Sidney Street, so – as befitted his background as a soldier and war reporter and his reputation as a man of action – he decided to see for himself. He was driven to Stepney, arriving a little before midday; he stayed there for almost three hours. 'It was a striking scene in a London street – firing from every window, bullets chipping the brickwork, police and Scots Guards armed with loaded weapons artillery brought up etc.', he recounted in a letter written the same day to the prime minister, H. H. Asquith.[17]

Wearing an overcoat with an astrakhan collar and 'placidly smoking a cigar', Churchill – conspicuous with his trademark silk top hat – arrived at the northern end of Sidney Street.

> With great daring Mr. Churchill walked along Richardson-street, Lindley-street, to Sidney-street, went beyond the firing line of the Scots Guards, and calmly surveyed the besieged house ...
>
> He had not stood very long at the corner of the street before a serious fusillade broke out.
>
> The Home Secretary stood unmoved while other spectators ran to cover.[18]

'This is a funny sight,' Churchill was heard to say. He took up a vantage point at the junction with Lindley Street – recklessly close to the action – and then across the road and a little further back, in an entrance alongside William Walker's beer shop, the Sidney Arms. Close by him was a *Daily Chronicle* reporter: 'Now and then [Churchill] would give an order, telling this line to advance or that to retire. Noticing the side door of our yard to be open, he shouted, "Close that door, or you will be shot."'[19] He was in his element.

Photographers captured the Home Secretary peering towards 100 Sidney Street – images which appeared all over the papers and were turned into postcards that sold in huge numbers. He clearly courted attention and enjoyed the thrill of the moment. The Home Office let it be known that while the Home Secretary had seen 'a good deal of active war' this was 'the first time he has witnessed street fighting, with the excitement of a great crowd, [and] the ricocheting of bullets within a limited space'.[20] Indeed, Churchill was one of the few people on the scene who was familiar with the Mauser pistol, of exactly the same sort the gunmen were using. He had bought a 'Broomhandle' Mauser, as the c96 model was known, in 1898 just a couple of years after it went into production and had used it – and killed with it – when on active service in Sudan. He had described the Mauser, in a letter home to his mother, as 'the best thing in the world'.[21]

Winston Churchill was fiercely criticized for putting himself in harm's way and for distracting the police and troops from their primary task of flushing out the gunmen. Basil Thomson, at the time a senior official at the Home Office and later the head of the Metropolitan Police Criminal Investigation Department, declared himself 'astounded' that the Home Secretary had ventured to the scene of a shoot-out.[22] It gave the impression of reckless self-promotion as well as leading to some confusion about who was in charge. A. J. Balfour, the Conservative Party leader, made political capital out of this breach of convention. 'He was, I understand, in military phase, in what is known as the zone of fire – he and a photographer were both risking valuable lives,' Balfour taunted in the House of Commons. 'I understand what the photographer was doing, but what was the right honourable gentleman doing?'[23]

A headline in the next morning's *Daily Mirror* read, 'Mr Churchill in Command'. At the inquest into the two men who died at 100 Sidney Street, Churchill insisted it was 'quite untrue' that he took charge of operations, but he conceded that he told the police to move onlookers further from the line of fire and was candid in stating, 'I think I am the highest police authority.'[24] The perception, however much Churchill may have denied it, was that the Home Secretary was present to direct the response to the incident. He came to regret the decision to venture to the scene, stating that it was motivated 'by a strong sense of curiosity which perhaps it would have been well to keep in check'.[25]

THE BURSTS OF gunfire came irregularly, followed by a lull. When shots were fired, they were almost always returned. The soldiers sought to draw fire to run down the gunmen's cache of ammunition. An *Evening News* reporter found a rooftop vantage point and set down an eyewitness account, which would have been read across London before the bodies of the two men had been retrieved:

> The crowd murmurs and heaves and shouts clamorously; the police are pressing them back. Again the volleys clang out with the sound of deadly peril ... the shots of the murderers come by turns from every window in the house; one imagines these wretches racing up and down the stairs, watching their chances. A policeman shows himself for a moment: bang from an assassin's pistol, and a faint puff of smoke from the ground floor window.
>
> I climb over the roof-top and look over the coping on the other side and see another sight which seems to me incredible. On the wet, muddy road, protected from the cold slush by a carpet of Yiddish newspaper posters, there are four soldiers. Three of them are stretched full length on the ground; the fourth is kneeling. Each has a loaded rifle in his hand ...
>
> And while I am writing these very words spurts of smoke are spitting out; from the first window on the first floor, from the second window on the first floor. A thundering reply from hidden soldiers.[26]

A *Daily Chronicle* reporter gave a vivid eyewitness account of the gun battle:

> The anarchists' house had the horrible fascination of a house of death. Bullets were raining upon it. As I looked I saw how they spat at the walls, how they ripped splinters from

the door, how they made neat grooves as they burrowed into the red bricks, or chipped off corners of them. The noise of battle was tremendous and almost continuous. The heavy barking reports of Army rifles were followed by the sharp and lighter cracks of pistol shots. Some of the weapons had a shrill singing noise, and others were like children's pop-guns. Most terrible and deadly in sound was the rapid fire of the Scots Guards, shot speeding on shot, as though a Gatling gun were at work.[27]

This was war reporting from the streets of East London.

According to an account Churchill wrote a decade after the event, active consideration was given to storming 100 Sidney Street in commando style, with police or troops simultaneously bursting through the front door, entering through a rear second-floor window and breaking through the roof. While this would almost certainly have led to casualties among those staging the assault, it could also have forestalled the very real prospect of civilian loss of life. Churchill recalled that he had suggested advancing up the staircase behind a steel plate or shield and that 'search was made in the

A Maxim gun in position on Sidney Street.

'A Devilish Kind of Courage'

Field guns on their way to Sidney Street.

foundries of the neighbourhood for one of suitable size.'[28] It seems a haphazard way of seeking to end the siege and was not pursued, but such was the desperation of the police that they sought additional support from the military.

A second and larger detachment of Scots Guards reached the scene at about 1.30 p.m. They were equipped with a Maxim gun, a formidably effective early form of heavy machine gun – a Russian-made Maxim model was still used by Ukraine's army in 2022.[29] More ominously, soldiers of the Royal Horse Artillery who had just had their midday meal were ordered to 'boot and saddle' and made their way from St John's Wood to Stepney, bringing at least two large horse-drawn field guns and wagonloads of ammunition. The *Daily Mail* published photographs both of Scots Guards with a machine gun mounted on a tripod and of a much bigger field gun being made ready for action.[30] Winston Churchill told the inquest that he hadn't summoned this much more formidable weaponry. 'I heard that a Maxim gun had arrived . . . I never directed anyone to send for a Maxim gun, nor did I send at any time for any further military force. The artillery came up as I was driving away.' It's a mystery who did requisition these heavy-duty guns – the head of the City of London

Police insisted it wasn't him. But by the time the artillery arrived, the stand-off was just about over and neither Maxim gun nor artillery was used – which, as one of the papers commented, 'was perhaps fortunate for the reputation of the authorities'.[31] In all, including a detachment of Royal Engineers from Chatham deployed to tunnel into the building if required, 124 soldiers were 'detailed for service' in Sidney Street. They fired five hundred rounds of ammunition.[32] If the gunfire from police and the two gunmen is included, it's likely that well over a thousand bullets were fired in the course of the siege, and perhaps double that number.

THE HOME SECRETARY had been at Sidney Street for a little more than an hour, and the shoot-out had lasted well over five hours, when the first wisps of smoke were seen escaping from the second floor of the building. The smoke slowly became thicker but it was the best part of an hour before flames were seen. The police had earlier turned down the fire brigade's offer to turn three large jets of cold water on the building to try to force the gunmen out.[33] Once a blaze took hold, the fire service was on the spot almost immediately with horse-drawn pumps – within three minutes of being called, according to the official account – but a senior police officer ordered the firemen not to approach the building or attempt to douse the flames. 'The origin of the fire had not been explained,' the coroner declared – and there is some evidence, inconclusive but not insubstantial, to suggest that the blaze may have been started deliberately to force the gunmen out of the house. Evening newspapers on the day of the siege reported that the fire had been started 'by (it is said) the order of the Home Secretary'. The *Daily News* the next morning carried a longer report citing telephoned messages by firemen to their senior officers that pointed strongly in the same direction, while also reporting that any suggestion 'that the police fired the house on the order of the Home Secretary is authoritatively denied'.[34]

The ripples created by the *Daily News* report led to what may well have been an uncomfortable encounter the following morning between Sir Edward Henry, the Commissioner of the Metropolitan Police – whose men were, of course, implicitly being held responsible

'A Devilish Kind of Courage'

Winston Churchill at Sidney Street amid Scots Guards, police and a fire officer.

for starting the fire – and the Chief Officer of the London Fire Brigade, Sampson Sladen. The fire chief stood his ground, sharing extracts from the service messages phoned in to Mile End Fire Station from fire alarm posts. At 1.09 p.m., just six minutes after the alarm was raised, the station received a message from a fire alarm point close to Sidney Street that the 'alarm [was] caused by Police smoking out burglars'. Eleven minutes later, a longer message was phoned through to the fire station: 'tell the Superintendent the Police have fired some premises in Sidney Street for the purpose of burning out supposed murderers. The Home Secretary, Mr. Winston Churchill, is present and has asked for the engines to be kept here to stand by.' Another half an hour on, a further message to Mile End laboured the same point: 'tell the Chief Officer the Home Secretary, Mr. Winston Churchill, is allowing a block of buildings to get well alight before any attempt is made to extinguish it.'[35]

The chief fire officer accepted that these phone messages were sent 'by the officers who first arrived and were in charge of the fire during the time of considerable stress and when accurate information as to the exact circumstances was difficult to obtain'.[36] But those fire officers on the spot were clearly convinced that the police had started the fire, because that's what they had gathered from the police officers who prevented them from getting to the burning building.

The testimony of the fire officers involved in tackling the blaze – set down in writing two days after the event, with a promptness that often eluded the police – underlines their sense that there was something irregular. Sub-officer W. H. Drew, one of the first on the scene within a few minutes of the alarm being raised, recorded that

> the Horse Escape [a horse-pulled wagon carrying a large retractable ladder] and steamer [steam-powered water pump to supply hoses] was turned out from this station, and on my arrival on the steamer within about 150 yards from the fire was stopped from proceeding any further by an Inspector of Police, who had already stopped the Horse Escape. Fireman Hodges who was in charge of the Escape informed me he had been told by the Inspector that the Police were trying to smoke out burglars from the building . . . I spoke to the Inspector who informed me that the Police had pulled the alarm as they required the presence of the brigade.[37]

There is just a hint here, though not explicitly stated, that the police called out the fire service to be in position to douse down a fire that they were intending to start. Station Officer A. E. Edmonds was at the scene just after Drew:

> I saw the premises were on fire and smoke issuing from the two upper floors, and the military and police firing at the burning house. I was stopped by the Police some distance from the fire and informed that I could go no further. I made some demur at this and a Police Official then told me that the Home Secretary was present. I spoke to him,

telling him I represented the Fire Brigade and wanted some instructions. I am not quite clear on the actual words he used, but I gathered that he forbid me to try to extinguish the fire the responsibility being his, the last words he said to me being, but 'keep your engines here'.[38]

Half an hour later, a divisional fire offer, C.C.B. Morris, reached the scene and took charge of the firefighting operation. By that time, the building was 'well alight on the three top floors. There was at the time a considerable amount of firing going on.' Morris was told that the Home Secretary was in charge of the operation and went up to speak to Churchill,

> asking him how long he proposed letting the house burn, pointing out to him that there was a risk of the fire spreading if allowed to burn much longer and that it would be necessary to order on more appliances. He told me it would be best to order on more engines but we were doing nothing as regards putting the fire out, until he gave orders.[39]

Later in the month, Churchill gave his own account to the coroner, explaining that

> [a] junior officer of the Fire Brigade (Station Officer Edmonds) came up to me where I was standing and said that the Fire Brigade had arrived, and he understood he was not to put out the fire at present. Was this right? Or words to that effect. I said 'Quite right: I accept full responsibility.' I wish to make it clear that these words refer to the specific question asked me, and that I confirmed and supported the police in their action. From what I saw, it would have meant loss of life and limb to any fire brigade officer who had gone within effective range of the building.[40]

There clearly would have been real risk to the firemen tackling the blaze, and Edmonds conceded at the inquest, 'I was grateful afterwards that I was stopped.' But Churchill's dealings with the fire brigade show how hollow were his protestations that he was not taking operational command. He was everyone's reference point.

Fire Officer Morris, a relatively junior officer and the brigade's 'officer of the day' on 3 January 1911, went on to serve as Chief Officer of the London Fire Brigade. He later reflected that if he had been more experienced, he would not have felt bound to follow the instructions from police and the Home Secretary. 'I never can understand', he wrote, 'why the then Home Secretary took executive charge of a situation requiring the most careful handling, as between the Police and the Fire Brigade.' When the brigade was eventually allowed to tackle the blaze, they approached initially from the rear and found that the rooms in the back extension were 'absolutely intact, not even filled with smoke'. But the front of the house was little more than a shell; the upper floors were burnt through and the flames were starting to spread to adjoining properties. In a long fire service career, Morris said it had been 'the only fire in London where I was able to watch the effects without any water going on, and it made me realize how quick and terrible a fire can be, even in a small street, if there is no Brigade to put water in at once.' It also made him ponder on the 'amazing bravery' of the two gunmen, even if they were 'brutal murderers'.[41]

But how did the fire start? According to C.C.B. Morris, the London Fire Brigade's considered view was that 'a gas pipe was punctured in one of the upper floors, and that the gas was lighted either at the time of the bullet piercing it or perhaps afterwards by a bullet causing a spark which ignited the escaping gas.'[42] It's also possible that the gunmen, exhausted and running low on ammunition, started the fire either as cover for an attempt to escape or as their funeral pyre. They 'had fought with a ferocity unequalled in the history of crime' and were 'not without a devilish kind of courage', in the words of a reporter on the scene.[43] They must have known that their chances of getting out alive were low.

Yet the possibility remains that the fire was started deliberately to bring an end to the siege, not least because the police were deeply anxious that the stand-off should not extend beyond sunset, which at that time of year would be at a little after four o'clock. Melville Macnaghten, assistant commissioner of the Metropolitan Police, was of the view that 'something desperate' would have to be done before darkness set in.[44] The issue was never subject to close scrutiny. The political attack on Churchill's handling of the shoot-out focused on his decision to be present. How the blaze started never greatly consumed wider attention, probably because public opinion would not have been too critical of police arson in the circumstances. Indeed, the police let it be known that they would have been willing to 'smoke out' the gunmen if absolutely necessary, but that it never came to that.[45] The determined insistence that the fire was not started deliberately by the police may well have been because any suggestion that the gunmen had been roasted alive might have encouraged revenge attacks by sympathizers of the dead men, so risking a cycle of bloody violence and cruel repression already being seen in other parts of Europe.

According to police officers on the scene, the fire took hold at the top of the building and then slowly consumed the lower floors.

The fire brigade trying to extinguish the flames at 100 Sidney Street.

Gunfire from the house continued as the flames grew more intense. Journalists at the scene reported that occasional shots from inside the besieged house continued until shortly after 1.30, more than six hours after the gunfire started; the police recorded that shooting persisted for even longer at the back of the house, which was out of view of press and public. 'The firing did not cease until the upper part of the house was entirely destroyed,' according to Superintendent Mulvany. 'The last firing was from the ground floor at the back.'[46] At a little after 2.15 p.m., a policeman kicked in the back door of the building. A dart of flame leapt out. The fire brigade could now start to train its hoses and extinguish the blaze. After a further half hour, firemen were able to enter the ground floor of the building. Most of the ceiling had fallen in and the building was unstable. A large piece of smouldering masonry, probably a hearthstone from an upper floor, fell as the building was being scoured for evidence, and injured five firemen. One of these men, District Officer Charles Pearson, suffered a fractured spine and partial paralysis and died from his injuries six months later; another fire officer was permanently disabled; a third was still receiving hospital treatment ten months later.

The bodies discovered in the burnt-out building were charred beyond recognition. A London Fire Brigade station officer said that as debris from the back room was being thrown into the yard, a 'bulky mass' was uncovered which he realized was human remains. 'There was no head. There appeared to be a stump of the neck and a bone of the arm protruding. Practically no clothes. No legs ... The body was in a half-upright position. I am therefore of the opinion that the body fell from one of the floors above.' Later in the day, as most of the debris had been cleared, a second body was found. 'There was no debris under it. The body practically laid on the floor,' another fireman deposed. 'I did not notice any head. I ... took hold of the right fore arm and a small piece about 6 inches long came away in my hand. There was no hand or wrist.' The absence of charred material under the body led him to believe that this man died where the body was found. Close to these remains, he came across a pistol; a second gun was found less than a metre away.[47]

Both were Mausers – the company's British agents later reported, having checked with the German manufacturers, that these guns had probably been supplied for retail sale in Finland.[48] Several days later a third automatic pistol, a Browning, was found amid the cinders. Other body parts were retrieved – six days after the shoot-out a police sergeant searching among the ashes found what he believed to be 'the fleshy part' of a thigh. He also found two keys. One of these opened the street door of Gardstein's lodging on Gold Street; the other was the key to 59 Grove Street. The police were initially convinced that one of the bodies was that of Peter the Painter.

A police surgeon, examining what was left of the two men, said the body that had apparently fallen from an upper floor was the first of the gunmen to die. Part of his skull had by then been retrieved, displaying a bullet wound that was the probable cause of death and which, given its position, would not have been self-inflicted. He also found evidence of an old fracture to a thigh bone that would have probably caused a limp, thus fitting the description of 'Joseph', or Sokoloff. The police surgeon told the inquest that as far as he could tell, and particularly going by the manner in which the tongue protruded from the mouth, the second man died by suffocation.[49] The jury came to the conclusion that this was Fritz Svaars, and that he had been suffocated by smoke during the fire. A verdict of justifiable homicide was recorded in both cases – and the jury added a rider recommending 'more stringent laws' to govern the entrance of 'criminal aliens' into Britain. 'The conduct of these two men is perhaps unparalleled in this country,' the coroner concluded. 'It seems impossible of explanation, except as an ample admission of their guilt of a capital crime, the despair of desperate men without hope.'[50]

The day after the shoot-out, Sidney Street became 'a sort of Mecca of the curious'. It was a continuation of the carnival. Crowds inspected the bullet marks; eyewitnesses, or those who claimed to have been present, rehearsed their accounts to anyone who showed an interest.

> Fashionable men and women drove up from the West-end. There was a long line of taxi-cabs outside Aldgate Station

Detectives and uniformed police in the bullet-pocked shell of 100 Sidney Street.

> ... City clerks, mothers and children from the suburbs, schoolboys ... but taking the day as a whole, the majority of the crowds were alien – every type of Jews, with Russians, Poles and Letts. They were intensely excited, jabbering in Yiddish and other tongues.[51]

The general view, of those in public life and on the streets of the East End, was that the two gunmen deserved their fate. There was little soul-searching about whether the men's lives could have been saved, or indeed over the finding that one of the men died from smoke inhalation. 'They are tigers and can only be treated as tigers,' thundered an editorial in the *Daily Mail*. 'Their character is not ours; they have no such respect for law and no such regard for humanity as is innate in almost every man of our race.'[52] But some voices were raised against the grain. Stepney's medical officer of health, Dr Danford Thomas – who was at the scene – was among the most outspoken. 'When you come to think of the matter it was really lynch law,' he commented. 'It seems extraordinary that, knowing the men were there, and were sure to be burned to death, no attempt was made even at the last moment to rescue them, or at any rate to put out the fire.'[53]

The cordoning of 100 Sidney Street succeeded, if only just, in avoiding police or civilian loss of life. Police, army and government joined forces in suggesting that the operation was a conspicuous success. The deployment of troops was clearly exceptional but – it was argued – so was the threat posed by desperadoes who cared little for their own lives and were armed with sophisticated weapons. While the gunmen were clearly both ruthless and reckless in their use of guns, they opened fire not at random but when they regarded themselves as cornered. But there was criticism of the decision to call in the army to deal with two armed robbers and some of it came from unexpected quarters. A newsletter issued by the Royal Irish Constabulary – a force which had borne the brunt of armed Fenianism – went in for the kill:

> Fifteen hundred armed policemen, two Companion of Guards, a Gattling [*sic*] Gun, and Mr Churchill, all engaged in attempting to capture a couple of common-place burglars whose motto was 'do not hesitate to shoot.' We have heard an immense amount of talk recently about the brave police of London, alleged to be the best force in the world. In this paltry affair they have cut a sorry figure ... The next time they find themselves suffering from funk in London, if they will send us a wireless message we promise to send

them a phalanx of Irish boys who will capture their men without firing a shot.[54]

The newsletter compounded the offence by suggesting that the London police 'turned a hose of scalding steam' on the house to disable the gunmen – for which there is no supporting evidence. The Royal Irish Constabulary was not noted for being a particularly gentle police force, but its bulletin made the barbed remark, 'It is not the duty of a police officer to inflict punishment.'

The Metropolitan Police took a different view. Melville Macnaghten, an assistant commissioner at the time of the siege, later harrumphed that he had no time for what he called 'irritating nonsense' from clergymen and others concerned that not enough was done to save the lives of the two gunmen:

> This is simply silly. The two men were wild beasts seeking to destroy, and it is the part, office and duty of police to turn the tables on all such dangers to humanity.
>
> I remember one hot weather in Bengal we suffered from an epidemic of mad dogs. Some I shot, some were clubbed to death by my servants: surely it mattered not how the end came so long as they were finished off somehow.[55]

The Eton-educated Englishman, who had spent sixteen years as a tea planter in India, seemed to be determined to kill off Latvian 'mad dogs' in whatever way he could.

Five days after the inquest, Svaars and Sokoloff – the latter still known only as Josef – were buried in the same cemetery as the two police sergeants who were shot dead at Houndsditch. The chaplain protested against being required to conduct a Christian committal service; the men in the coffins might also have been unhappy at that prospect. 'I have been chaplain here for twenty-five years come Lady-day,' the clergyman told a reporter from the *Daily Express*, 'but I would rather resign the post than perform the rites of the Church of England in such a case.' The two men were interred in an unmarked and unconsecrated section of the cemetery. The chaplain refused to say a prayer at the graveside and the only people present as the coffins were placed in a common grave were the undertaker's assistant and the gravediggers.[56]

8
'The Cossacks of Bourgeois Journalism'

The Home Office was so starved of news from Scotland Yard about the course of the shoot-out in Sidney Street that civil servants were obliged to turn to the evening papers. At eleven o'clock in the morning a senior official setting down by hand the latest information relied on a few column inches in the early edition of one of London's best-selling newspapers: 'It appears from the "Evening News" that the men "Fritz" + "Peter the Painter" have been located in a house off Commercial Road.' The civil servant also clipped and kept the article from the *Evening News*; it's usually the final edition of a newspaper that is held in the archive, so this is useful evidence of the first take of the story. 'SUPPOSED ASSASSINS AT BAY ... FUSILLADE OF REVOLVER SHOTS', ran the headline, and the report began, 'Over 700 police are surrounding a block of buildings situated immediately at the back of the Anarchist Club in Jubilee-street.'[1] The newspaper stated that 'revolver shots are being fired frequently and indiscriminately' and undermined the one hard piece of information received at the Home Office: that Sergeant Leeson had been shot dead. A jotting alongside the cutting confirmed that the police had been a little too hasty in writing off one of their own. A Home Office check with the London Hospital revealed that Leeson had been 'shot through [the] chest [but the injury was] "not dangerous"'.

The armed siege in the East End was one of a series of high-octane dramas that fuelled the growth of the popular press. The *Daily Mirror*'s publication on its front page in May 1910 of a photograph of King Edward VII on his deathbed, obtained through dubious means, led to record sales for a single edition of more than

2 million copies. Dr Crippen's arrest on board ship for the poisoning of his wife, and then his execution by hanging in the grounds of Pentonville Prison six weeks before the siege, caused a sensation, which the mass-circulation papers eagerly nourished. For exponents of a more urgent and image-led style of journalism, a news event with drama, crime, guns, anarchists and aliens was tailor-made. On top of that, the siege was just 5 kilometres (3 mi.) from Fleet Street and lasted long enough for journalists to get to the scene and witness some of the action.

The reporters who hurried down to the East End found whatever vantage point they could. Some, to judge by their copy, got access to rooms and attics from which Scots Guards and armed police were firing on the besieged house. Several found a more elevated, and rather safer, spot to look down on the action. Philip Gibbs was part of a posse of journalists on Sidney Street who decided to break the police cordon to make for the local pub – though not, on this occasion, for a drink:

> We were determined to see the drama out. It was more sensational than any 'movie' show. Immediately opposite was a tall gin palace – 'The Rising Sun'. Some strategist said, 'That's the place for us!' We raced across before the police could outflank us.
>
> A Jew publican stood in the doorway, sullenly.
> 'Whatcher want?' he asked.
> 'Your roof,' said one of the journalists.
> 'A quid each, and worth it,' said the Jew.
> ...Twenty of us, at least, gained access to the roof of 'The Rising Sun.'
>
> It was a good vantage point ... It looked right across to the house in Sidney Street in which Peter the Painter and his friends were defending themselves to the death – a tall, thin house of three stories [sic], with dirty window blinds.[2]

Other reporters gathered on the roof of another pub, the Three Compasses, at the northern end of Sidney Street. The popular press relied on a more vivid style of reporting – not simply description or analysis, but what it was like to be there. This more personalized style of reporting went hand in hand with the advent of the byline, so that news articles were not simply anonymous or by 'our correspondent' but were credited to a named reporter. This was still the exception rather than the rule, but the *Daily Express* on the morning after the siege had on-the-spot pieces from three bylined reporters.[3]

London's evening papers were the first to seek to introduce the 'new journalism' that had proved so successful – and profitable – in the United States. This took advantage of the invention of the Linotype press and the availability of cheap newsprint made from wood pulp, which together made possible the printing of hundreds of thousands of copies of a paper an hour. The halftone process of printing photographs allowed grainy but often starkly dramatic images to appear in the daily press, heralding the end of woodcut images, of staff engravers and – more gradually – of newspaper sketch artists. The popular press went for cheap cover prices, large advertisements and prominent headlines. Two other technological innovations, the typewriter and the telephone, also began to revolutionize how journalists worked. And an agenda that gave prominence to crime, sports and gossip gave a huge boost to circulation, as did a new generation of press barons.[4] Alfred Harmsworth (who became Lord Northcliffe in 1905 and later Viscount Northcliffe) began his career as a newspaper magnate when still in his twenties with his purchase in 1894 of the *Evening News*. The evening press was already ahead of the morning papers in 'enterprise, brightness and alertness', in the view of Kennedy Jones, the journalist Harmsworth brought in to edit the *Evening News*. 'The very first essential for an evening journalist is exceptional quickness – quickness of perception, quickness of decision, quickness of execution,' he declared.[5] The paper's coverage of Sidney Street reflected all those aptitudes. By 1911, the paper had a circulation of 300,000 and published five or six editions a day. And it made money.

For evening papers, a sensational news story that broke at breakfast time, too late for the morning titles, was an opportunity to achieve maximum impact and sales. There was keen competition between London's principal evening papers, which included, as well as the *Evening News*, the mass circulation *Evening Standard* and *The Star* and the more restrained *Pall Mall Gazette*. 'To-day London is the scene of sensational events unprecedented since the Gordon riots of 1780,' began the *Evening News* front-page story of its final edition, referring to week-long anti-Catholic riots which were eventually dispersed by the army with heavy loss of life.[6] The paper carried four photographs from Sidney Street on its inside pages. Both *The Star* and the *Evening Standard* managed to get photographs from the scene on the front page of their final editions.

If the *Evening News* was the advance guard of the new style of popular journalism, Harmsworth brought that to the morning papers with the launch of the *Daily Mail* in 1896. This also sold at a halfpenny and was 'Britain's first morning daily newspaper aimed squarely at the mass market'.[7] At the time of Sidney Street, the *Daily Mail* persisted with devoting its front page to advertisements – a custom *The Times* (which also became part of the Harmsworth empire) maintained until the 1960s – while its rival, the *Daily Express*, established in 1900, pioneered news on the front page with headlines designed to attract street sales. The *Daily Mail* devoted four richly illustrated inside pages to the siege the following day, including a breathless hour-by-hour account of the drama. By contrast, *The Times* put the story on page eight – its customary spot for breaking news – and carried no photographs.

Sidney Street came as the popular press was on the cusp of changing from artists' representations to illustrate news stories to reliance on photography, and not simply portraits but action photographs. The *Weekly Graphic* devoted the front page of its edition after the siege to a drawing of detectives shooting from an alleyway, which the paper declared was 'sketched on the spot from our special artist' – though the depiction of a shoot-out in the hours of darkness undermined this claim. Drawings often were clearer in reproduction on newsprint but they didn't have the immediacy and authenticity of the news photograph. William Hartley drew wonderful courtroom drawings of some of the Houndsditch defendants and witnesses, but the pendulum was swinging away from artists' sketches.[8] And an older style of line drawing – which made no pretence of being drawn from life but was a re-creation, usually of a crime scene – was beginning to feel dated. The weekly *Illustrated Police News* gave over its front page after the Houndsditch killings to a highly stylized drawing of 'one of the gang found dying by the police in an East-End garret'. Not only was the artwork a throwback to Victorian melodrama, but the information was unreliable – Gardstein had been dead for several hours before police came across his body.

Daily Mirror front page, 4 January 1911.

The most ardent British exponent of the use of the news photograph was the *Daily Mirror*, which Harmsworth had launched in 1903. Under his proprietorship, the paper developed the dictum, according to its editor, Alexander Kenealy, 'Give it hot, give it strong, and give a lot of it.' The first edition of the revamped paper under Harmsworth's ownership declared, 'The Daily Mirror is the first illustrated halfpenny paper in the history of journalism... Our pictures do not merely accompany the printed news. They are a valuable help to the understanding of it.'[9] On the morning after Sidney Street, the *Daily Mirror* published twenty photographs from or about Sidney Street, along with a drawing and a map. The front page was given over to a photograph of two Scots Guards lying prone on the cobbled surface of Sidney Street and directing their rifles towards the besieged building. While the definition in the image was poor, the reader was helped with labels: 'window from which burglars fired', 'police fired from these windows', and a vague – and perhaps enhanced – silhouette on the other side of the no man's land was helpfully labelled 'armed police'. The coverage spread over ten pages. It was a visual feeding frenzy.

The more established titles held their own, however, when it came to scoops. A *Daily Telegraph* reporter by the name of Ashmead-Bartlett managed to get into the house next to 100 Sidney Street once the blaze was extinguished. There he found Rebecca Fleishman, whose family were the principal occupants of the besieged house, 'practically in a state of hysterics', and escorted her to his home in West London. 'A young gentleman took me away,' Mrs Fleishman later recounted, perhaps somewhat disingenuously; 'he did not tell me where he was taking me. I was taken there naked, that is to say, I only had a skirt on me and a coat.' Once at a distance from the maelstrom, and apparently encouraged by her brother, she related to the reporter a tale which took up a full two columns of the paper. As well as a detailed account of the inception of the stand-off, Mrs Fleishman recounted innuendo-laden tittle-tattle about her tenant, Betsy Gershon, in whose room the two gunmen had taken refuge: Gershon's husband had left her; she wore a wedding ring when she rented the room but had ever since left it off; she was visited by 'a tall dark man with big moustaches'; she 'professed' to be a dressmaker. Fleishman also voiced suspicions that her tenant was an anarchist and an atheist. The *Daily Telegraph* had outflanked the police in getting, and publishing, evidence from a crucial eyewitness.[10]

The competitiveness between titles led to the reporting as fact of news that was wrong: that Peter the Painter was undoubtedly in 100 Sidney Street and had perished in the flames; that the two men who died had turned their guns on themselves. Some of the errors – perhaps arising from conversations with over-excited police officers, but howlers all the same – are almost comical. Several papers reported prominently that 'bombs' had been found in debris at 'the anarchists' fort' at 100 Sidney Street. They had to recant a few days later and explain that these were metal cylinders used for stamping out serrated leather buttons. The most bizarre editorial misstep was in the *Daily Mirror*, which published a grainy photograph of a door, explaining that this was 'a secret door' in the back wall of the anarchists' club on Jubilee Street 'through which the assassins escaped before the battle of Sidney-street'. From the back of the club to the rear of Sidney Street would have been little more than a hundred yards, but there were buildings in the way and there was never any suggestion of anyone moving directly from one to the other, not least because the club has closed down several weeks before the siege. Three days later the *Mirror* acknowledged that the picture was 'of merely an ordinary door' exposed during renovation work at the former club.[11]

Within four days of the siege, the publishers of the *Daily Chronicle* published a sixteen-page special titled *The Battle with the London Anarchists*, published using cheap newsprint and selling at a penny. This declared itself to be the 'only complete account of the Houndsditch Tragedies and the Historic Siege of Foreign Anarchists in the East End of London'. It included fifty or so photographs from the siege, portrait photographs and drawings, along with a detailed account largely based on the paper's reporting. It told the story of 'the most melodramatic series of crimes that have ever taken place in the history of London': 'No sensational novelist, no storywriter of crimes and adventures, has ever imagined a tale of anarchy, crime and bloodshed, so thrilling, so wild in its incident, as this amazing affair that has happened in the heart of London.'[12]

This was sensational journalism at its potboiling best (or worst). Publishers found other ways of making money out of the incident. It came during the heyday of the topical postcard. Before the

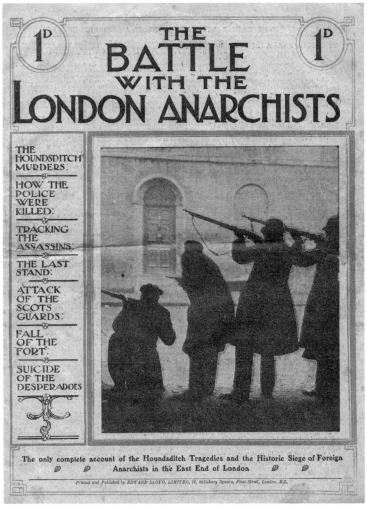

The hastily put together penny pamphlet issued by the *Daily Chronicle* group on 7 January 1911.

widespread use of telephones, the postcard with a halfpenny stamp was the customary means of conveying a short message, especially locally at a time when towns and cities had several postal deliveries a day. Postcards featuring photographs of Winston Churchill in Sidney Street, of Scots Guards on the street taking aim and of the 'anarchists' house' on fire, images which had already appeared in the daily papers, sold in tens of thousands and were often kept as souvenirs. Among them was an image that has become iconic: Churchill peering towards the action, flanked by Scots Guards and armed police, while on the low roof just above him is a youngster looking directly at the camera smiling and, by the look of it, waving.

The papers faced competition from a new medium for which the shoot-out in Stepney ushered in the era of the action newsreel shown in cinemas within hours. The newspaper reporter Philip Gibbs was struck to see, while covering the siege, a 'cinematograph operator, standing well inside Sidney Street . . . winding his handle vigorously, quite oblivious of the whiz of bullets'.[13] As many as five competing newsreel companies – Andrews, British Pathé, Gaumont, Warwick and Cooperative (which had hitherto specialized in Shakespeare productions) – were able to get to the scene. The film taken by the three of these fledgling film producers survives, amounting to a little over fifteen minutes of footage. Their images were shaky and at times blurred, and of course the newsreels were silent and in black and white, but they conveyed the drama of what the British Film Institute (BFI) describes as 'still one of the most spectacular events ever captured on film'.[14]

The competing newsreel companies displayed different strengths, down in large part to the ability of the camera operator to get the best vantage points. Gaumont was particularly successful in getting film of repeated puffs of smoke or debris, demonstrating the vigour of the exchange of gunfire across Sidney Street. It also secured telling shots of the determination with which the police, many of them wearing capes, pushed back the crowd of exuberant onlookers. Pathé got a scoop in capturing footage of Winston Churchill looking on from a street corner, talking animatedly, gesticulating and then walking determinedly out of shot, apparently towards the scene of the

Widely circulated postcard depicting Winston Churchill at Sidney Street.

siege. It also filmed a Scots Guard taking aim with a rifle and, more remarkably, a man in a bowler hat, probably a police detective, appearing from a back yard entrance and raising his revolver as if to open fire. Pathé also got dramatic footage of mounted soldiers riding along one of London's main roads, with a tram heading in the opposite direction, taking field artillery to Stepney. Andrews's film operator managed to join some of the print journalists on the roof of the Rising Sun, a particularly good spot to film the spread of the smoke and flames that engulfed 100 Sidney Street and the belated attempts of firemen to stem the blaze. All the footage reflected the huge throng that crowded as close as they could get to the scene of the action: a press of bodies, mainly men, in exuberant mood – some holding up children so the youngsters could get a view; small groups of young women wearing their best hats; crowds surrounding the horse-drawn fire tenders and gathering round as injured firemen were carried out of the charred site of the siege; women and children standing at doorways, more excited than anxious, some covering their head with a shawl; clusters of onlookers at windows and on balconies. One shot depicted a photographer with a substantial handheld camera taking photographs of the crowd – one section of the news media keeping tabs on another. It's a visual record that would have been unthinkable even a few months earlier.[15]

The newsreel originated in France and was introduced to Britain in the summer of 1910. Initially, a reel taking a few minutes to screen was part of a varied cinematic bill in theatres. Within a few years, it developed a settled format of four to six topical stories covered in about five minutes and issued twice a week to match the routine change in the cinema programme.[16] Sidney Street was rare in being an action story, rather than a planned event, which was in reach of the cameras – perhaps the first big breaking-news story to be captured on film in this way. The newsreel companies gave their short films titles such as *The Great East End Anarchist Battle* and *Battle of London* and they showed urgency and initiative in getting the film to an eager audience. The footage was shown that same day in both the matinee and evening shows at the Coliseum and in the evening performances of two other central London theatres. 'Cinematograph pictures containing every detail of the battle were being shown even as far away as Richmond before five o'clock in the afternoon,' the *Daily Express* reported.[17] Edward Marsh, Churchill's private secretary, was astonished – and thrilled – to see himself in a newsreel showing at the Palace Theatre just off Shaftesbury Avenue:

> I make a most gratifying appearance as almost the central figure of 'Mr. Churchill directing the operations', at the Palace, which is nightly received with unanimous boos and shouts of 'shoot him' from the gallery – why are the London music-hall audiences so uniformly and so bigotedly Tory? you would have thought a stray Liberal must occasionally find his way in by accident – but it seems not.[18]

The story was told that audiences, when seeing Churchill on screen, would shout, 'Oo let 'em in!' – referring both to the Liberal government's perceived laxity in regulating immigration and Churchill's personal opposition to the Aliens Act brought in by a Conservative government in 1905. That may have been an accurate reflection of music hall sentiment, but the tale was probably apocryphal.[19]

The media response to the Houndsditch police killings included some of the most grievous antisemitism to appear in the mainstream press. A Sunday newspaper, *The People*, was the worst offender. It carried a cartoon showing a swarm of rats with semitic features and labelled 'Undesirable Alien' who had been told to 'Clear Out' of other countries making their way unimpeded into the UK through the gaps in a barred gate bearing the words 'Aliens Act'. The cartoonist was Edward Huskinson, editor of the society magazine *The Tatler*.[20] The same edition of *The People* carried a scurrilous piece of doggerel, 'The Lessons of Houndsditch', which read, in part,

> Have we forgotten Tottenham? I pointed the moral then
> That the country ought to be rid at once and for all
>   of the dangerous men,

'England for the Alien!', *The People*, 25 December 1910.

Nothing was done to clear them out; we let the demons stay,
And – three heroes are lying in their graves who might have
    lived today.

We may catch the murderers or may not. If we do I only
    hope
We shan't turn sickly and plead that they may escape
    the hangman's rope.
I only wish we could lash them first, for the villains all
    fear pain,
And hang them later to make quite sure that they couldn't
    offend again.

But I think it's time to plead once more to get rid of
    the cursed breed
Of Alien Jews who seem to have been the authors of
    the deed.
Remember Tottenham! Foreign Jews were the coward
    murderers there,
And it's pretty certain that aliens held the guns on
    the Houndsditch stair.

What's the good of an Alien's Act, when we let the
    alien scum
Swarm into England in droves and herd in every city slum.
I would give them all – aye, rich and poor – one day, not
    a moment more,
To clear out, and hang them if they were found again
    on British shore.[21]

Both cartoon and verse seem designed to normalize a particularly virulent form of anti-Jewish prejudice.

This crude racism was accompanied by a vilification of anarchism and anarchists, which made no distinction between the small number of desperadoes and gunmen who claimed some allegiance to anarchism and the much larger number who deplored such violence and expressed their criticism of government and society more temperately. Within the East End Yiddish-speaking anarchist movement – who felt scapegoated as Jews, as immigrants and as anarchists – there was resentment at the manner in which the press represented all anarchists as would-be killers. In the aftermath of the Houndsditch shootings, and before the Sidney Street siege produced an even louder crescendo of virulent and sensationalist journalism, the *Arbayter Fraynd* or 'Worker's Friend' – London's main Yiddish anarchist weekly – published a forceful criticism of the press coverage. The article drew a striking comparison with the Cossack troops, which were renowned as brutal suppressors of revolutionary movements across the Russian Empire:

> It is impossible to describe briefly all the lies, allegations and calumnies that the Cossacks of bourgeois journalism have tossed around . . . about the foreign anarchists in general and about the Arbayter Fraynd Club in particular . . .
>
> But there is no doubt that the real source of the absurd and silly allegations is the political police, and that the highly developed bourgeois reporter-factory provided the prescribed tone for the credulous reader.[22]

There is no doubt that anarchists were themselves partly responsible for their bad press: some activists had carried out bombings, shootings and stabbings in several European countries and further afield that were designed to outrage and scare those with power and wealth, and the Latvian expropriators in London had banded together as anarchists even if they were outlaws as much as ideologues. Practitioners of propaganda by the deed, of course, relied on 'the Cossacks of bourgeois journalism' to spread word of their actions and to disseminate a sense of alarm and terror. But the *Arbayter Fraynd* article had a point: much of the press coverage of Houndsditch and Sidney Street sought simply to condemn rather than to report and explain.

Alongside the racism and the xenophobia displayed by some sections of the popular press was a determination by some papers to investigate rather than castigate. The writer and reporter Philip Gibbs was among the more adventurous. Along with his colleague J. P. Eddy, he sought lodgings in the house on Grove Street where Gardstein had died but they were, unsurprisingly, rebuffed. They then found rooms in the home of a master tailor at 62 Sidney Street, and used that as a base to explore, and write about, the Jewish East End. Gibbs's articles in the *Daily Chronicle* appeared under the title 'Among the Aliens'. He came across the anarchist club, now meeting in a Russian hotel in Whitechapel, where Rudolf Rocker was addressing those assembled. In a hotel bathroom he was given a basic introduction to anarchism by 'a well-dressed, rather good-looking and pleasant-eyed lady' he named as 'Mrs Rocca' – that is, Milly Witcop, Rudolf Rocker's partner:

> She spoke English perfectly, and in the presence of half a dozen men who crowded in to listen, we had an argument lasting at least an hour, on the subject of anarchy. She began by disclaiming, for the anarchists in London, all knowledge of and responsibility for the affair of Peter the Painter and his associates. They were merely common thieves. But it was laughable, she thought, what a panic fear had been caused in middle-class London by the killing of a policeman or two ... Why all that agitation over the deaths of two guardians of property, when there was no agitation at all, no public outcry, no fierce clamour for vengeance, because every night men and women of the toiling classes were being killed by the inhuman conditions of their lives, in foul slums, in over-crowded bedrooms, in poisonous trades, in sweated industries, as the helpless slaves of that capitalistic system which protected itself by armies of police? The English people were the world's worst hypocrites. They hid a putrid mass of suffering, corruption, and disease, caused by modern industrialism, and pretended that it did not exist.

Gibbs conceded that he was 'hopelessly outargued by this brilliant, extraordinary, and dangerous woman'.[23]

The distinctly old-school and right-of-centre *Morning Post* conducted a more formal interview with Rudolf Rocker, discovering not a 'wild revolutionary' but 'a man in [his] forties, intelligent and mild mannered'. Rocker was pleasantly surprised that his views about incidents such as the Houndsditch shootings were reported fully and accurately:

> I have no hesitation in saying that the present situation in Russia is directly responsible for these crimes. There is no freedom for the Press in Russia, no freedom for the workmen to combine. Some Russians become desperadoes through circumstances. They have no respect for human life – no respect for their own lives, in fact. Most of them are Letts [Latvians]. In the Baltic provinces the reaction was more extreme than in other parts of Russia.[24]

The Times also cited the views of Rocker and his colleagues in a tolerably well-informed, if unsympathetic, account of the anarchist movement in London. This explained anarchism's espousal of revolt and highlighted a more recent turning of the tide against 'expropriation' as anarchists 'found that their ranks were being filled by thieves, who stole for their own benefit'.[25] The paper also gave space to a long letter critical of the newspaper's reporting from an avowed anarchist, the pseudonymous John Pagan, who complained of the 'malicious misrepresentation of a humane ideal, an ideal worthy of our consideration and respect'.[26] This was journalism providing a platform for cogent and relevant voices normally excluded from the public sphere.

The Times was also one of several papers that offered expert analysis of the repression in tsarist Russia and the plight of the Baltic provinces in particular. On the morning after the Stepney siege, it published a well-informed account of the political impact of two waves of migration from Latvia and neighbouring areas: the first, after the outbreak of the Russo-Japanese War in 1904, was of young men seeking to avoid conscription; the second, three or four years later, was of revolutionaries who, after a period of violence and disorder, fled the newly assertive tsarist authorities:

> When one considers the record of the Anarchist groups in Russia during the two or three years of open disorder, little wonder remains that they should give us some taste of their quality when permitted to settle here. Their crimes could only by the broadest stretching of terms be called political. They robbed banks; they levied wholesale blackmail; they murdered freely.

The article also offered an antidote to those demanding suppression of the anarchist movement. 'The Anarchist club is not a centre of danger. It is rather a useful spot in which the men of the movement can be found. The real peril comes from the groups that work apart from any centre.'[27]

Newspaper editorials and the overall slant of the reporting argued that the Aliens Act needed to be revised to make it more effective in excluding, or deporting, migrants regarded as undesirable, and in particular those with a propensity to crime or the use of guns. 'If fresh proof were needed that the time has come to exclude the foreign Anarchist and criminal from our midst it is here in this disgraceful record of this Houndsditch gang,' the *Daily Mail* argued. 'The ordinary British criminal is rarely or never a wanton murderer or a bloodthirsty miscreant. If he is caught at his trade by the police he surrenders with a fair grace and cherishes no malice. But these foreign desperadoes stick at nothing.'[28] It's one of the few occasions when the popular press championed the 'ordinary' British robber.

The 1905 Aliens Act, complained the *Daily Express* the day after Sidney Street, was 'lamentably weak and insufficient'. The paper instituted a campaign for legal redress. The next day it complained that criminal aliens could evade the working of the Aliens Act by travelling to Britain in a small ship or paying for other than the cheapest tickets:

> These absurdities must now be swept away, and we must have an Aliens Act which really will prevent the landing of notorious Anarchists, determined criminals, miserable paupers, and diseased persons. No sane conception of

hospitality or freedom can contemplate the right of refuge for foreigners who are, or who may become, a peril to the community of Britons.[29]

It returned to the theme for a third successive day, asserting that 'our shores will not really be safe until we follow the example of our neighbours and institute the passport system.'[30]

The demand for stronger regulation of immigration extended to the establishment press. The *Daily Telegraph* commented that the 1905 Act 'may prevent the dumping of some human refuse, but not the importation of Anarchist ruffianism' and it had in any event been administered with 'culpable laxity'. The paper believed that the 'impression upon public opinion has been so grave, the demand for action is so imperative, that we have little fear this time of an official attitude of perplexed procrastination ending in mere futility'.[31] Some Conservative politicians expressed themselves more bluntly, and there was a clamour for legislative action. Stepney Borough Council called for a more restrictive Aliens Act and for immigrants to be registered for five years after their arrival. The mover of the resolution lamented that Stepney had been 'inundated by people who had been called the scum of Europe'. Several other London borough councils backed this appeal.[32]

One of the few media voices to urge caution was the *Jewish Chronicle*, which argued that the root of the issue lay in 'Russian barbarism' and misgovernment. 'The heart of the alien problem in London lies in the Government offices in St Petersburg and in those of the provincial satraps. The way to protect the lives of the London police is to exert influence for the prevention of the brutalising of Russian men.' It warned that hasty legislation to restrict alien immigration wouldn't stop political violence:

> There was no ring which the law could place round the United Kingdom through which a Russian anarchist could not find a loop-hole of admission. If any sort of amendment, strengthening, or extension of the Aliens Act would, with any certainty, keep out of this country alien criminals

and really undesirable immigrants – Jews or non-Jews – we would urge it in the best interests of the class of aliens whose freedom of entry into this country we wish so ardently to see maintained.[33]

Whatever the intellectual force of that argument, it was overwhelmed by the drumbeat of demands for something to be done.

The pressure for stricter immigration rules was made greater by a series of observations and recommendations by coroners and inquest juries. Two years earlier the foreman of the inquest jury into the policeman and schoolboy killed in Tottenham stated that

> it was an inconceivable scandal that any Government should allow these criminals into this country ... They earnestly beseeched the ministers in power to take such steps as would remove from Great Britain the odium and stigma of being the last asylum and refuse [sic] of these criminal desperadoes of the Continent.[34]

The shootings in the East End prompted a flurry of similarly strongly worded pleas for tougher regulation. The City coroner conducting the inquest into the death of one of the police sergeants shot at Houndsditch stated that 'the present Aliens Act (1905) fails absolutely so far as the exclusion of criminal aliens is concerned.' He urged a system of registration, fingerprinting and compulsory personal reporting of new immigrants, a complete ban on aliens possessing 'deadly weapons' and stiffer penalties – perhaps including flogging – for anyone (alien or otherwise) possessing such weapons while committing a serious criminal offence.[35] A few weeks later, the inquest jury into the deaths of the two gunmen at Sidney Street also recorded the hope 'that this occurrence may be the means of more stringent laws being passed to govern the entry of criminal aliens into this country'.[36]

H. H. Asquith's government was already beleaguered by a series of crises to which it had failed to give an adequate response. These included the stridency of the campaign for women's suffrage, a more militant and syndicalist-inflected trade union movement and increasing political polarization across Ireland. On top of that, two general elections were held in 1910 – the only other year that has happened is 1974 – on the issue of 'peers versus people', after the House of Lords blocked Lloyd George's 'People's Budget', which proposed higher taxes on the wealthy and the introduction of a tax on land. The second of those elections jostled for prominence on the front pages alongside news of the Houndsditch shootings. Asquith's government was twice re-elected, but only just, losing its previously ample majority.

British Liberalism was strongly committed to the right of asylum for political refugees and to a tolerant attitude towards immigrants escaping political or religious oppression. The government didn't want to be stampeded by the popular press into restrictive legislation, but it had emerged weakened from the twin elections of 1910 and so couldn't simply stonewall in the face of a chorus of criticism. Winston Churchill's initial response on the day of the Sidney Street siege was that a fresh look at immigration legislation might be required. 'I think I will have to stiffen the administration and the Aliens Act a little,' he told the Prime Minister, 'and more effective measures must be taken by the police to supervise the dangerous classes of aliens in our midst.'[37] Writing two days after the shoot-out, Edward Marsh, Churchill's private secretary, confided, 'I expect Winston will bring in a pistol Bill, which seems a better way of dealing with the crux than trying to stiffen up the Aliens Act. The criminal aliens seem to be just the ones who have the money.'[38] Something needed to be done, but nothing too draconian.

Churchill briefly gave consideration to introducing legislation that would have been deeply illiberal, including an attempt to find a way of excluding criminal aliens before they had committed a crime. But the bill he introduced in the spring of 1911, the Aliens (Prevention of Crime) Bill, was a modest measure which, among other things, required alien immigrants to have a licence to own a pistol and increased the penalties for illegal immigration. The government also offered qualified support to a much more restrictive private member's bill brought in by a Conservative MP which proposed mandatory registration of alien immigrants and removed the exemption for ships carrying fewer than twenty steerage-class migrants. Both measures faced opposition from backbench Liberal MPs and Labour parliamentarians. The bills never emerged from their Parliamentary committee stage; they were not so much rejected as crowded out by more pressing matters.[39] Whether the failure of this proposed legislation was – from the government's point of view – by chance or design is difficult to say; probably a bit of both. The pressure for action on immigration had begun to abate, and Churchill was preoccupied by a wave of industrial unrest which led him to deploy troops in Liverpool. In October 1911 he was appointed First Lord of the Admiralty and immigration law was no longer his problem or indeed a priority for the government. The Tottenham, Houndsditch and Sidney Street shootings, for all the noisy demands of the popular press, coroners and Conservative politicians, led to no fresh legislation to restrict immigration or limit the right of asylum.

The introduction of tougher immigration rules had, however, been delayed rather than stopped. A day after war was declared in August 1914, Parliament passed the Aliens Restriction Act requiring foreign nationals to register with the police and providing in some instances for the power to intern and to deport. This measure was aimed at Germans and other nationals of enemy countries, but it was applicable to all foreigners residing in the United Kingdom (though not to those from Ireland or from British colonies). While war was the catalyst for this more rigorous legislative approach, the earlier furore over immigrant anarchists and criminals helped to prepare the ground. The regime this legislation established was continued after the war. The 1919 Aliens Restriction (Amendment) Act, which among other things replaced the 1905 Act, continued the requirement for foreign nationals to register with the local police and introduced penalties for incitement to sedition and for promoting industrial unrest. The following year the Passports Service was established in Britain as part of an international initiative to introduce standardized travel documents to monitor and regulate the movement of people. The era of relatively unhindered travel across international borders was over.

9
Acquitted

The scoresheet of the legal proceedings against those accused of involvement in the Houndsditch murders was, from the police's point of view, dismal. Eight people were charged; the cases against four defendants were dropped before the Old Bailey trial; the most serious charges were abandoned during the trial; all but one of the defendants were acquitted of all charges; and the one conviction, for a relatively minor offence, was promptly overturned on appeal. Not a single enduring guilty verdict was achieved. No one was convicted of responsibility for the most grievous loss of police life in London's history. It was, in the judgement of a London evening paper, a 'fiasco'.[1]

This was mainly because those most likely to have fired the fatal shots – Gardstein, Svaars and Sokoloff – were dead, and their most wanted co-conspirators, notably Max Smoller and Peter the Painter, evaded arrest. But it was also a reflection on the case the prosecution put together and the difficulties the police faced in lining up credible witnesses. The 'chief trouble' was 'not so much to know who had been concerned as to get legal evidence against them', lamented Detective Inspector Fred Wensley of the Metropolitan Police:

> Among the crowd of foreigners from whom we were driven to seek information was the usual number who professed to know a great deal. Their news, when sifted, was proved to be either nothing but pure imagination or exaggeration of unreliable gossip that had grown as it has passed from mouth to mouth. This class gave endless work and trouble. Then there were others who might have been helpful

– tradespeople and immediate neighbours – but who were afraid of the likely consequences to themselves if it became known that they had aided us. A third group were those more closely associated with the suspects as friends or acquaintances – usually compatriots who were unwilling to help against their fellow countrymen.

Whatever the varying motive of these people, they could seldom be pinned down and held to a statement. They were liable to trade on their ignorance of the English language. They would either assert that they had not understood a question or that we had misconstrued an answer.

Wensley even surmised that if the two men who died at Sidney Street 'had been captured in different circumstances without arms in their hands, it is probable that they would have been acquitted'.[2]

Fred Wensley's recollection carries more weight than other police reminiscences. He was one of the key detectives in the Houndsditch investigation, a considerable figure who went on to enjoy a nationwide reputation. And the East End was his manor. At the time of the Sidney Street siege, he and his family lived just a couple of minutes' walk away in the backstreets of Stepney and he had even picked up a smattering of Yiddish.[3] He mused that on his way home, he may have unknowingly walked past the house where some of the gang were hiding. With his daughter's help, Wensley kept a meticulous cuttings scrapbook of all the cases he had cracked in the East End: murders, knifings, rapes, robberies, sex trafficking, gang violence, protection rackets, unlicensed clubs. He kept a close eye on local organized crime; Arthur Harding, one of the East End's most persistent offenders, regarded 'Weasel' Wensley as his main adversary.[4]

Wensley's complaint of unhelpful witnesses had some justification, but it was also true of many of the cases in the East End in which he managed to secure convictions. The Houndsditch prosecutions were blighted by other problems: the police didn't seem to be sure themselves who among the gang did what and where; they weren't clear who was in the gang and who was a friend or hanger-on; and above all, they didn't have reliable identification evidence to support the charges they decided to pursue. As a result, the prosecution case arising from the police killings was in perpetual retreat.

Police coordination wasn't helped by rivalry between London's two forces. The City of London, the square mile that constitutes the financial district, had (and has) its own police force, which was not answerable to the much larger Metropolitan Police. Houndsditch was, in the words of one of the police officers involved, a 'small and squalid section of the East End', but it lay just within the City; Sidney Street was in Met territory. The two forces had separate chains of command, but on such a high-profile case the City Police knew it needed to rely on the expertise and resources of its vastly bigger neighbouring force. Fred Wensley and his Met colleagues, with their intimate knowledge of the East End, were brought into the Houndsditch investigation from the start. But Wensley also became embroiled in another landmark case in London's criminal annals – and one which impinged on the police murders.

On the morning of New Year's Day 1911 – two weeks after the Houndsditch shootings and two days before the Sidney Street drama – the body of Leon Beron was found in bushes on Clapham Common. The dead man was a Jewish migrant from Eastern Europe who lived in Jubilee Street just a few doors from the anarchist club and owned and rented out several insalubrious properties in Stepney. He had been bludgeoned and stabbed to death and his wallet was empty. The case attracted huge attention and banner headlines. The police believed that Beron had been lured to his death by Steinie Morrison, another East End Jewish migrant, tall and elegant, and a thief. Both Beron and Morrison patronized the Warsaw restaurant at the bottom end of Brick Lane, where Gardstein and his friends were also said to gather. At the trial, a defence witness suggested that Beron was a police informant who had been killed to prevent him from 'grassing' on the Houndsditch killers. Gashes on both of Beron's cheeks were said to be the letter 'S', denoting the Polish word for spy. Neither judge nor jury was swayed. Morrison was convicted of murder and sentenced to death, though the Home Secretary, Winston Churchill, commuted the sentence to life imprisonment. Morrison continued to protest his innocence and staged several hunger strikes, which probably contributed to his early death in jail ten years later. While there is strong evidence that Morrison was involved in Beron's murder, he is unlikely to have wielded the murder weapon.

Leon Beron was reputed to be a 'fence', a dealer in stolen goods, and there has been much speculation over the decades that he was used by the Latvians to sell on any items they stole and had been primed to receive the jewellery from Harris's safe in Houndsditch. While the coincidences of timing and location are remarkable, there's no firm evidence of a link between Houndsditch and the Clapham Common murder. Beron and Morrison were certainly not political émigrés. Wensley and his fellow police officers were convinced the two crimes were not connected, and they were probably right.

While the City and Met police worked together well, there was a point of tension in the Houndsditch investigation. The City of London Police were adamant from the start that the perpetrators were anarchists acting out of motives that were in part political. The poster bearing Gardstein's mortuary photograph issued by the City Police six days after the shootings was explicit that the two wanted men, Fritz Svaars and Peter the Painter, were 'both anarchists'. The Commissioner of the City of London Police, William Nott-Bower, stuck to this line in his memoirs, saying that those responsible for the police murders were an 'armed gang of Russian Anarchist Burglars'.[5] The Metropolitan Police, however, was reluctant to accept that the crime was in any sense political. This may have been in part so that any moves to deport suspects were not snagged on the continuing right of asylum. It was also because of the implication that the Met's Special Branch, the only police unit responsible for political surveillance, may have failed in its purpose of preventing political violence. This lay behind a circumlocutory letter from Melville Macnaghten, the Metropolitan Police assistant commissioner responsible for Special Branch, to the head of the City Police. It was prompted by translations of letters and pamphlets seized during the Houndsditch investigation that made reference to

Liesma, the Latvian anarchist group with which many of the gang were associated.

> The so-called 'Leesma' (Flame) group of Letts [Latvians], according to our information, came into existence within the past two years and consisted of eight or nine members. They had no regular place of meeting and were almost unknown to members of the recognised Groups. None of the persons concerned in the Houndsditch crimes were known as Anarchists although some of them frequented Jubilee Street and other meeting places. They appear to have formed part of a section of foreign criminals who used the term 'Anarchy' to cover their otherwise nefarious callings. Their real object, it would appear, was not the furtherance of an anarchical movement or conspiracy, but plunder and robbery for personal gain.
>
> The Houndsditch crimes have been repudiated by Anarchists, and persons competent to speak for the anarchist movement in this Country, and I cannot find that there has been any expression of sympathy with the murderers from Anarchists here, or from the Chief Anarchist centres on the Continent.[6]

Macnaghten was covering his own back, and none too convincingly – while also suggesting that the Metropolitan Police had been keeping tabs on the Liesma group even though they weren't anarchists.

Whatever Special Branch files there were about those suspected of the Houndsditch murders haven't survived. And there's no echo of the outcome of any covert surveillance in the City of London Police records – with one exception. A Met police officer, Edward Searle, wrote by hand a letter to a friend and fellow policeman whom he addressed as 'Old Jim'. The recipient appears to have been PC James Martin, one of the City of London force present at the shootings. Searle had served with the Met in Whitechapel for seven years but transferred to Peckham just three months before the Houndsditch shootings. He was prompted to write because of likenesses published in the press of those sought in connection with the murders. He thought he recognized one of the men as a regular speaker at open-air political meetings at Philpott Street in Stepney. 'I used to attend all these meetings and report on them as I had a fair knowledge of the Yiddish,' Searle wrote. '[S]ome of his speeches, I expect, are recorded at Scotland Yard.' He was clearly worried about being indiscreet, stating, 'Now Jim I <u>do not want your people to let our people know</u> I have written to you re these people' – though the recipient could pass on word to his 'chief'.[7] Martin must have done so – for otherwise how could a private letter have ended up in the police archive – though to what effect we don't know. It confirms that the police took some trouble to keep an eye, and an ear, on at least some East End anarchists.

THE BULK OF the police work was chasing leads in the East End and across London, but the suspects were all fairly recent migrants to Britain. Police forces in other parts of Europe knew much more about some of those involved in the Houndsditch robbery attempt than the two London police forces leading the investigation. The informal links already in place with overseas police forces were activated to try to secure leads, information, names and photographs. There were political and diplomatic sensitivities to consider. The Home Office turned down an offer from the head of the detective department in Riga, the Latvian capital, to come to London to assist in the search for the murderers. The Metropolitan Police believed that such a visit 'would prove embarrassing and would be unlikely to lead to any useful results'. A visit from a senior police official in a force accused of torture and worse and from a country that was a byword for autocracy and repression was deemed unacceptable. But the British government made clear that it was eager for less visible collaboration.[8] A month after the Houndsditch shootings, the British consul in Riga passed on to London four photographs supplied by the police in Latvia. They depicted Latvian revolutionaries, several of whom were, or had been, in London.[9]

The London police turned for assistance to the police force in the Russian capital, St Petersburg, and received tip-offs from

Russian officials in Paris, where the Okhrana, the tsarist secret police, had one of its biggest foreign offices. The most useful tie-up was with the police in the French port city of Marseilles. By 13 January, the London police had assembled details of where Peter the Painter had once stayed in Marseilles which they sent on to the police there. A week later, the Marseilles police responded with information and, more valuably, two photographs of Peter the Painter. By the end of the month, these were on 'wanted' posters widely distributed by the City of London Police, with prominent mention of a £500 reward on offer. The photographs – showing a well-dressed and well-presented young man, with suit, tie and wing collar, neatly cut hair and carefully curled moustache – remain the defining images of one of London's most celebrated anti-heroes.

The police also enlisted the help of the imperial Russian consulate in London, especially for translation. That, of course, was as good as sharing information with the Okhrana. The police also had some access to the Russian network in London of informers and secret agents, which was probably more extensive than any contacts Special Branch might have developed. There are just occasional glimpses of this concealed world in the police archive. Take this terse and curious letter, marked 'confidential', from the Russian Consul General to Police Superintendent Ottaway at the end of January 1911:

> I received from that gentleman, whom I introduced to you, when he was in London, a letter asking me to tell you that any direct relations of the Police with that other gentleman, whom you know, must be stopped. Therefore I should be very much obliged if you would arrange that no direct intercourse of that sort would take place. That person must not call upon you or at the Police Station and no Police Officer should call upon him. The only way would be to arrange interviews at public places, like railway stations, restaurants and so forth. If my services, as confidential interpreter, are needed, I am at your disposal, but again only under the circumstances as above.[10]

It's as if one of Joseph Conrad's secret agents was drafting the note. The tone is not at all diplomatic and suggests irritation that the police might be in danger of jeopardizing a Russian 'asset'. What we don't know is who that informer was and what intelligence they had to share.

Those arrested in connection with the Houndsditch shootings were promptly brought to court. Rosa Trassjonsky and Luba Milstein were initially charged with offences including being accessories to murder. A few days later, Osip Federoff, Jacob Peters and Yourka (or Zurka) Dubof, 'all young and distinctly of foreign appearance', appeared before the same court charged with murder. Some evidence was presented at these remand hearings, both from police officers and eyewitnesses. The only procedural difficulty was over language. The magistrate, Sir W. P. Treloar, wanted to be sure that those charged understood the offences of which they stood accused and could follow the proceedings, leading to an almost comical exchange with one of those in the dock:

> Sir W. TRELOAR. Do you understand what this man has said, Fedorof?
> Fedorof. No, no.
> Sir W. TRELOAR. Do you understand what I am saying.
> Fedorof. No. (Laughter.)

The swearing-in of a court interpreter – variously described as interpreting in Yiddish and in Russian – didn't entirely resolve the problem. At the next hearing, there was an awkward stand-off, with the interpreter at one point saying he couldn't continue if he was to be constantly interrupted. It transpired that a representative of the Russian consulate was audibly seeking to correct the translation. At the next hearing, there was a similar scene with one of the defence solicitors complaining that the interpreter was 'hopelessly incompetent'. The same interpreter had been present at some of the police interrogations, which must cast some doubt on the accuracy of the witness statements.[11]

The purpose of the committal proceedings at Guildhall Police Court in the City of London was not to establish the guilt or innocence of the accused but to determine whether the prosecution case was sufficient to merit a full trial. This was an exhaustive process, with 22 days of hearings spread over more than three months. At this stage, the prosecution had to demonstrate not that the accused were guilty but that a jury might reasonably return a guilty verdict. So the bar was low, which makes the manner in which the prosecution case got tripped up quite startling.

Rosa Trassjonsky (centre left) and Luba Milstein (centre right) in court, 5 January 1911.

The main prosecuting counsel was Archibald Bodkin, an old-school lawyer who later rose to become the Director of Public Prosecutions. He argued that the Houndsditch robbery attempt was 'a long concerted and very carefully planned scheme', in which nine or ten people were involved. He suggested that as many as 22 shots were fired by at least three of the Houndsditch robbers. But the crucial factor was identification. Who was present at 11 Exchange Buildings, the base point for the attempt to burrow into Harris's jewellery shop? Who fired the shots? Who knew that a robbery was being planned and that guns would be carried? The unreliability of the evidence was reflected in the testimony of seventeen-year-old Bessie Jacobs, who lived at Exchange Buildings. At a police station identity parade, she initially picked no one out, but later said that, once he had put his hat on, she recognized Jacob Peters as someone she had seen several times near the scene of the attempted break-in. But in court, when the defendants were asked to put on their hats, she decided she had made a mistake and it was another of the accused, Osip Federoff, that she had seen. It was hardly evidence on which conviction for a capital offence could be made.[12] A few of the witnesses were required repeatedly to deliver their evidence – at the inquests (there were two for the police officers killed at Houndsditch because they died in different jurisdictions and a separate hearing for the two men killed at 100 Sidney Street), at the committal hearings and then at the full trial.

The arrests of Nina Vassileva, John Rosen (the 'Barber') and Karl Hoffman in early February 1911 increased the number of defendants to eight. The police had some success in getting usable testimony from the defendants. On 5 February, while being held at Bishopsgate Police Station, Rosen approached a police constable and indicated that he had information he might be willing to share. Later that day he made a fresh statement to police declaring that the testimony given on his arrest three days earlier – that he had never been to 59 Grove Street and knew none of the other defendants – was not true. He gave chapter and verse about his friends, about the gathering in Grove Street on the afternoon of the Houndsditch shootings, and about later meetings and conversations with two of his fellow defendants, Hoffman and Vassileva. He recounted how Hoffman had told him that Fritz had said that Max had shot Gardstein. That was hearsay twice over, but at least it was a break in the stonewall denial from other male defendants. Rosen's revised statement was not an admission of guilt, but it must have encouraged the police to believe that they were on their way.[13]

Once he was locked up in Brixton jail, John Rosen told his co-defendants that his testimony was intended to help them. That's not how they saw it. Later in the month, Hoffman and Dubof used a convict who was working as a cleaner to pass notes written in Latvian between their cells. He alerted the prison authorities. The notes were seized and translated – they still survive in the City of London Police archives. In part, the two defendants were trying to get their story straight. But they also expressed shock about Rosen's willingness to inform on his colleagues. 'Look Boy,' Hoffman said to his comrade, 'the Barber has spoken very much about us in order to come through with [a] whole skin.' Dubof agreed that it was 'awful that the Barber has said so much'.[14]

The breakthrough didn't lead anywhere. The evidence of culpability was weak and the prosecution case began to collapse. On 22 February, Bodkin told the magistrate's court that the evidence against Luba Milstein was not sufficient to justify her further detention. She was the first of the eight accused to be discharged. When the prosecution case closed a couple of weeks later, two more prisoners were discharged. The magistrate ruled that 'there was not sufficient evidence against Trassjonsky and Hoffman on which a jury could convict.' At the next hearing, Osip Federoff was also told he was free to go. At the conclusion of the committal hearings, the four remaining defendants – Nina Vassileva, John Rosen, Jacob Peters and Yourka Dubof, all in their mid-twenties – were sent for trial charged with conspiring to break and enter Harris's jewellery shop; Peters, Dubof and Vassileva also faced charges of 'feloniously harbouring, comforting and assisting' George Gardstein (who was of course dead) knowing that he had committed murder – that is, being accessories to murder after the fact; and Peters and Dubof alone were charged with the murder of Sergeant Tucker.

The prosecution went to great trouble to prepare its case, even arranging for a police constable to assemble a wooden scale model of Houndsditch and Exchange Buildings (which the City of London Police still has) to demonstrate the layout of the murder scene. The signed witness depositions ran to 632 handwritten pages (a more manageable 216 pages when typed up). More than 140 exhibits were prepared – ranging from bullets recovered from bodies to photographs seized from suspects' rooms, piping and tools retrieved from Exchange Buildings, and the police helmet of Sergeant Bentley with a bullet hole clean through its brim.

THE OLD BAILEY trial got under way on 1 May 1911, four and a half months after the shootings. The presiding judge was Sir William Grantham, a former Conservative MP who had spent a quarter of a century as a high-court justice and had a reputation for rash remarks. He had attracted public attention in the aftermath of the Sidney Street shootings when he commented that it involved 'two Anarchists, that was to say two Socialists of the very worst type – men who did not acknowledge God or anything . . . Though he thought what had happened in the East-end was most disgraceful, he hoped it would be a warning to people not to disregard religion.'[15]

Mr Justice Grantham was 75 years old and this was one of his last cases. The transcript suggests that he was at times confused, inattentive, hard of hearing and ill-tempered.[16] His obituary later in the year described him as a 'convinced Churchman and a Tory of the early Victorian school' who was 'prone to assert his views unadvisedly' and whose 'summings up to the jury were apt to disclose too much of his personal feelings'. As a result, the obituary added, 'his judgments were at times reversed on appeal.'[17] Grantham's conduct of the Houndsditch trial bore out all these castigations.

The prosecution case suffered a sharp setback on the first day at the Old Bailey. Archibald Bodkin made the opening statement for the prosecution, arguing not that either of the men charged with murder necessarily fired the fatal shots but that in law all those who

Acquitted

combined together for an unlawful purpose leading to murder were equally culpable. The judge wasn't impressed by this argument. Grantham said he had read the witness depositions and he ruled that

> there was no evidence that either Dubof or Peters fired any shot . . . The charge against them was one of constructive murder. He thought it right to say at this stage of the case that he should feel it his duty to tell the jury that in his judgment it was not a case in which they would be justified in finding them guilty of murder.

The jury were directed to find the two men not guilty on the most serious charge facing them.[18]

The opening day also saw the key prosecution witness, Isaac Levy – the man who witnessed the fatally injured George Gardstein being helped away from the scene by two armed men and a woman – take the stand. Under cross-examination, he revealed that when he first rushed to Bishopsgate Police Station, he didn't mention that he had been confronted by two men with guns. 'I was so excited and terrified that I did not know what I was doing.' He had identified Peters and Dubof as the men who pointed the guns at him, but under cross-examination his testimony fell apart. The following morning, the judge intervened to state that Levy's testimony was 'so unsatisfactory' that, in the absence of corroborating evidence, he could not allow any jury to convict on the basis of his identification. In Vassileva's case, he said, the identification evidence was stronger but the prosecution could not demonstrate that she knew a murder had been committed. The prosecution was obliged to drop the charge of being accessories to murder. By the end of the second day at the Old Bailey, the only charge outstanding was conspiracy to break and enter Harris's jewellery business.

The judge clearly felt that the setting aside of any charges directly relating to the most serious police murder in London's history required some explanation. He took the unusual step of addressing the jury (and so, of course, the reporters present) directly:

> Having gone through very carefully the whole of the evidence in this case, I am strongly of opinion that the three men who were really the chief murderers – at any rate, the men who we know were shooting – have each of them met his doom. That is my view; I may be wrong. One of them – Gardstein – was clearly one of the men shooting at the policemen. In my view the other two men who were in the house were the two men who burned in Sidney Street ... I may be wrong, but that is my view. It is rather satisfactory to know that at any rate the three chief men engaged in it have met their doom, though perhaps not in the way some of us would have liked.[19]

The message from the Old Bailey was that although the murder charges had been abandoned, that didn't mean the killers had got away with it.

The trial continued at the Old Bailey for another nine sitting days. Both judge and jury visited the site of the attempted break-in. Court time was also taken up in a discussion about an echo in the courtroom, which prompted the judge to spend his lunch break trying, and failing, to find the acoustic problem of which defence counsel complained. There was another acerbic intervention from the bench when Jacob Peters, giving testimony in his own defence, mentioned that he attended publicly funded English lessons but gave up, complaining that because 'most of the instruction was given in Yiddish he learnt more Yiddish than English'. The judge testily expressed the hope 'that the London County Council would be made aware of that. Ratepayers could hardly be called upon to pay for people being taught Yiddish.' Grantham's sense of humour was also somewhat arch. When the prosecuting counsel explained that he wasn't suggesting that the sole woman among the defendants scaled the 2-metre (7 ft) walls dividing the backyards of the properties on Exchange Buildings, Grantham responded, 'Whether she did or not, all I can say is that she is certainly not an Englishwoman. I do not know any young woman who would not climb over this wall. (Laughter.)' At one point, Nina Vassileva's lawyer asked a police witness to read out a description of Peter the Painter, which prompted the judge to remark: '"Surely you do not think the jury capable of believing that your client . . . is 'Peter the Painter'? (Laughter) . . . She hasn't got a moustache, you know." (Laughter.)' And when a witness clearly on edge, Isaac Levy, accused a defence counsel of trying to 'bamboozle' him, the judge's bon mot was to muse out loud which was worse, looking down the barrels of two pistols or being cross-examined in court.[20]

When it came to the substance of the trial, much of the evidence was circumstantial – that the defendants had been seen with the dead men or around Exchange Buildings. It was guilt by association. Some of these identifications suggested prodigious feats of recall by the witnesses, and the evidence associating Jacob Peters with either the crime spot or the gang members was particularly weak. Aside from Isaac Levy's unreliable testimony, none of the evidence against the three men linked them to firearms or ammunition or located them inside 11 Exchange Buildings. Dubof and Peters were both able to put forward several witnesses in support of their alibis for the night of the shootings. Against Vassileva, the evidence was stronger – her fingerprints were found on bottles inside the house in Exchange Buildings, and the identification evidence from neighbours and others was convincing. Her panic-stricken behaviour after the shootings added to the impression that she had been complicit in the robbery attempt.

The three men all took the witness stand as part of their defence. The defence lawyers went to town on the identification evidence: one said the police identity parades had been 'a farce'; another argued that Rosen bore such a strong resemblance to Fritz Svaars that one could easily be mistaken for the other. Nina Vassileva, alone among the defendants, did not take the witness stand and so avoided cross-examination. The only witness her lawyer called was to vouch for her good character.[21] The judge's summing up, as reported in the press, was notable for its strictures against two prosecution witnesses. If PC James Martin – who fell to the ground when the first shots were fired at Exchange Buildings – 'had shown greater courage and a greater desire for duty in this case . . . they would have been in a better position to know what happened'. He also censured Isaac Levy, the tremulous tobacconist who stumbled on the scene, for not pursuing the armed men carrying Gardstein.[22] This was hardly priming the jury to deliver a guilty verdict.

After retiring for just twenty minutes, the jury found Dubof, Peters and Rosen not guilty and they were discharged. Vassileva was found guilty of conspiracy to break and enter. The judge, addressing the sole remaining prisoner, said that

> there could be no doubt that she was implicated in the transaction, but he was quite willing to believe that she had no intention of adding murder to the crime of attempting to break into the safe. Gardstein was about as desperate a man as ever set foot in this country... It was a very bad case. He sentenced Vassileva to two years' imprisonment without hard labour.[23]

But he went along with a specific request made by the jury and agreed not to recommend Nina Vassileva for deportation. The court had heard hearsay evidence that she feared death if she returned to Russia, and whatever her culpability the jury didn't see it as a capital offence.

At the close of the Old Bailey trial, the judge was allowed to keep one of the guns found amid the embers of 100 Sidney Street. 'The burnt Mauser will be a most interesting memento of the celebrated Houndsditch murders trial,' William Grantham wrote from an address in Eaton Square. He also asked for, and got, the metal stock or support that was found which allowed the pistol to rest on the shoulder as it was fired. 'Of course I hold them at your service, if you ever get a chance of catching any of the others,' Grantham wrote to the head of the City of London Police, knowing that a further trial was exceptionally unlikely. He added an extraordinary postscript: 'I think the trial ended quite as well as we could have expected.'[24] His comments are an acknowledgement that while it may have been essential to be seen to stage a trial after such a grievous and much-publicized crime, the evidence simply wasn't there to convict.

This wasn't the end of the court hearings. A little more than a month after her conviction, Nina Vassileva's appeal came up before the Lord Chief Justice. Her lawyer argued that the judge's summing up at the Old Bailey had been inaccurate and so had misdirected the jury. The appeal court agreed. It was particularly concerned about Mr Justice Grantham's suggestion that the compelling evidence that Vassileva had lived for a while at 11 Exchange Buildings demonstrated her guilt. 'It seemed to them' – the appeal bench ruled – 'that the jury ought to have been asked to consider the independent question whether she might not have been living there quite innocently. In all the circumstances they felt bound to quash the conviction.'[25] After four months in Holloway jail, the last of the Houndsditch defendants was freed.

The Old Bailey jury was right on the basis of the evidence presented to acquit the men in the dock. The appeal court was arguably rather generous in allowing Nina Vassileva's release. But most of those who faced charges arising from the Houndsditch affair were fortunate to avoid conviction and a long jail sentence. And certainly the justice system was not vengeful in its treatment of those accused of a crime that had shocked the nation.

So what did happen at Houndsditch? There is no certainty, but here's the most probable scenario. At the core of the group responsible for the attempt to rob Harris's jewellery business in Houndsditch, and so for the triple police murder, were Latvians who were associated with the Liesma anarchist group. They teamed up with some Russians who had the skills and a criminal track record to make the enterprise more likely of success. As well as George Gardstein, who was shot in the back by one of his comrades, Fritz Svaars, 'Joseph' Sokoloff, Max Smoller and Nina Vassileva were at or close to Exchange Buildings when the shots were fired. The men carried guns, at least three of which were used. Justice Grantham, for all his evident failings, was right in stating that Gardstein, Svaars and Sokoloff probably fired the fatal shots. It is possible, as Svaars alleged, that it was Max Smoller who accidentally shot Gardstein – and the fear of recrimination from his comrades may explain Smoller's almost immediate vanishing act. It is also possible that Svaars came up with this story to avoid any personal blame as well as to pin responsibility on someone who was disliked and a relative outsider in the group.

There is a contrary view that needs to be mentioned. Donald Rumbelow, who as a junior police officer rescued the police files relating to the Houndsditch killings from destruction, has suggested that Jacob Peters was the principal gunman.[26] There is some contradiction in the testimony of police officers who survived the shootings, one of whom believed that Gardstein was the man who opened the door to Sergeant Bentley and then retreated up the stairs while two stated that Gardstein was the man who entered the ground-floor room from the rear and opened fire. But none of these police officers identified Peters as a gunman or indeed as present at Exchange Buildings at the time of the shootings. And neither the judge nor the jury was impressed by the fairly thin evidence implicating Peters. The likelihood is that Peters was not part of the group, though he may well have known of the robbery his cousin was planning.

Of the others charged, Yourka Dubof, John Rosen 'the Barber' and Karl Hoffman were all in on the robbery plan and assisted to different degrees. Osip Federoff was on the fringe of this group, though he was probably aware of what his colleagues were planning. Rosa Trassjonsky was seen at Exchange Buildings and was probably to some degree complicit in the crime; Luba Milstein probably knew that her partner was planning a robbery but wasn't involved. Peter the Painter was not at Exchange Buildings and did not actively take part in the robbery attempt, but he knew and approved of the plan. It is probable that part of his role was to take some of the proceeds back to Latvian émigré groups elsewhere and to funnel money to buy arms and to help prisoners and their families in the Russian Empire.

10
Nina, Luba, Rosa

All the émigrés who opened fire at Tottenham, Houndsditch and Sidney Street were men. The story of those encounters is often told with an overwhelmingly male cast list as if any women in the narrative were simply in the wrong place at the wrong time. Yet three of the eight people charged in the aftermath of the police killings at Houndsditch were women; two of them were anarchists; one, perhaps two, of these three were complicit in the Houndsditch robbery and aware that their comrades were armed. Alone among the accused, a woman defendant was convicted and sentenced to jail before being released on appeal. For all three women, the violence in which they were swept up changed their lives utterly, and in one case tragically.

The revolutionary groups and radical nationalist movements that sprang up across Russia and its empire towards the end of the nineteenth century recruited women as well as men. While women were in a minority, it was a conspicuous minority. Among the many photographs seized by the London police as they searched for the perpetrators of the Houndsditch shootings – almost all, frustratingly, unlabelled and undated – are a few which show women among groups of what appear to be young revolutionaries. One among them depicts what seems to be a band of women activists, all dressed in matching style. Some of these photographs include Otilija Lescinska, more widely known as Tija, who – while not involved in the London shoot-outs – was an important figure in the armed Latvian left-wing movement, both in the Baltic and while living in London.[1] In the aftermath of the Sidney Street siege, a Russian official based in Paris got in touch with the City Police to share intelligence. He advised that there were about fifteen anarchists in the group believed responsible for the shootings, of which several were women. He provided a description of one activist in particular: a cigarette maker called Anna who lived on Sidney Street and was hiding somewhere in West London.[2] From the level of detail provided, this woman had either been under surveillance or been informed on by a comrade. Whether or not the information was accurate or relevant, the prominent role of women within groups committed to expropriation was seen as unremarkable.

Within the anarchist movement in the East End – which provided, perhaps unwittingly, the social infrastructure amid which the Latvian expropriators were able to operate – there were again a number of prominent women activists. Milly Witcop, Rudolf Rocker's partner, was the most high-profile of these, but there were others, including Milly's sister Rose Witcop, Millie Sabel (or Sabelinsky) and Naomi Ploschansky (later Nellie Dick), a particularly energetic young activist who took the lead in establishing an anarchist Sunday school. The Jubilee Street Club didn't simply admit women: women were welcome and felt comfortable there, as reflected in how regularly they came along. The movement combined a rejection of the role of the state in regulating personal relationships with a disapproval of an exploitative attitude towards women. Rudolf Rocker and Milly Witcop made quite a stir when they were refused entry to the United States in 1898 because they were not married and had no intention to marry.[3] At the same time, Rocker expected a respectful attitude towards women. In his memoirs, he recounted the story of a married anarchist from the Baltic, 'something of a dare-devil', who badly treated a woman comrade and got her pregnant. 'I was furious at this blackguardly behaviour,' Rocker stormed. 'So were most of our comrades.'[4]

The conduct of the Latvian exiles did not always live up to Rocker's standards. There was certainly a tolerance of free love, and sexual relationships that were neither lasting nor monogamous. Naomi Ploschansky recalled many decades later that some of the men involved in the Houndsditch robbery attempt sought to portray themselves to women as Robin Hood-style anarchists 'taking from the rich to give [to] the poor. This money was to help the movement or something, which was a lot of baloney.' But it served a purpose. 'The Jewish girls I guess had a free love idea. And so they went to live with them.' Ploschansky herself was not a puritan. In 1913 she met an anarchist and educationalist from Liverpool, Jim Dick. They lived together for a couple of years before marrying and then, in 1917, emigrating to the United States, where both were seminal figures in libertarian education and the modern-school movement. Ploschansky recalled that she was apprehensive of telling her anarchist parents that she had married because they might laugh at her:

> they didn't believe in it any more than I did, though they were married legally ... I was afraid to tell them because I didn't want them to feel that I had changed my opinion. I hadn't changed my opinion about it. I just felt it was necessary at that time to do it.[5]

One of the letters seized by police offers a glimpse of the attitudes of at least some of the Latvian men. 'About the girls you recommended me to, they are of course very reasonable,' one wrote from New York to a comrade in London: 'secret sweethearts, I like them very well + cannot say one bad word about them. The only thing I cannot understand is how they can be content with this awfully degrading life.'[6] Among some of the group, their lives revolving more around guns and robbery plans than political principle, there was a swagger which was reflected in attitudes to women. That's evident in the witness statement of Bessie Jacobs, a seventeen-year-old who lived with her parents in Exchange Buildings a few doors from the house used to try to break into Harris's jewellery shop. A few weeks before the shootings, she saw a man she later recognized as Gardstein – she had been taken to the mortuary to confirm the identification – adjusting the street door at 9 Exchange Buildings. She had a clear recollection of the words that passed between them: 'as he was passing me he looked at me and said "good morning baby". I said to him "who do you think you are talking to". He replied "It's alright miss, I am speaking to my friend" ...I did not see the person he referred to as his friend.'[7] As chat-up lines go it was fairly innocuous, but it suggests a cocksure young man who thought a lot of himself.

Arthur Harding, an East End criminal, was both a rival and an admirer of the East European gangs with which he rubbed shoulders in Spitalfields. He recalled Gardstein as 'a rather good-looking young Russian', describing him as 'the gaffer, the top man ... He spoke English not too badly. He was a nice chap.'[8]

> We young men who were always to be found in Brick Lane knew all these aliens and their girls better than the police. For one thing, we knew they were not Jews. We were told they were on the run from the Russian secret police; that fact alone gained them our sympathy. They were supposed to be anarchists, and belonged to a club in Jubilee Street, which was also a spieler [an illegal gambling den]. They were doing a little burglary to get funds for their political aims.
>
> They always marched in the roadway with their women folk in the middle of them; they numbered as many as twelve or fifteen people, men and girls, who all seemed blond.
>
> ... We were on nodding terms, they knew we were the same kind as themselves; we tried to become friendly with the girls who were good-lookers, gypsy style.[9]

Harding's memoirs are at times self-important and unreliable but he offers a window into the street culture amid which the Latvians and their allies operated.

NINA VASSILEVA HAD style. Even when helping her wounded lover away from the site of the Houndsditch shootings, she was strikingly attired. An eyewitness recalled that she was wearing a fur toque or brimless hat and had a large muff to keep her hands warm (or perhaps to conceal what she was holding). She was 'rather a nicely shaped and nice looking woman'.[10] He seems not to have got such a good look at Vassileva's face – he initially picked out another

Photographs of Nina Vassileva taken on her arrest.

woman at the police identity parade but was told of his mistake and given a second chance. When the same witness gave evidence, Vassileva shouted out, 'It is lies . . . He is a lying witness' – but her protestations were unconvincing.[11] The police had initially described the woman they were seeking as '5 ft 4, slim build, fairly full breasts, face somewhat drawn, eyes blue, hair brown'.[12] Their mugshots of Vassileva capture a look of confident defiance, a glower rather than a gaze. That attitude perhaps explains why, alone of those charged, she made no statement to the police, did not take the witness stand and made no comment of substance during the trial.

Nina, or Lena, Vassileva had been in London for longer than most of the rest of the group and she had a better grasp of English. When she was questioned by a police inspector, she said she could understand him as long as he didn't 'speak quick'.[13] She also spoke Latvian, Russian and Yiddish. The police recorded that she was 23, a Russian from Dnipro or Ekaterinoslav (now in Ukraine), and had come to Britain in the latter part of 1906. She worked for several months in domestic service at a musician's home in Dalston and then got employment as a cigarette maker, at times in a workshop and otherwise working from home. She told police that her father was dead – her lawyer suggested that he had been a chef in the palace at St Petersburg. She wouldn't say where her mother lived. There's no indication that she had family in Britain. A passport in her possession was issued in the Courland district of Latvia in 1905 in the name of Minna Grislis, a Lutheran Christian born in 1884. The information, as so often, is contradictory, but the likelihood is that Vassileva was a Latvian and a political émigré and her fluency in Yiddish – which appears to have been her first language – suggests that she was Jewish.

After leaving domestic service, Nina lodged for a while at 29 Great Garden (now Greatorex) Street in Spitalfields; it's not clear whether she already knew her fellow lodger, George Gardstein, or whether they met during the fairly brief time that they stayed in the same house. When her landlords, the Perelman family, moved to a house in Wellesley Street in Stepney, Vassileva was on sufficiently good terms to move with them. The friendship soured, however, and Perelman told the police that he had asked Vassileva to leave after she had a quarrel with his daughter. She seems to have had an aptitude for falling out; she was not on talking terms with Luba Milstein and alone among those who faced trial was not welcome at the rooms in Grove Street that Milstein shared with Fritz Svaars and Peter the Painter. While at Wellesley Street – according to Perelman's testimony – Vassileva was visited by Svaars, Gardstein and another of the group, John Rosen (the 'Barber'). Yet another key figure, Yourka Dubof, took a room in the house. The lodgings that Nina Vassileva moved to in April 1910 were not far away, on Buross Street, just off Commercial Road and a short stroll from Sidney Street. Another of the group, Karl Hoffman, had worked for the landlord there and introduced her as a potential tenant. That's where she was arrested, a month after the Sidney Street siege.

Nina Vassileva was an active member of the group that attempted the Houndsditch robbery. She was not a hanger-on or a moll. But she was the lover of one of her comrades. 'Gardstein was her sweetheart and she is now wearing black for him,' Fanny Gordon, the landlord's wife at Buross Street, told the police. 'She told me that he was her young man and that she was going to marry him.'[14] Fanny's husband, Isaac Gordon, told the court that Vassileva had shed tears over the post-mortem photograph of Gardstein in the papers and commented admiringly to him, 'Do you know what a man he was'. She told him that the dead man 'was a particular friend of hers'.[15] The Gordon family went to the mortuary to see the body found in Grove Street. All recognized the man as Nina Vassileva's boyfriend. Twelve-year-old Polly Gordon said she'd seen him in Nina's room and knew him as Johnny. Vassileva's defence at her trial was in part that she had been under Gardstein's influence, and – her lawyer conceded – 'it was admitted that she was living with [Gardstein] as his mistress.'[16] Vassileva never publicly acknowledged the relationship and late in life told an enquirer that Gardstein had instead taken up with Masha, a woman she had introduced him to. Nina Vassileva and Masha Sticking were close friends. Vassileva said that she had got the fur and muff that she was spotted wearing immediately after the Houndsditch shootings from her friend, and there is an elegant portrait photograph of Masha – one of the few in the archive that is labelled – with a smart fur hat, stole and muff. Masha was certainly fond of Gardstein and distraught after the Houndsditch shootings.[17] It's quite possible that both women were Gardstein's lovers, but the close bond between Vassileva and Gardstein was certainly personal as well as political.

In the weeks running up to the Houndsditch robbery attempt, Nina Vassileva spent very little time at her room in Buross Street. For two or three weeks she stayed with Masha Sticking, who needed nursing through a spell of ill health. She then told her landlord that the manager at her cigarette factory was unwell and she was taking over the role temporarily and living on site. That was a ruse. She was staying at 11 Exchange Buildings, the base for the group's attempt to burrow their way into Harris's jewellery business on Houndsditch. She took on the role of housekeeper – she slept downstairs in the cramped building while the men bedded down upstairs. Exchange Buildings was a cul-de-sac and there were no passers-by, but the neighbours kept a curious eye on the new tenants. Not all identified the woman among the tenants as Vassileva, but the weight of evidence is compelling. Among those who recognized Vassileva was Joseph Da Costa, who worked at 1 Exchange Buildings:

> I saw her take the shutters down from windows on the room on the ground floor every week-day morning and put them up again in the evening. It was shortly after 9 am that the shutters were taken down and about 5 pm that they were put up. I recognize her by her face, which I had many opportunities of seeing.[18]

The two had also spoken; shortly after moving in at No. 11, Vassileva asked him if he would clean the windows. He was better placed than most to make a reliable identification. Alone among those charged, Vassileva's fingerprints were found in 11 Exchange Buildings. This form of criminal evidence was still new – Scotland Yard's Fingerprint Bureau had been opened only in 1901 – but it was sufficient to convict her.

One detail in particular points to Vassileva's complicity in the planned robbery. Her natural hair colour was described as fair, or blonde, or golden, but before moving in to Exchange Buildings she dyed it black, seemingly to frustrate identification of her as an associate of the robbers. Da Costa and several other witnesses commented on the striking difference in her hair colour from the 'quite black' shade she sported while in Exchange Buildings and the much lighter colour of her hair before and after. Vassileva's landlords, the Gordon family from Latvia, saw her for the first time in several weeks on the evening after the shootings. Her hair was still black and that gave them quite a shock. She was also clearly anxious. She asked the Gordons' daughter to buy a paper and read to her the reports of the shootings. Polly Gordon testified, 'It stated in the paper the height the woman was and what jacket she wore. I saw [Vassileva] measure herself with a yard stick in her own room.'[19] She burnt her black hat (Mr Gordon managed to save the two feathers) and a blue blouse and skirt and started adding letters and papers to the flames. 'I have heard the police are going to search all houses and they would find them,' she told her landlord. He told her that she was creating a bad smell and must stop.

The following morning, Isaac Gordon entered Vassileva's room while she was still in bed. She said she was miserable and ill. 'It would be better if they had shot me instead of the man they have shot. He was the best friend I had,' Gordon recalled her as saying. Later in the day, she gave him for safekeeping a parcel containing photographs, papers, her passport and some books.[20] He took them to his son-in-law's, who persuaded the older man not to risk being caught up in a police murder, and they both then went with the package to Arbour Square Police Station. At ten o'clock that evening, Detective Inspector Wensley, accompanied by two sergeants, went to Buross Street to talk to Vassileva. She didn't give a lot away. Asked whether she knew the men responsible for the Houndsditch shootings, she replied, 'Perhaps I do, perhaps I don't.' The police searched her room but found no guns or cartridges or other incriminating items. She was not arrested but the police arranged to keep her under observation.[21] 'It depends upon circumstances,' Wensley observed at the Old Bailey, 'whether we leave a woman at liberty to watch if men who are wanted come and see her.'[22] Isaac Gordon's son-in-law got the impression that the police were satisfied that Vassileva was not the woman they were looking for, and she continued to lodge with the Gordons in Buross Street.[23]

Vassileva appears to have had two immediate preoccupations: to get the black dye out of her hair and to get out of London. She used a sponge and chemicals to try to cleanse the colour out, buying repeated pennyworths of white or acetic acid from a local shop – where again her change of hair colour caught attention – to rinse out the hair dye. Rosen 'the Barber' called on her as she was washing out her hair and, according to his indiscreet evidence to the police, she admitted to him that she was the woman who had been living in Exchange Buildings. In a mood of despair, she sought out an old acquaintance, an East End doctor, Mengle Freedman, who had been a tenant in the house where Vassileva had once been a domestic servant. They attended the same Russian concerts. She called at his surgery on Whitechapel Road and explained that she felt very depressed because of the police inspector's visit and the arrests made following the Houndsditch shootings. She seemed to want the doctor to provide an alibi. When she was rebuffed, she commented dolefully, 'I have no more friends.'[24]

Nina Vassileva's hair quickly returned to its natural colour but she was less successful in making her escape. On Tuesday, four days after the shootings, she packed up her clothes and gave them to Mrs Gordon, declaring, 'I must go away from here and make you a present of all the things I leave behind ... London is not the place for me, I must go to Paris.' She handed back her front-door key and the Gordons weren't expecting to see her again. By the evening, she was back at 11 Buross Street. 'I cannot get away to Paris as everything is closed to me, and wherever I go there are Detectives following me,' she told Fanny Gordon. Fanny's husband remembered Vassileva also saying, 'If I go to Russia I shall be killed and if I stop here I shall be hung.' Her comrades had either made their way hurriedly out of London or gone to ground; her lover was dead. She was left to fend for herself. No wonder that she was – according to Fanny Gordon – 'very miserable'. For three weeks Vassileva barely went out. Then she went away for a week, apparently to stay with friends, and was eventually arrested on the day she returned, 7 February, which suggests that the police were on the lookout for her. Inspector Fred Wensley, the arresting officer, described her as 'a tall, self-possessed girl'.[25] She was also a touch stroppy. At the police station her handbag was searched. It contained a sealed envelope. When asked what was in it she replied, 'I found it in the street.'

The evening after her arrest, Vassileva took part in the first of a series of identity parades at Bishopsgate Police Station. Twenty-three potential witnesses inspected the line-up, including Nicholas Tocmacoff, who was now openly assisting the police – nine touched her on the shoulder. Vassileva's robust attitude was undimmed. When she was given the chance to change her place in the line-up, she declined: 'I am quite satisfied where I am standing; if people identify me they will do so wherever I stand.' At the close of the parade, she declared that she had no complaint about how it was conducted but added, entirely reasonably, that she 'would like to know what she had been identified for doing'.[26] She managed to secure legal representation. A younger lawyer, William Crocker, came across Vassileva when his father was helping to prepare her defence. 'I remember seeing her sitting patiently in our waiting room,' he recalled.

> She wore a voluminous dark skirt down to her ankles, a severe cotton blouse, a stiff stand-up linen collar and a flat straw 'boater'. There was nothing of the revolutionary about her, nothing to hint at the strain through which she had passed. She looked for all the world like a rather timid nursery governess seeking a post.

For those perhaps expecting a firebrand femme fatale, it was a touch of a let-down.[27]

When the Old Bailey trial of the four Houndsditch accused got under way on 1 May 1911, Vassileva was accused of 'harbouring a felon guilty of murder' as well as of conspiracy to break and enter and to steal – an initial charge of involvement in the murder wasn't pursued. The first and most serious charge of harbouring was withdrawn on the prompting of the judge. But based on the fingerprint evidence, she was found guilty of conspiracy to break and enter. She was the only person ever convicted of an offence arising from the Houndsditch killings, and she must have reflected on the acute injustice of that. No one ever suggested that she fired the bullets or encouraged anyone else to do so.

Vassileva was sentenced to two years' imprisonment, but the judge was swayed by an explicit and unusual recommendation of the jury against her deportation. 'It was stated on behalf of Vassileva that she was a political refugee from Russia, but that she had always borne a good character; she seemed to have come under the influence of Gardstein, with whom she was living, and his associates,' according to the official proceedings of the case.[28] Justice Grantham commented that without the jury's recommendation 'he should certainly have deported her.' The verdict and sentence prompted Vassileva to make what seems to have been her most substantial courtroom interjection, declaring through an interpreter that 'the only fault which might be found with her was that she had tried to screen a very wrong man; she was not guilty.' She added, 'I say that you find me guilty because I lived with a man, and you find him guilty, but it has not been proved.'[29]

Just six weeks after her conviction, Nina Vassileva's case came to the Court of Appeal with the Lord Chief Justice presiding. He found that while it was 'undoubtedly' established that Vassileva was at 11 Exchange Buildings 'for several days in some capacity or other as wife or housekeeper', there was no evidence that she had been party to the attempt to break into the jeweller's premises. And the appeal court ruled that the judge had been wrong to tell the jury that she had been involved in hiring the house and to suggest that simply her presence at No. 11 was evidence of guilt:

> in the opinion of this Court, beyond her presence at No 11, and the presence at No 11 of the persons who were there for an illegal purpose, there was no direct evidence against her. She appeared to have been a respectable girl, a cigarette maker. Unfortunately it could not be disputed that she lived with Gardstein as his mistress. Much has been said about the falsehoods she is alleged to have told, but many of her statements were made when she was being charged with the murder of a Policeman. It would be dangerous to draw an inference from her falsehoods.[30]

The conviction was quashed. Nina Vassileva's appeal had been successful and there was no scope for a retrial. The anarchist monthly *Freedom* argued that justice had been done. 'It was an abominable thing to think she should suffer because of her relationship with one of the dead men. Now she is free; and so ends the terrible tragedy of Houndsditch – for the present.' The appeal court's decision also marked the final and complete collapse of the prosecution case in the most grievous police shooting in London's history: 'eight prisoners were arrested and every one had now been released,' commented the *New York Times*. 'If Peter the Painter is where the

London papers reach him, he must gloat over the last scene of the tragedies which he ... brought about.'³¹

It's striking that the appeal court described Nina Vassileva as 'respectable' even though, in the words of the Lord Chief Justice, 'her standard of morality might not have been high.' She also won some approving words from her landlord, Isaac Gordon, who had first alerted the police to her suspicious behaviour. 'Vassilleva [*sic*] was a perfectly respectable young woman,' he declared from the witness box at the Old Bailey. 'She was quiet and well-behaved, regular in her coming and going, and friendly towards the witness and his family.' A manager of a tobacco company gave evidence that Vassileva's character was 'very good'.³² All these commendations were offered even though she was the unmarried partner of a man who was incontestably a gunman, robber and anarchist expropriator. The defence argument that Vassileva was a good woman led astray by a bad man seems to have been accepted. She was industrious and self-reliant; and without any family to support and protect her, she was vulnerable. The Lord Chief Justice saw these qualities and circumstances as outweighing her radical politics and her choice of partner.

Nina Vassileva also won the regard of Rudolf Rocker and his partner Milly Witcop, the key activists in the Yiddish-speaking anarchist movement in the East End and the founding figures of the Jubilee Street Club. 'A few of our comrades had met her when she had sometimes come to the Club, to our public meetings,' Rocker recalled.³³ 'It came out that Muronzeff [Gardstein] had been associating with other women as well, had in fact been deceiving Nina Vasileva [*sic*] as he had deceived Malatesta.' Witcop undertook to see Vassileva in prison and the police – who kept a close eye on all who came to visit the Houndsditch defendants – listed her as coming to Holloway jail at least twice in April 1911. 'When Milly arrived the poor girl stared at her in amazement and burst into tears: "You come to see me! Then I am not forsaken by everyone!"' Rocker recorded. Rocker and Witcop were deeply unhappy with the initial verdict and sentence meted out to Vassileva: 'It seemed odd. For if she had known what [Gardstein] was doing the sentence should have been more severe. If she hadn't, two years was a lot for having an affair with [Gardstein].'

Once Vassileva's appeal was successful and she was released, she found herself with no money and nowhere to stay. She turned to Rudolf Rocker and Milly Witcop for help. 'We hadn't really known her before. It was the first time she came to our door. I doubt if Milly hadn't gone to see her in prison whether she would have thought of coming to us,' Rocker set down in his reminiscences. 'We told her she could stay with us till she found work, and could get a room elsewhere. She stayed with us nearly a month. We sometimes talked about [Gardstein]. She always said that she had never had any suspicion of what he was doing.' Rocker was pleasantly surprised that the press left Vassileva alone. 'Even the sensational papers which had featured her case, behaved decently in that regard.'[34]

Nina Vassileva turned for help to get her life back on track to the Jewish Association for the Protection of Girls and Women, an organization that sought to help vulnerable women immigrants. They managed to find her a job, but it was a hard slog to get back her working tools and other possessions seized by the police. A letter in Vassileva's own hand listing the items she wanted returned demonstrates clear handwriting and a confident signature, as well as a colloquial command of English. A lawyer was engaged on her behalf, and the association turned to one of its well-placed allies to make a personal appeal to the head of the Metropolitan Police. Blanche Sitwell, writing to Sir Edward Henry in November 1911 from one of London's smartest addresses in Knightsbridge, pleaded on Vassileva's behalf: 'She has got employment and will I trust now do well – but of course she cannot earn much and I understand that she is a good deal handicapped by not having yet got back her clothes and effects from the police.'[35]

That seemed to work. She received her passport, photographs, books and jewellery and other items. Even then, she was told that her fur muff and stole had been handed to her former landlady. A watch and a ring were retained as they were said to be part of the proceeds of a robbery at a jeweller's shop at Wrocław (now in

Poland, at that time Breslau in Germany) – they were still held by the police half a century later.[36]

As with so many of the East European migrants attracted to anarchism before the First World War, the success of the Bolshevik Revolution in Russia in 1917 provided a new lodestone for Vassileva. In subsequent years, she took a job at the London office of the Soviet Trade Delegation, a role which suggested pro-Soviet sympathies, and was employed by Arcos, the All-Russian Co-operative Society. Into this narrative another Sidney Street veteran intrudes. In 1920, John Ottaway – after 29 years at the City of London Police, including eleven as detective superintendent – joined the fledgling British Security Service, MI5. 'The recreations listed by Ottaway on joining indicated that he came from lower down the social scale than most other officers: cricket and tennis rather than hunting and field sports,' according to MI5's authorized history.[37] Ottaway became the head of the agency's three-person observation section, responsible for shadowing suspects and conducting sensitive inquiries. In 1925, he followed a suspect to the offices of Arcos in Moorgate and, after a protracted anti-espionage operation, Special Branch, accompanied by intelligence officers, raided the Arcos office in May 1927. It was the first big raid targeted at Soviet espionage in Britain. Nothing particularly incriminating was found, but the government had already decided to break off diplomatic relations with Moscow and used the raid as the pretext to do so.[38]

In 1929 Arcos returned, taking six floors in the newly built Bush House, described at the time as the world's most expensive building and later to become synonymous with the BBC World Service. Newspaper reports spoke of the Soviet trade organization 'reinvading London'. Two years later, a Special Branch officer called on the City of London Police – he was seeking to confirm that Nina Wasillewa, working for Arcos at Bush House, was the same person as Nina Vassileva of Houndsditch notoriety. The Home Office had been told that 'she is an undesirable alien and ... she was concerned in a notorious crime in London about twenty years ago.' An MI5 note the following year records that she had been dismissed from Arcos.[39] But she wasn't deported. In old age, she lived in a small flat

Undated photograph of Luba Milstein.

on Brick Lane, no more than half a mile from the site of the Houndsditch shootings. She was tracked down there in the summer of 1959, 'white-haired, blue-eyed, her striking features still echoing the flaxen beauty of fifty years earlier'.[40] She died in February 1963 in the hospital where Sergeant Robert Bentley had succumbed to bullet wounds more than half a century earlier. Her death certificate recorded that she was a spinster of unknown occupation and gave her age, incorrectly, as seventy.

WHILE NINA VASSILEVA was in all probability a political refugee and a revolutionary activist, Luba Milstein was a lovestruck youngster. She was a teenager when she took up with Fritz Svaars and became swept up in the Houndsditch killings. It was both an exhilarating and a deeply unsettling time for her. Milstein told police that she was born near Kyiv, her father was dead and her mother was living in Mile End. When she gave evidence in court, she gave the oath on Jewish scripture. Milstein had been in England for about two years. She was introduced to the Jubilee Street Club by a friend and went there not because she was an anarchist but because she was able to meet Russians and converse in her own language. She met Gardstein there, and through a friend became acquainted with Fritz Svaars, who – to judge from some of the surviving photographs and the testimony of friends – was one of the more dashing and charming of the Latvian émigrés.

Within a couple of months of meeting Svaars, Luba Milstein moved out of the family home and into his room nearby in Newcastle Place – she didn't give her mother her new address. They had been together for about five months at the time of the Houndsditch murders. When Peter the Painter came from Paris, they took a bigger place, two first-floor rooms at 59 Grove Street in Stepney, which were found for them by a friend and shopkeeper, Reuben Frankel. Peter slept in the front room, where Milstein also kept her sewing machine and sometimes worked; Luba and Fritz had the back room. Luba comes across as young and besotted. 'I will remember this evening all my life, as long as I shall live,' read a postcard she had written and which was retrieved by the police.[41]

Although she was working and sometimes paid the rent on behalf of Fritz and herself, there was a profound imbalance in the relationship. Milstein told the police she didn't have a front-door key. 'I was not married to him, but we lived together as husband and wife,' she recorded in a witness statement.[42] Numerous other witnesses gave testimony that they believed that Luba and Fritz were married, or at least that they behaved as if they were.

Fritz Svaars was indeed married – but not to Luba Milstein. When he became a political refugee, he left his wife behind in the Baltic. It's not clear whether Luba knew that her lover was married or that he was hoping to emigrate to Australia – she told police she didn't even know Fritz's surname. But word of Fritz's London lifestyle certainly percolated back to Latvia. Among letters that the police seized and translated was one that appears to be from Fritz's sister, Lisa, advising him 'not to carry on with a Jewish Girl, as you already have a wife'.[43] Milstein's protestations of ignorance about her partner's plans to carry out an armed robbery are not entirely convincing. There are suggestions that she was kept in the dark because some were worried that she wouldn't be discreet. But she saw Svaars and Gardstein with guns and she must have got a sense of what her partner and his friends were up to.

Although leaving home at nineteen and taking up with Fritz Svaars must have caused consternation within her family, Luba continued to work as a skirt finisher at her brother's business. Her friend and workmate Rosa Trassjonsky, seven years older, seems to have taken the role of confidante and support, which must have been of increasing importance when Milstein began to realize just how deeply her lover was implicated not simply in the Latvian resistance but in revolutionary expropriation. The bond between Luba and Rosa must have helped sustain them both when they were lumbered with the task of caring for a dying man. Milstein didn't cope too well – after all, her lover was one of those who had taken to his heels and she must have wondered whether she would ever see him again (she didn't – Fritz Svaars died at 100 Sidney Street a little more than two weeks later). Amid all the shock and the distress, finding a doctor and trying to destroy potentially incriminating photographs and documents, Trassjonsky had the kindness and empathy to give Milstein her room key and send her to rest at 10 Settle Street, just a few minutes' walk away. When, a few hours later, it was clear that Gardstein was dead, the two women were deeply anxious that they would take the blame. They agreed to go to the police but, according to Trassjonsky, changed their minds because 'we could not speak English.' In the end, Trassjonsky remained at Grove Street while Luba spent the next few hours moving around, helping those implicated in the robbery to make good their escape, even giving Peter the Painter half a crown (12½ pence – about £15 in today's money).

Milstein was at a room on Havering Street in Shadwell for much of the day after the shootings. One of the men who lived there came back with an evening paper and had just enough English to share the main points of the front-page report but not the detail. This was the first time that she understood what had led to Gardstein's bullet wounds. She picked up that a woman was wanted in connection with the murders and panicked and assumed it was her (when of course it was Nina Vassileva). At one point she was considering fleeing the country. Milstein spent the night with a friend. On the Sunday morning, two of her brothers found her and, in the afternoon, Jack Milstein, one of the brothers, accompanied her to a police station, telling the officer on duty, 'This is the young woman the police are looking for.' The initial police questioning of Luba Milstein didn't get very far. Her stock reply was: 'I don't know, I no speak English.'[44]

Rosa Trassjonsky was already in police custody. Three days later both were charged with being accessories to murder, assisting in the escape of the two men who carried Gardstein back to Grove Street and conspiring to rob Harris's jewellery shop. The following morning, a photograph of Trassjonsky, being led into court between a detective and a female warder, took up a large part of the front pages of the *Daily Mirror* and the *Daily Graphic*. Luba Milstein's name was also prominently reported and her photograph featured in the coverage of subsequent court appearances. She spent the next two months in Holloway jail before being discharged by the magistrates' court, at the prosecution's request, for lack of evidence. *The Star* gave a vivid account of the scene when Milstein was told she was free to go:

> The interpreter explained the decision in Russian, and Luba rose, smiling.
>
> Chief Inspector Ottaway nodded to Luba's brother, seated with a friend in the gallery at the rear of the court, and a constable conducted her across the well of the court and handed her to her brother.
>
> All the other prisoners turned round and gazed upon the released prisoner.
>
> Luba, her arms grasped by her brother and his friend, was still smiling, until she reached the outer door, when she broke into a fit of hysterical crying.[45]

Prosecuting counsel commented approvingly that Milstein has acted on 'good and judicious advice' and given a full account of her connection with those who were the focus of the investigation – words that can hardly have been well received by the remaining defendants. It may not be a coincidence that her most detailed and candid statement to police was made just five days before the charges against her were dropped.[46]

Luba Milstein's letters to her family from jail had varied from furious protestations of her innocence, to pleas for a good lawyer, to requests for more reading matter, particularly books in Yiddish and a Russian translation of Oscar Wilde's *De Profundis* ('from the depths'), which presumably appealed because it was written in a prison cell. 'It seems to me that I will never come out + I ask myself why?' she wrote to her mother. 'What wrong have I done to the world that I have to suffer so much + why am I punished, because I was wronged by a bad man, + just because I was fooled + dishonoured by a murderer, who wore a mask of a gentleman.'[47]

There was another recipient of Luba Milstein's prison letters – Sima Traeberg, an eighteen-year-old friend and perhaps a relative. Milstein wrote a short note to her friend in Yiddish soon after being moved to Holloway:

In short, I am now in jail. That is, I was arrested – for what I can't tell you . . . I can only tell you that I'm in no way guilty, I haven't committed any crime and I hope the truth will save me and I think I will be set free, because I'm innocent . . . How long I will sit here, I don't know. I think they're holding me because they think I know where the real guilty parties are . . . I told them everything I know but they don't believe me and who knows how long I will have to sit here.[48]

Milstein expressed concern that she might be deported and advised her friend to delay plans to come to England. But for whatever reason, Sima Traeberg made the journey to London and stayed with Milstein's family. In a series of letters to Sima, inevitably translated and read by prison officials and police, Luba agonized over her turbulent relationship with Fritz Svaars. She had time to reflect, on both the high points – 'I loved him so much' – and the low, declaring that 'at times I wished I was dead.' While she clearly resented the time Svaars spent with his close friends, and the camaraderie he shared with them, from which she felt excluded, there's nothing to suggest a repudiation of his use of guns or his expropriatory form of political activity. But there is a hint of some momentous personal news: 'my health was not so good, I understood what was the matter with me, Fritz seemed to have understood what was the matter with me.'[49]

Milstein was expecting Svaars's baby. It must have been a harrowing pregnancy, with a father who had died under such circumstances. Naomi Ploschansky recalled that she was asked by the family's lodger, an acquaintance of some of the Houndsditch group, to visit Luba during her pregnancy, but her mother forbade that. The baby, Alfred, was born later that year, and at the start of the following year Milstein sailed with her child to New York. The police seem to have been taken by surprise by her departure – with her went perhaps the best prospect of securing convictions if any of those still wanted for their alleged role in the police killings should surface. In 1913, Luba Milstein was joined in New York by one of her co-accused and a close friend of Fritz Svaars, Karl Hoffman; they lived together for almost half a century. Alfred took his stepfather's original name of Dzirkalis, anglicized to Driscoll, but was not aware of his real paternity until he was thirty. Driscoll told the historian Philip Ruff that his parents, whatever their one-time anarchist sympathies, were both enthusiastic supporters of the Soviet Union until they died. Luba Milstein lived into her eighties – her granddaughter is a distinguished artist.[50]

IF LUBA MILSTEIN'S is a survivor's story, her friend Rosa Trassjonsky was not so fortunate. Indeed, of all those caught up in the Houndsditch shootings, the fate of Rosa (or Rosie, and also on occasion Sara) Trassjonsky is among the most tragic. It destroyed her life. She was probably on the periphery of those involved in the attempted robbery. But she was Luba Milstein's best friend and on good terms with some of the group, and she tended Gardstein, a dying man deserted by his comrades, in the closing hours of his life. She was arrested and charged, and appeared in court and in the papers, and although she was discharged, her life never returned to its earlier rhythm. Her room was searched and notes, postcards and photographs were seized, and the letters she wrote from jail were intercepted and translated before being posted, and these very personal documents offer a rare and intimate insight on a troubled life.

By Trassjonsky's own account – and she was not always the most cooperative of witnesses, on one occasion refusing to sign a police statement based on her testimony – she was at the close of 1910 aged 26 or perhaps a little older and from a small town in a part of Russia bordering Poland (and now in Belarus). She was brought up in a Jewish family and spoke Yiddish; her mother had been married three times. 'For my mother's sins I am suffering,' she told the police.[51] She had left Russia two or three years earlier, spent a few months in London, then moved to Paris for eighteen months, returning to London a few months before her arrest. She initially stayed with her aunt in the East End, then took a room – a back room on the second floor the size of which was probably reflected in the paltry rent of 3s 6d (17½ pence – or today's equivalent of £22)

Photograph of Rosa Trassjonsky taken on her arrest.

a week – at 10 Settle Street in Whitechapel, one of the very few buildings associated with the Houndsditch events still standing. Her landlord told police that she frequently received letters addressed to her from Paris and Liverpool.

Rosa Trassjonsky found a job as a skirt finisher at a workshop in Mile End run by Luba Milstein's brother. That's where the two women met and they became firm friends. Rosa's landlord told the police that Luba called for Rosa on most mornings; Luba's landlady said that Rosa was 'in and out every day and evening'.[52] The tenderness of that friendship may have been one of the few bright spots in a fairly bleak life. 'I am a single woman, I have no children, I have no money,' Trassjonsky told the police – or at least that was what she was recorded as saying – adding rather conveniently, 'I have no objection to be expelled from the country to the place I came from.' Trassjonsky was protective towards her younger friend. She refused to tell the police the name of Milstein's lover, though it was hardly a secret, and insisted she would make a point of not telling them anything that they didn't already know. She certainly had attitude. As for the documents she was in the course of destroying when the police found her in the room next to the one where Gardstein's body lay, Trassjonsky told the police – not very convincingly – she was doing this because Milstein had asked her to without giving a reason. 'I shall not tell you whose photos they were I destroyed,' she was reported to have declared. 'I thought she was asking me to do so because she was living with a man.'[53]

The police wanted to establish whether Rosa Trassjonsky shared the politics of Peter the Painter and his colleagues. She insisted that she had never come across the men while in France. But there are loose ends to her testimony. Her passport was in a different name, that of 'Sara (Davidowna Tuiwewna) daughter of David Tuwie Treschau' (and it bore the ominous endorsement that it was 'valid only in such places where Jews are allowed to reside', which points to what she was trying to escape). She was also known as Rose Selinsky, the name by which the newspapers reported her arrest; some said that she had another name, Kershofski. There are many reasons why she may have used multiple identities – operating clandestinely as a revolutionary is certainly one of them. The police recorded that she had a deformed fingernail, right shoulder blade and left hip (which could possibly have been the scars of torture).

Rosa Trassjonsky appears to have been involved in the left-wing groups that emerged across the Russian Empire after the failure of the 1905 Revolution. The historian Philip Ruff has uncovered evidence that in the following year, she was active in an anarchist group in Białystok, now in northeast Poland and then under Russian rule. The city had a particularly large Jewish population and in June 1906 was convulsed by a brutal anti-Jewish pogrom in which dozens died. Trassjonsky was arrested in September 1907 and in police photographs was named as Sorka Treshchanskaya.[54] Among the photographs seized by police from her room in Whitechapel were two with inscriptions in Yiddish dated April 1908, one of a young man and the other of two women, both given to her as keepsakes on her departure from Russia. Another photograph, of a studiouslooking young man, bore an inscription in Russian: 'May this card, Rosa, be a memento for you of the suffering we lived through and may a new era begin – of happiness and love ... Paris. October 9th 1910.'[55]

In London, police investigating the Houndsditch police murders received two separate tip-offs, one from a Special Branch officer, suggesting that Rosa Trassjonsky was a revolutionary activist. She was certainly a habitual visitor to the Jubilee Street Club, where – according to Rudolf Rocker – she 'had been regularly attending the weekly meetings and social evenings'. The *Arbayter Fraynd* and *Germinal*, another of Rocker's anarchist journals, were among the literature found in her room. 'People who knew more about her than we did said she worked in a tailoring workshop, and lived poorly and honestly by her meagre earnings. We never found out how she had got to know the Houndsditch murderers. Quite possibly she had met them in our Club.'[56]

While some of the identifications of Trassjonsky by witnesses appear unreliable, she seems to have been seen with those involved in the Houndsditch robbery attempt more than can simply be explained by her friendship with Luba Milstein. Nina Vassileva – someone Milstein kept at a distance – was among her circle of friends. She may not have been directly involved in the robbery attempt, but her links with those responsible were more than simply social. One later account went further, asserting that Trassjonsky was Peter the Painter's 'sweetheart', though without offering any evidence.[57] Certainly, the police search of her room uncovered letters to Peter, including from his girlfriend, as well as to Luba Milstein and to Fritz Svaars. But these may have been placed with her for safekeeping or carried by Milstein when she spent a few hours in her friend's room during the torrid night following the Houndsditch shootings. Trassjonsky's landlord made a point of stating that she never had male visitors; and as Peter the Painter appears not to have been a womanizer, it's unlikely that they were in an intimate relationship. Indeed, Milstein, in lamenting her own folly in getting involved with a gunman, told the police, 'If we had known what kind of people we inter-mixed with we would not have stayed with them. At least this girl (Rosie) didn't do so.'[58]

As we've seen, Rosa Trassjonsky kept her composure much better than her friend did during the harrowing night when Gardstein was dumped on them and then died. But interrogation, arrest, detention in Holloway jail and appearing in court took a heavy toll. When first detained, the women were allowed to exchange pencilled notes in Russian – they survive alongside a translation provided by the Russian consulate. Luba addressed her friend affectionately as Rosochka. 'Lyuba! If anyone is not guilty it's you, dear,' Rosa replied. 'No matter what happens to me, you must stay brave and healthy. You're young and you'll survive everything. I kiss you so hard.'[59]

Rosa Trassjonsky was right: Luba was young and survived, and whatever trauma she bore did not stop her making a fresh life for herself; Rosa was not so lucky. A couple of days after the exchange of scribbled notes, Luba Milstein wrote in some distress from the prison hospital at Holloway to her brother, 'I feel myself very bad . . . Rosie is also in hospital, she lost her senses, I cannot bear it, I am afraid I also will become mad.'[60] Trassjonsky was indeed retreating into a tormented world of confusion and paranoia. She wrote from prison an agonized letter to her parents in Russia:

> Just a week ago . . . a letter was received from you in which you write that you think that I am mad, just the following morning I was arrested, and I am accused of murder, in which I am not guilty, but I cannot prove it . . . I would eagerly like to see one of you . . . I kiss you. Your daughter Sara Rosa.[61]

She received no reply, and three weeks later, in some exasperation, she wrote again. 'I know that you suffer owing to [me] being in prison,' she told her family, 'but I suffer more':

> You know that I have always been weak + nervous + therefore when I was arrested I lost my senses + thought that from every side I am shouted at that I killed him. I heard

nothing else. I felt + I know that I am innocent + that has driven me mad, thinking that everybody is shouting at me that I killed a person. Afterwards I was taken to a hospital. I feel better now, but am not quite well . . . I am still young but agony, hunger, cold, misery + illness, these are the things which have always surrounded me since I was 13 years old. I have not had a single day in my life in which I could say that I feel quite well, as the usual pains in my side + headaches were always with me + are with me even now.[62]

She went on to recite how during her childhood she witnessed her father shouting at and hitting her mother, who in turn smacked and punched her and her siblings. 'I know many more things but I will not write to you now.' It's a letter that must have been as painful to write as to receive. She needed love and support and got neither.

In jail and in the dock, Trassjonsky must have felt desperately alone. She had to ask Milstein for help to get fresh underwear and bed linen. She was discharged for lack of evidence against her on 8 March 1911, a couple of weeks after her friend. There was now a chance for her to resume her old life. That didn't happen. Her aunt, who seems to have been her only relative in London, either wouldn't or couldn't help and neither, it seems, did anybody else. When the ten-yearly census was recorded in early April, Trassjonsky was among the hundreds of destitute inmates of Mile End Workhouse. Within days her plight moved from bad to worse. She was admitted to the vast, forbidding, Colney Hatch Asylum in North London, opened in 1851 and at its zenith holding more than 2,000 patients. She was initially recorded as suffering from 'melancholia' and then 'mania' and was given a black eye by a fellow inmate, an injury sufficiently serious that it was recorded in the monthly log.[63]

In June 1911, London County Council (LCC) applied for a court order to pave the way for Trassjonsky's deportation under the 1905 Aliens Act as an alien pauper. She wasn't well enough to attend court but the order was granted all the same. An Islington businessman contacted the police to offer Trassjonsky light work in his factory and somewhere to live until she was well enough to fend for herself. That prompted the police to check on Rosa's well-being. The response they received from the LCC Asylums Committee was grim: 'Sara Rosa Trassjonsky is insane, of suicidal tendencies, and has to be tube fed, and her condition is of such a nature that she may never recover sufficiently to be deported from this country.'[64]

Eighteen months later, the police files record a striking act of kindness. A package was handed in for forwarding to Rosa Trassjonsky at Colney Hatch. It was a perfumed sachet bearing the note 'Xmas, 1912. To the nurse who so kindly tended "Carl Gastin, alias Gardstein during his last hours".' After careful consideration, the police – having removed the brown paper wrapping, which remains in the London Metropolitan Archives – passed on the package to the asylum with the request that it be handed to Trassjonsky 'if she is in a condition to receive it.' We don't know whether she was, or what she made of the present. The giver chose to be anonymous – but we now know that it was Gardstein's lover, Nina Vassileva.[65]

From then on, Rosa Trassjonsky fades from the official record. The Colney Hatch registers got her name wrong – she was repeatedly listed as Rosie Trannjonski – an error that persisted through her long years on the asylum ward. Rudolf Rocker wrote that she 'was sent to a lunatic asylum where she committed suicide soon after', but in fact she was still living when Rocker's memoirs were published almost half a century after the Sidney Street siege.[66] Trassjonsky remained at Colney Hatch through two world wars and was discharged only in 1960, and one must assume was entirely unaware that in that year her character, played by Nicole Berger, was the female lead in a feature film based on the Sidney Street shootout. After so many decades in an institution, Trassjonsky was unable to live independently. She was informally readmitted to the asylum and died there of broncho-pneumonia and senility in 1971. Her death certificate recorded incorrectly both her first name and her surname, and gave no place of birth and her date of birth simply as '1884'. Her occupation was given as 'retired felling hand', felling being the stitching of seams, a trade she had not pursued for sixty years. She had been well and truly forgotten.

11
Who Was Peter the Painter?

'Of "Peter the Painter" not a trace was ever found,' Winston Churchill recorded a few years after the Siege of Sidney Street. 'He vanished completely.'[1] That was not quite true. Peter the Painter was never tracked down and he remains in many ways an enigma. But his identity is not as shrouded in mystery as the standard police and official account suggests. The London police never publicly revealed the identity of Peter the Painter, the man for whom they put out reward posters and identified as wanted for the most serious police murders London has ever endured. From the police's public comments, you might imagine that the story of Peter the Painter is as puzzling as the identity of the East End's 'most wanted', Jack the Ripper. In fact, the superintendent leading the police case was satisfied by the end of the following year that he could put a name to Peter the Painter. But the police kept quiet. They didn't want the embarrassment of having to reveal that their evidence was not sufficient to secure his extradition back to Britain, nor perhaps the prospect of another trial in London with the likelihood of another acquittal.

In August 1912, Scotland Yard received a letter from Kyiv offering help – in return for a reward – in arresting 'the principal offender' among the Russian revolutionaries who had committed criminal acts in London. The letter, translated by a Special Branch officer, said that the wanted man had returned home to his relative, Johan Shakle, in Courland in Latvia, but had since moved on. 'I have recognized the face, and know where he is living at present,' the writer declared, 'and if you have any power of extradition in this case, I am willing to place myself at your service.' The letter reached

Superintendent John Ottaway at the City of London Police, who clearly regarded the information as reliable while being suspicious of the motive. He noted,

> The man referred to is no doubt 'Peter the Painter' against whom the evidence is insufficient to extradite.
>
> It may be in the interest of the accused that [the] writer desires to know what action the police intend taking in the matter and in the circumstances I respectfully suggest that no reply be sent.[2]

A few months later, Russia's Consul General in London wrote to Ottaway to share information from the Russian Foreign Office (perhaps in this case a euphemism for the Okhrana secret police) that pointed in the same direction as the earlier intelligence:

> Peter the Painter has been now identified as being possibly the peasant of the Province of Courland, district of Goldingen[,] Evan Evanovitch (Janis Janisoff) Jakle, alias Jaklis. He was born on the 19th July 1883, his father is called Evan Evanovitch, his mother Margaritha, he has a brother called Karl, and sisters, Anna, married to a man called Sakee, Mary, Catherine and Milda, all the above named live on a farm called Kounen, in the district of Talsen.
>
> Janis Jakle or Jaklis is wanted by the Police in Golding[en] having absconded and evaded Military Service. He is known to be at present in Germany, but his whereabouts are not established.
>
> I beg to inform you of the above so that you may take advantage of the information at your discretion.[3]

This was a detailed identification and the information was broadly accurate. Peter's mother, Margarieta, was from Kuldiga (then known by the German name of Goldingen) and he had been educated there. The family rented a farm known as Kule or Kuhlnen near Talsi (then Talsen). His date of birth was right and his siblings were named as reported. And on the crucial point, Janis Jaklis – more correctly rendered as Zaklis – was indeed Peter the Painter.[4] But the London police did not take up the Russian government's invitation to 'take advantage of the information'. Indeed, this potential breakthrough in tracking down a wanted man again received a muted response. The Consul General's letter was acknowledged but no further action appears to have been taken. The lack of determination to chase down the man widely held to be the driving force of the gang responsible for the murder of three policemen is striking.

More than thirty years later, the City of London Police briefly returned to the issue of Peter the Painter's identity. A reporter who had covered the Siege of Sidney Street, J. P. Eddy, had over the years become a successful lawyer, a King's Counsel and also a Recorder or part-time judge. In October 1945, he addressed a lawyers' dining society, the Crimes Club, on the subject of Peter the Painter. Ahead of delivering his lecture, Eddy called on the City Police, leaving a letter asking whether Peter the Painter was ever traced and whether he could see any items relating to the Houndsditch murders retained by the police. The latter point was quickly approved, but as to the identity of the wanted man, a superintendent scoured through the records and came across the communications from the would-be informer in Kyiv and the Russian Consul General in London and recorded that 'the wanted man was undoubtedly' Jakle or Jaklis. That information does not seem to have been shared with Eddy, and certainly there's no whisper of Peter the Painter's real name in the published version of his talk.[5] Even after the lapse of so many years, the police were unwilling to admit that Peter the Painter's identity was not a mystery, and that they never had the means of securing either extradition or conviction.

THE NAME OF Peter the Painter was first mentioned to the police by a key witness, Nicholas Tocmacoff. He had been at 59 Grove Street on the afternoon of the Houndsditch shootings and was detained when he called back there the following day. He was only held for one night, but before he was released he had signed a witness statement in which he spilled as many names as he could remember. In the original of this statement, the words 'the Painter' were in some cases added by hand – perhaps to distinguish this Peter from Jacob Peters and also from Tocmacoff's roommate, Peter Pinkovski. However Peter styled himself, it would have been in Russian or Latvian, not English. And whatever language Tocmacoff used to communicate with the police, it wasn't English. His police interpreter was a Dutch-born constable in the City of London force, Homme Walthuis, who seems to have devised the exceptionally resonant English version of the sobriquet by which the wanted man was known. It wasn't invented but a rendition into English of a Latvian or Russian nickname, but it was the police that coined the name by which this fugitive has been known ever since.[6]

On Monday, 19 December – three days after the shootings – the police had names and descriptions for some of those they most wanted to question. Among the details published in later editions of the *Evening News* was:

> PETER: Surname unknown; known as 'Peter the Painter'; aged twenty-eight to thirty; height 5ft. 9in. or 10 in.
> Complexion sallow, skin clear, eyes dark, hair medium, moustache black, medium build.
> Very reserved manner.
> Usually dressed in brown tweed suit, large dark stripes; black overcoat, velvet collar rather large; rather old, large felt hat; shabby black lace boots.
> Believed to be Russian Anarchist, frequents club and institute, Jubilee-street. Resides Grove-street.[7]

It was the first public appearance of this assumed name. There's no doubt that the rhythm and alliteration of the name made it immediately memorable, as well as bearing an echo of Jack the Ripper. The name both damned Peter and added to his allure.

A week after the murders, the City of London Police issued 'wanted' posters offering a £500 reward for information leading to the arrest of Fritz Svaars and Peter the Painter. It declared, 'Both are Anarchists.' A third person, an unnamed woman, was also being sought. The posters featured a post-mortem photograph of George Gardstein, the Houndsditch gunman who had died in the rooms shared by Svaars and Peter the Painter in Grove Street. The story was reported that Peter the Painter had evaded arrest by minutes when police raided the house in Havering Street where he had briefly taken refuge. The name was beginning to lodge. On 28 December, *The Star* reported that a man was found sprawled on the ground in Acton calling out, 'I am Peter the Painter.' He was fined five shillings (25 pence) for being drunk and disorderly.

After the Sidney Street siege, the police were clear almost immediately that one of the bodies found in the burnt-out building was that of Fritz Svaars. The *Evening News* reported that the police were 'satisfied that the second body is that of the other assassin, "Peter the Painter."'[8] The following day the paper reported that there was a 'mystery' about Peter the Painter's fate. The day after, the *Evening News* carried a front-page report asserting that 'City Police now accept the theory that "Peter the Painter" is at large, but it is now not supposed that he played as great a part as the others in the murders.' The sense that Peter the Painter had again escaped, Scarlet Pimpernel-like, added to his reputation. 'Peter the Painter is a personality of seemingly impenetrable mystery,' the *Daily Mirror* reported. 'Apparently nobody knows his real name or much of his history. Nobody has seen him since the night of the crime. He is believed to be still hiding in London – but where? And who is sheltering him?'[9] The *Daily Mirror* developed this theme the following day, describing him as 'the most sought-for individual' and 'the mystery man of the plot' about whom the only certain thing known was 'that he is armed with an automatic pistol, which he will probably not hesitate to use when his hiding-place is found':

> Having attained a position of unenviable eminence, 'Peter the Painter' has become a sort of popular hero in the East End, especially among the juvenile section of the inhabitants, and it is extraordinary what a large number of people there are now who claim his acquaintance . . .

The little boys in the streets discuss 'Peter the Painter' while squatting in the doorways of mean houses, and many a brick wall bears a chalk representation of the redoubtable Peter as delineated by imaginative youngsters.[10]

This was a personality cult in the making. The *Morning Post*, more credulous than sensationalist, talked to one of these so-called acquaintances, 'a young East End lad', who asserted that 'Peter the Painter was nearly always drunk, and I knew him well by sight, and so did my mother ... He was a funny chap, especially when he was drunk, and on one occasion he threw my friend off a bicycle, and they had a fight.' The paper also fed popular prejudice and indignation, giving credence to the youngster's description of the small community of Latvians as 'all violent, ignorant, dirty people ... They are, in fact, just like animals.'[11]

By mid-January 1911, the police believed they had reliable information about Peter the Painter's stay in Marseilles two or three years earlier. They had an address, the names of two associates and the surname they believed he went by at that time, Piatkow (or Piaktow). The Marseilles police replied within a week. In May 1908, they had searched a house occupied by five apparent refugees, among them Peter Piatkow, who had papers indicating that he was born in Pskov, a Russian city close to the Baltic states, in June 1883. He moved around a lot in Marseilles. One address was known as an anarchist haunt and the manager of another boarding house where he stayed described him as 'a very violent character' – though another informant put forward a very different picture, of a man who worked hard, didn't drink or go out with girls and was vegetarian.[12]

French police officers tracked down one of the Marseilles associates mentioned by the London police, who had indeed been a close friend of Peter the Painter and stated that Peter had worked as a painter in the docks and elsewhere, was probably from Courland in Latvia and had used an assumed name. With a touch of deception, the Marseilles police managed to get their hands on photographs of Peter the Painter for long enough to have them copied. These were two high-quality portrait shots apparently taken

One of the photographs of Peter the Painter provided by the Marseilles police.

a few years earlier in the United States. The Marseilles police sent copies to London and these formed the basis for the 'official police portrait' of Peter the Painter that appeared on the front page of *The Star* on 26 January, and for the poster bearing both photographs and again offering a £500 reward, which was issued by the City of London Police four days later. By then, the police had uncovered another name used by the wanted man, Schtern. That poster with the photographs of a handsome, smartly dressed and self-confident Peter the Painter added to the air of intrigue and, by providing a face to accompany the name, further burnished his standing in popular folklore. It was, however, a touch misleading. When Pavell Molchanoff – an old comrade in France – had met up with Peter the Painter in London, he was struck that Peter's beard had gone, though he still had a (perhaps less flamboyant) moustache.

The London police tried, with some success, to trace more details of the movements and associates of Peter the Painter before he came to London. They discovered that by the close of 1909, he had moved to Paris. He stayed at an address in rue Danville until moving to London the following autumn and by this time had become fluent in French. The police found a letter addressed to P. Piatkow in Paris on Gardstein's body. They also seized correspondence to Peter the Painter, including postcards sent from Kyiv by his girlfriend, Anna Schwarze. 'I kiss you with all my heart – your black girl – I am yours with all my body,' one card ended (the word *schwarz* means 'black' in German).[13]

WHEN PETER THE PAINTER moved to the East End of London, he moved in with Svaars. They were comrades-in-arms, and Peter enjoyed status from his prominence in the armed movement in Latvia in 1905 and 1906. Fritz may also have had a debt of honour to his old friend, who sprang him from detention and so may have saved his life. Once installed in 59 Grove Street, Peter the Painter kept a low profile. He didn't, it seems, take a job or otherwise support himself; he played musical instruments in his room (the police found a violin, a mandolin and a tambourine); he may have helped paint stage scenery for an amateur theatre production and perhaps helped to prepare the stage for a balalaika performance. Tocmacoff recounted that he saw Peter painting a picture, but he doesn't seem to have been a diligent or productive artist. A couple of Peter the Painter's associates commented to police how reserved he was and Vassileva suggested in an unguarded moment that he wasn't trusted sufficiently to have led the Houndsditch robbery. From the testimony of associates – not always candid, of course – he doesn't emerge as a leader or driving force. While the photographs used by police suggest a debonair and well-presented young man, he was different in style from both Gardstein and Svaars: he was not brash, nor the sort of man to whom eyes turned. If he had a gun, he didn't flaunt it.

Although we know that Peter the Painter was Janis Zaklis, he remains an opaque figure. It's not simply the manner in which he eluded the police in London and the uncertainty about what happened to him later. We know what Peter the Painter looked like and where he stayed during his brief sojourn of ten weeks or so in London, but we have nothing in his own voice from that time – not even through the filters of interpreters and police statements. And the comments others attributed to him amount to nothing more than a few insubstantial remarks. He clearly came to London with a purpose – we can't be sure whether that was personal or political, but probably both. Amid the eddies of information and disinformation, nothing is certain, but it's likely that Peter the Painter had a role in preparing the way for the Houndsditch heist. The November 1910 issue of the Latvian anarchist journal *Briviba* listed Peter the Painter, using an old assumed name from his time in Latvia, as the treasurer of the Liesma group in London.[14] He may well have been lined up to take some of the proceeds out of the country and feed it to other Latvian groups and to the political project of which they were part. But he was probably not the mastermind of the operation that he has sometimes been portrayed as.

For the police, the most urgent task was not filling in Peter the Painter's back story but finding him. Detectives were said to be watching the docks at Liverpool in case he should try to board a transatlantic liner. Fanciful identifications were reported, some well-meaning and others malicious, from across London and beyond. He was reported, on slender evidence, to have a cast in his left eye and to be an 'inveterate' snuff-taker. The newspapers had some fun with the persistent and contradictory rumours about the wanted man's whereabouts. In early February, *The Star* reported that the 'elusive personage Peter the Painter' was in Switzerland; a month later, he had jumped from a ship as it docked at Antwerp and disappeared.[15] The police received vexatious letters, some partly in Russian, signed 'Peter the Painter', again an echo of the Jack the Ripper case a generation earlier. In the following months, reports of sightings came in from across the world. A sheriff in Illinois who had seen a photograph of the suspect in a paper wrote to say, 'This man Peter the Painter I think is here. He represents himself to be a Minister, and is preaching in School-Houses ... I will keep [a] tab on him the best that I can, until I hear from you.' A British official, with commendable understatement, noted it was 'highly improbable' that this was the wanted man.[16] News of other possible sightings came from Winnipeg in Canada, Sydney, Naples and Brussels, while someone took the trouble to share the news that Peter the Painter was on his way to India.[17]

It's not at all clear where Peter the Painter was once he had managed to cross the North Sea a few days after the Houndsditch shootings. There are suggestions that he spent time in several European countries and that he perhaps returned to London for a few days in April 1911 – though that would have been reckless, especially with the trial linked to the Houndsditch police murders about to get under way. The Russian intelligence already cited from December 1912 locating Peter the Painter in Germany is the last semi-reliable information on his whereabouts. The failure to secure convictions at the Old Bailey was a stark reminder to the police and the prosecuting authorities that the case against the Latvians and their associates was weak. There was nothing to suggest, in spite of the notoriety he gained, that Peter the Painter was present when the three police officers were shot dead, or that he used or owned firearms. As the judge declared during the Old Bailey trial, 'There is no evidence to show that the man who was called "Peter the Painter" was one of the murderers. I may be wrong, but that is my view.'[18] It was a curious observation given that the man he was talking of was not among the defendants, but on this occasion Mr Justice Grantham wasn't wrong. If Peter the Painter had been in the dock at the Old Bailey, he too would almost certainly have been acquitted. There was no purpose in maintaining the police search.

Some senior figures in the London police responded to the dearth of evidence against the most high-profile of their suspects by suggesting that he hadn't been involved. Sir Melville Macnaghten, assistant commissioner of the Metropolitan Police, asserted in his memoirs, which were published only four years after Houndsditch and Sidney Street,

> I do not believe that [Peter the Painter] had anything to do with the case, nor do I think that he was in England at the time of the tragedy. He had, however, lived with Fritz some weeks before, and was undoubtedly a pal of the party. But, in my opinion, he chiefly owed his notoriety to the aid of 'apt and artful alliteration.' In other words, his name was attractive and looked well in print.[19]

The police had distributed his details to the press complete with the alliterative name they had devised; they had issued the 'wanted' posters bearing his likeness. They created the legend of Peter the Painter. One of the country's most senior police officers was now suggesting they had got it all wrong. There were even whispers that Peter the Painter may never have existed. This was delusional. The police had ample evidence of his presence in Grove Street, and of at least the start of his panicked flight after the police murders. Whatever Peter the Painter's level of complicity, he couldn't simply be painted out of the picture.

Another tale gained traction that Peter the Painter was a police informer – working not for the London police but for the tsarist Okhrana. An early iteration of this story appeared in the *New York Times* when it reported on the appeal court's quashing of Nina Vassileva's conviction in July 1911. This declared without equivocation, or indeed attribution, that Peter the Painter was 'an agent provocateur of the Russian Government'. The paper's reporter suggested obliquely that the manner in which Vassileva's conviction had been promptly overruled fitted with indications that Downing Street had taken steps 'to call off the detectives' pursuing Peter the Painter.[20] It was a good conspiracy theory and the Russian authorities would certainly have liked to have an agent inside the Liesma or 'flame' group. But there is no supporting evidence. The London police tried and failed to arrest Peter the Painter, seeking help from the Russian and French police forces. When it became painfully clear that they didn't have a legal case likely to secure his conviction, there was little point devoting resources to a lost cause. It was humbling for the police to fail to bring to justice a man they presented as a prime suspect in the murder of three police officers, but there's no need to invoke a conspiracy theory to explain their shortcomings. Nevertheless, the notion that one of Britain's 'most wanted' was a secret agent proved too tempting for some writers. A history of Britain's secret service published in 1969 recycled the story, but without any fresh evidence of substance and while managing to conflate the Houndsditch and Sidney Street shootings into a single incident in a manner which doesn't inspire confidence in the hypothesis put forward.[21]

Peter the Painter never broke surface after he left London. Some of his relatives believed that he moved to the United States. Basil Thomson, who was head of the Metropolitan Police's Criminal Investigation Department during the First World War, suggested that Peter the Painter died in the United States in 1914 – but that seems to be based on a deeply unreliable tale that the wanted man was actually Peter Pilenas, the brother of an interpreter for the London police.[22] There were more persistent reports that he had settled in Australia, where John Rosen made a new home and where Fritz Svaars had aspired to live. On a few occasions, Australian police believed that they had found the fugitive. Some of these communications between police forces could be a touch cloak-and-dagger. In July 1917, the London police received a telegram stating that it 'is believed that Peter Piatkow, alias The Painter, is located in Melbourne'. The Melbourne police wanted fingerprint details and word of any distinctive marks of identity. Superintendent Ottaway of the City of London Police drafted a telegram in response: 'Peter Piatkow Heartsunk Fernplant Nioposnuff Marblerub Angleshot Flavorum Enomobarch Flavodo Extradition …'. Happily, the copy in the archive also includes the decoded message: 'Peter Piatkow

Have not Fingerprint impressions nor any distinctive mark Not to be arrested for me not sufficient evidence for his Extradition.'[23] However you transcribe the coded communication, the message was: even if this should be Peter the Painter, there was nothing to be done.

One of the more remarkable accounts of Peter the Painter's purported Australian afterlife came from Ben Leeson, the police officer seriously injured at Sidney Street. Leeson viewed Peter the Painter as an 'elusive arch-villain' and indeed 'the master-mind, who, backed by the Red Terror, plotted and nearly carried into execution a reign of anarchy and terrorism in the heart of the world's greatest metropolis'. Once Leeson was discharged from hospital, he made a personal trip to Australia to recuperate. He told the bizarre story in his reminiscences of how, in Sydney,

> whom should I see in the booking-hall of the Central Station but 'Peter the Painter' himself! I knew the 'Painter' well by sight, for previous to the Houndsditch and Sidney Street affairs he used to frequent the saloon-bar of the King's Head public-house at the corner of Grove Street and Commercial Road; in fact, there was at one time a photograph of him hanging in the bar.

Leeson went on to recount how he and the man he believed to be Peter the Painter shared an otherwise empty train compartment. 'It was an awkward situation,' he recorded with exceptional literary restraint. The two men engaged in some small talk but neither gave any sign of recognizing the other and eventually Leeson got off at his intended destination.[24] The tale is, of course, nonsense from start to finish and, much like Leeson's insistence that 'the hand of Stalin' was behind the shootings at Houndsditch and Sidney Street, it seems to have been intended to boost sales of memoirs by an aggrieved former police officer with a penchant for presenting fiction as fact. It simply demonstrates that a generation after Sidney Street, Peter the Painter still had a place in the popular imagination. The suggestion that Peter the Painter ended up in Australia, however, is plausible. The historian Philip Ruff, who talked to some of

Peter the Painter's distant relatives, believes that the fugitive may have settled there in 1913 and some years later started a family – but there's no hard evidence.[25]

There were other curious, and more ominous, tales about Peter the Painter's new identity. In 1927, when the British authorities became concerned about Soviet espionage activities and raided the London offices of the Russian trading enterprise Arcos, they came across a cypher clerk, Anton Miller, in the throes of burning documents. In the aftermath, Moscow came to the conclusion that Anton and his brother Peter Miller, who worked in the same cypher department, were security risks. Both were Latvians and operating under assumed names. According to MI5 records, the Soviet authorities seem to have believed that Anton Miller was Peter the Painter, and that the British authorities had discovered this and were blackmailing him to act as a spy. The British files are littered with mistakes and misconceptions but they document that the Miller brothers were eventually ordered back to Moscow and shot. In 1932, an MI5 informant, having compared in detail photographs of Peter the Painter and those of Anton Miller taken almost twenty years later, concluded they were the same man. This can't be quite as easily dismissed as Ben Leeson's tale of his train companion, but seems to be unlikely.[26]

There's another much-repeated myth that places Peter the Painter, some years after his flight from London, as a Soviet Communist insider. The East End anarchist leader Rudolf Rocker recorded in his reminiscences that

> in the early days of the Russian Revolution, [Peter the Painter] appeared in Russia, and was appointed by the Bolshevik Government as an official of the terrible Cheka, becoming one of its most notorious agents. Our comrade Alexander Shapiro, who had seen Peter in London, met him in Russia, working as an agent of the Cheka.[27]

The Cheka, an abbreviation of the All-Russian Extraordinary Commission, was the first incarnation of the Soviet secret police, and is often used as a generic term for all the secret police units that operated under Soviet Communism. It was an institution that came to be even more feared than the tsarist Okhrana. Peter the Painter never worked for the Cheka, but Rocker's tale was not an invention. He had simply confused two Peters. It was Jacob Peters, one of those tried and acquitted at the Old Bailey, who returned to revolutionary Russia and rose to a senior rank in the secret police. Alone of those caught up in the Houndsditch affair, Jacob Peters achieved a grisly eminence.

Jacob (or Jectat or Jekabs) Peters was, by his own account, from Courland in Latvia, though Russian seems to have been his first language and he was a member of a Russian library while in London. He was aged 24 at the time of the Houndsditch shootings. At his trial at the Old Bailey, Peters recounted how in Latvia he had worked variously as a grocer's assistant, as a dock labourer and in a butter factory. He became an activist in the Latvian Social Democratic Party, and for several years undertook unpaid propaganda work in the army under the name of Svornoff. That led, by his own account, to a court martial, but after eighteen months in detention he was acquitted. A British intelligence report drawn up a few years later suggested that Peters's activism in Latvia included 'confiscating money from banks, factories etc, where it was a question of just a revolver and confederate' – which is entirely possible but unproven.[28] Fearful that he faced arrest for articles he had written for a left-wing journal, he fled to Germany with the intention of heading on to the United States. But he was short of money and, after travelling to Denmark but failing to find work there, he came to London in October 1909 and trained to be a tailor's presser. One of his employers gave evidence that he was a very good workman but spoke little English.

Peters's mother was Liza Svaars and he was Fritz Svaars's first cousin. Peters had stayed with his cousin at Great Garden Street when he first came to London, but they constantly rowed. The two lived close by but didn't see a lot of each other, and when they did it was – it seems – mainly to pass on family news. Peters was unusual among those charged after the Houndsditch shootings in not having gathered at 59 Grove Street earlier in the day. And he had an alibi for the shootings – he had complained to his landlady that mice were nibbling his food and on that evening he was repairing and setting a mousetrap.

On questioning at his arrest on the evening of 22 December 1910, six days after the Houndsditch shootings, Jacob Peters exclaimed, 'It is nothing to do with me. I cannot help what my cousin Fritz has done.'[29] That's a comment which is likely to have increased the police's suspicions rather than allayed them. He told the police that the basis for his differences with his cousin was political: 'he is an Anarchist. I am a Social Democrat.'[30] He was secretary of the London branch of the Latvian Social Democrats. He was also a member of Britain's own Social Democratic Party, the successor of which was a decade later the main constituent in the founding of the Communist Party of Great Britain – the police found his membership card of the SDP's Shoreditch branch.[31] He explained that he was so well known as an activist that he used a different name to get work. While in Brixton Prison awaiting trial, Peters wrote to a friend and comrade – no doubt knowing that the authorities would translate and read all correspondence – lamenting the political innocence of the London police: 'I think that when you have read in the newspapers that I am charged because I am a member of an Anarchist Club, you will laugh because you know I am an energetic enemy of Anarchists.'[32]

The Latvian Social Democrats repudiated any suggestion that they had been involved in the shootings at Houndsditch and Sidney Street. A statement issued in Brussels declared, 'we have nothing in common with robbers and hooligans who so frequently are influenced by Russian secret agents.' The party insisted that they had taken part in a congress of Russian Social Democrats in London in 1907 which decreed that party members were to have nothing to do with 'expropriators' and that the Latvian Social Democrats had since then 'acted vigorously against any one palliating or excusing such means of carrying on our struggle'.[33] It seems that after Peters's arrest, his party was not entirely satisfied that he had kept sufficient distance from anarchists and took action against him. The authorities received information suggesting that Peters

Jacob Peters, perhaps taken at his wedding in 1916.

was expelled from the Latvian Social Democrats group in London but was later reinstated.

Jacob Peters's family links to Fritz Svaars and his profile in the small world of Latvian revolutionaries in London probably explain his arrest, and the unreliable identification evidence of Isaac Levy suggesting that he was one of the gunmen was sufficient to place him in the dock. It's quite possible he knew of the robbery plan and perhaps in some manner assisted it, but he was not a core member of the group and was very probably not at Exchange Buildings on the night of the shootings.

In the aftermath of his acquittal, Jacob Peters took up with May Freeman – who seems also to have been politically on the left – and they lived together in Islington in North London. She knew that Peters had been a defendant in the Houndsditch trial, later recounting that her boyfriend 'told me everything, so that I should not marry him in ignorance of his record'. In December 1913, when May was nineteen, they had a daughter, Little May or Maisie. They married in 1916.[34] Peters's activism continued unabated and during the First World War the level of surveillance was much increased. He was a prominent member of the Nosere group of émigrés, many of them apparently Latvians, which met at the Communist Club in Fitzrovia. In this deeply factional world, he sided with Lenin's Bolsheviks.[35] On 1 May 1917, Peters – clearly excited by the pace of political change in Russia and its empire – headed back home, initially to Riga. He had been summoned to assist the incipient revolution. He got swept up in the Bolshevik rise to power and was in Petrograd and a key actor during the October Revolution.

By the following year, Peters had emerged as the deputy head of Lenin's newly established Cheka secret police. A British diplomat and spy, R. H. Bruce Lockhart, came across Peters in Moscow in 1918, when the revolution was fighting for survival and the Bolsheviks were struggling to maintain supremacy. He considered the Latvian to be ruthless and fanatical but also with a sentimental and chivalrous side. When the Bolsheviks acted decisively against 'Black Guard' anarchists in Moscow, raiding the mansions they had taken over, Peters – who had once declared himself an 'energetic enemy' of anarchism – demonstrated what that meant in practice. He took Lockhart to the scene of one raid, with bodies of young anarchists strewn around amid the decadence and destruction. Peters later reminisced to the British diplomat about his imprisonment in Latvia under the tsar and showed his nails 'as proof of the torture which he had undergone'. He also spoke of his time in England, and Lockhart – after a brief spell of detention – happily delivered a letter from Peters to his wife in London.[36] As the crushing of opponents of Lenin's Bolsheviks became more intense, news reports described Peters as 'the man who spends his time in signing decrees for execution during the Moscow Reign of Terror'. A British intelligence document in June 1919 portrayed him as 'Russia's greatest murderer'. He was deeply complicit in what became known as the 'Red Terror', seizing the wealth of the new administration's enemies and suppressing any rival groups.[37]

When Jacob Peters started to attract international notoriety, the *Daily Express* tracked down May Peters, 'a good-looking young woman', at her home in Islington. She insisted that Peters was 'a kind husband and father' and that the allegations against him were 'unthinkable'.[38] But May Peters was herself under scrutiny. In May 1919, a well-connected Conservative MP, Henry Page-Croft, wrote to the Home Secretary with what he said was confidential information, that Mrs Peters 'married a Russian whom she states is Peter the Painter of Sidney Street fame'. This canard that her husband was the wanted anti-hero crops up several times in the files and may have swayed the view of officialdom when she needed help. The letter alleged that May Peters was promoting strikes and spreading left-wing propaganda. 'She is a loose woman openly advocating Bolshevist principles including free love, to which, unfortunately the daughter of my informant has fallen a victim.'[39]

She was initially reluctant to follow her husband to Russia, even once the war had ended and the Bolshevik authorities offered to arrange a passage for herself and her daughter. But in March 1921, she headed to Moscow – and very quickly regretted it. Jacob Peters had a new wife and family. May Peters secured a divorce and asked for permission to return to Britain. In July 1922 a left-wing Labour MP, Neil Maclean, took up her case.

> Mrs Peters speaks no Russian and has a very hard time to maintain herself in Moscow under this handicap. The Russian authorities regard her as English, but the English Mission in Moscow persist in regarding her as still Russian and refuse to grant a passport. So she can neither get a passport from the Russian authorities nor the English authorities.

An official memo that was drawn up in response to the MP's plea was concerned less about her nationality than with her political sympathies:

> She is a member of the I.W.W. [Industrial Workers of the World] and of the notorious International Socialist Club, from which she was threatened with expulsion for immorality. While she lived in this country she associated entirely with extremists and is alleged to have been concerned in the Sydney [*sic*] Street affair. There is no proof or even hint in our records that her interest in politics has abated . . .
>
> In view of the above, the Commissioner of Police recommends that the alleged view of the English Mission be upheld and that her return to this country should be opposed.[40]

She should, in effect, remain stateless because of her husband's notoriety and her own political views and perceived lifestyle. There was no suggestion that she had ever committed any criminal offence, just the miasma of being seen as an undesirable person. There was no substance to the Sidney Street slur; she wasn't living in London at the time (the 1911 Census records her as a seventeen-year-old live-in domestic servant in the home of an auctioneer in Weybridge) and only met Peters after his acquittal.

Six years later, in 1928, May Peters was still in Moscow and still asking for a British passport. She supplied her birth and marriage certificates to support her request for naturalization as a British subject. 'Do you know of any reason . . . why she should not be given facilities to come to the United Kingdom if she can get out of Soviet territory?' asked a British official in Moscow in a memo to London. Guy Liddell, then based at New Scotland Yard and later a senior figure in MI5, replied cautiously,

> I dare say she has had a pretty difficult time in Russia. Now that people there are beginning to feel the pinch, she probably thinks that she would be better off over here. Her political record in this country prior to her departure for Russia does not appear to be a very serious one, and if, as seems possible, she has had enough of the Soviet system, her testimony might have beneficial effects in this country. There is, on the other hand, the possibility that the

intention may be to send her here for some special political purpose.[41]

This was at a time of continuing concern about a Soviet spy ring in London. The Home Office said it couldn't help May Peters get out of Russia, but once she had left Soviet territory she could be given a visa to come to Britain – though her naturalization would depend on proof that her divorce was regarded as valid by the British courts.

She wasn't able to get out. Appeals to the Home Office from her sister the following year prompted an official at the Foreign Office to repeat the false accusation that May Peters 'is the former wife of the notorious "Peter the Painter"'. Almost two decades after Sidney Street, her fate was still clouded by this confusion. In July 1930, Peters called at the British embassy in Moscow. She had formally taken out Soviet nationality so that she was no longer seen in Moscow as a British subject and intended to apply for a Soviet passport. 'Mrs Peters, who was decently dressed and looked fairly well, though thin, was much affected by the possibility of returning to the United Kingdom.'[42] She never made it home. Jacob Peters, who served the revolution loyally and was at one time a close friend of Lenin, succumbed to Stalin's terror. He was arrested in November 1937 as part of an alleged Latvian conspiracy and was shot and executed the following April. May Peters died in 1942. After the war, their daughter, Maisie, secured work at the British embassy in Moscow, which was as close as she got to returning to the land of her birth. She had an affair with a member of the British Military Mission in Moscow which led to her being accused of spying and sentenced to a labour camp. Maisie Peters was released in 1956, at about the time her father was posthumously rehabilitated along with many of Stalin's victims. She died in Moscow nine years later at the age of 51. Her family in Britain requested her ashes – even this was denied.[43]

12
The Anarchist Aftermath

For the anarchist movement in Britain, the violence at Houndsditch and Sidney Street, and the angry response to it, was a moment of peril. The press, political leaders and many others in public life denounced anarchism as the corrupting ideology that had led to shoot-outs in the streets of London. Anarchists were once again demonized. These were by far the most serious acts of violence in Britain ever linked to anarchism and anarchists. The all-too-obvious likely consequences were increased surveillance of anarchist meetings and activity and the prospect of police action and possibly deportation against any émigrés who were seen to be in any way associated with the actions of the Latvians. Anarchists couldn't simply say: nothing to do with us. The evidence that some of those involved in the Houndsditch robbery attempt had regarded themselves as anarchists, and their frequenting of the Jubilee Street Club, couldn't be wished away. By and large the anarchist response was to suggest that the gunmen weren't really anarchists; that even if they were, that doesn't mean that anarchists support armed robbery and the shooting of policemen; and that the real culprit was Russian despotism, which had brutalized its citizens and turned advocates of social justice into outlaws.

In its issue after the Houndsditch murders, the anarchist monthly *Freedom* devoted its front page to an article posing the question 'The Houndsditch Tragedy: Who Is Responsible?' It detailed the cruelty and ruthlessness with which the 1905 uprising in Latvia was put down and argued that some of those subject to such oppression 'would be inevitably driven to the desperate acts we have just seen in Houndsditch'. The tragedy was 'the desperate work of the Tsar's victims' and could perhaps have been provoked by a police agent. The article also issued a complaint commonly voiced in anarchist propaganda, that any awkward or dissident voice was often diminished or dismissed by the establishment as anarchist extremism. 'Indian Nationalists want their own Government: they are Anarchists! Portuguese Republicans kill Dom Carlos: they are Anarchists! Burglars in Houndsditch shoot the police: they are undoubtedly Anarchists! And if Lord Rosebery should, as he threatens, defy Lloyd George's taxation with physical force, it will be laid to the door of the Anarchists.'[1] This was good knockabout rhetoric but didn't address the issue of how at least some of those associated with anarchism sought recourse to semi-automatic weapons and armed robbery.

Freedom Press went on to issue a leaflet in response to 'the outburst against Anarchism and Anarchists' intensified by the gun battle in Stepney. This argued that the press was deceitful in implying that aliens were habitually criminal, asserting rather tellingly, 'No nation has sent forth more of its own people as aliens over the world than Great Britain.' The article conceded that the gunmen were 'probably revolutionists from the Baltic provinces of Russia' but lambasted the press for so eagerly raising the cry of 'Anarchist!' It went on to argue, less convincingly, 'Even if some of the people concerned were Anarchists, it would not prove they were burglars because they were Anarchists, any more than ... Crippen [was] a murderer because he was a Roman Catholic.'[2]

The *Arbayter Fraynd* was more directly in the firing line, as the press made so much of the gunmen's familiarity with the Jubilee Street Club, which took the Yiddish-language weekly paper's name. 'Anarchism and anarchists have no relationship with individual thievery,' the paper declared. It made many of the points and rhetorical arguments that *Freedom* also rehearsed, notably about the culpable vengefulness of the forces of Russian imperialism. But in an issue dated just three days after the siege, it paid a tribute of sorts to the two gunmen who had died:

> Both of the men in Sidney Street who held out for twelve hours against an entire army were certainly no ordinary

human types. You might have the most earnest opinion about their behaviour but even their most bitter opponents must admit – they displayed a desperate courage. If two soldiers had managed to defend themselves this way, monuments would be erected in their honour and the newspapers would not cease to tell of their deeds. Who can deny that under other circumstances the same people would have probably been good and useful members of a free society and their energies would have had an entirely different outlet?[3]

This was a generous epitaph for Svaars and Sokoloff – they did indeed display a degree of valour, but they were also armed robbers who opened fire to evade arrest.

The following month, the *Arbayter Fraynd* had something of a scoop. It persuaded one of the most prominent anarchists of the time, Errico Malatesta, to write for the paper about the two shoot-outs.[4] He had been an unwitting associate of George Gardstein, the gang member who suffered fatal injuries at Houndsditch, and as such was implicated – in the police's view at least – in the murder of the three policemen. In the immediate aftermath of the incident at Sidney Street, the *Evening News* tracked down Malatesta, 'the brains of the anarchist movement', in his lodgings in rooms 'over a wine-shop in Islington', where he spoke 'volubly in a heavy foreign accent'. The paper gave prominence to his clear-cut repudiation of expropriation:

'It is deplorable, this taking of life,' [Malatesta] said. 'It is a mistake, foolish, useless, criminal.

But what in the world has it to do with Anarchism? The men were not Anarchists, but burglars and murderers, and they should be called burglars and murderers ...

... Anarchism does not include the robbery of safes and the shooting of policemen who frustrate it.

'Nor must you believe in the criminals who call themselves Anarchists to lift themselves to a higher plane.'[5]

Writing for the *Arbayter Fraynd*, Malatesta reiterated that 'both the theory and practice of robbery is contrary to the political standpoint of the anarchists.' Indeed, he argued that as 'enemies of the capitalists, we can't allow ourselves to have any sympathy for the robber, who has no other wish but to become a capitalist himself'. He addressed directly the death of the two gunmen in Sidney Street:

> these robbers were Russians – fugitives, from Russia, perhaps. It might also be the case that they had occasionally gone to an anarchist club for public meetings, when the club was open to everyone. Naturally, the capitalist press exploited this in order to declare war on the anarchists. Listening to the bourgeois journalists, you'd get the impression that anarchism's dream of justice and love between people was in reality nothing but thievery and murder, and it is certain that through their lies and deceptions, they have succeeded in alienating from us many people who would have otherwise been on our side and who we really would like to have with us.[6]

That was part of the problem facing anarchists. Their association in the popular press and public perception with gunmen and violence consigned the movement to the margins of political activism and debate.

Malatesta's unwitting role in the preparations for the Houndsditch robbery came close to leading to his deportation. The police were able to trace an oxygen cylinder that the robbers brought with them in their attempt to break into the jewellery store and then crack open the safe. The company that supplied the cylinder gave the police the business card of the man who had bought the items: 'E. Malatesta & Co. Electricians and General Engineers – Cycles and Motor Cycles Built and Repaired – Metal Work'. Malatesta had a basement engineering workshop with a furnace in a street off City Road in Islington where, he told the police, 'I have been making experiments in the brazing of metals by means of oxygen and coal gas.'[7]

He was brought in for questioning and explained that the day before the attempted robbery, he had sold on for £5 some of the items he had bought from the suppliers on Farringdon Road: the oxygen cylinder – which weighed 25 kilograms (55 lb) and had a capacity of over 1 cubic metre (40 cu. ft) – along with a pressure gauge, a valve and up to 18 metres (20 yd) of rubber tubing. The buyer was a man in his late twenties 'who spoke bad French' and gave the name Lambert and said he needed the equipment for a lantern show. Malatesta arranged to have the cylinder refilled and all the items were collected the following day, just hours before the start of the attempt to burrow into the Houndsditch jewellery shop. A 'young English lad' aged about eighteen loaded the items on to a costermonger's barrow and wheeled them away. Malatesta confirmed that these were the same items that police retrieved from Exchange Buildings after the shootings in which the three policemen were killed.

The Italian anarchist also revealed another, more enduring, association with the gunmen. According to his witness statement, about a year before the Houndsditch robbery attempt, Malatesta met a man in his early twenties at the Jubilee Street anarchist club who was introduced to him as a 'comrade' and whom he came to know simply as 'the Russian'. Malatesta said he couldn't remember who made the introduction, but Rudolf Rocker recalled that one of the more prominent of the Jubilee Street anarchists, Siegfried Nacht (also known as Arnold Roller), acted as an interpreter in conversations between the two and suggested that the younger man make use of Malatesta's workshop.[8] This man 'was I understand a Russian Political refugee and an engineer', Malatesta told the police. 'During the past 12 months he has used my workshop to do any little job he has had. Sometimes he would come two or three times a week. I last saw him on Friday afternoon at my workshop.'[9] That was the day of the attempted break-in at Harris's jewellery business. When taken by police to the mortuary at the London Hospital, Malatesta recognized the man on the slab, George Gardstein, as his engineering acquaintance. This was deeply incriminating, leading to the supposition that Gardstein prepared some of the tools and equipment used in the robbery attempt at Malatesta's workbench.

Malatesta was only held by the police for a few hours. He was called upon to see if he could pick out anyone in an identity parade at Bishopsgate Police Station – and returned there twice in February on a similar mission – but didn't recognize anyone.[10] He was a cooperative informant, and the police must have reflected that a conspirator in armed robbery was unlikely to have left his business card with the company providing him with the tools for the job. On Malatesta's release, his friend Rudolf Rocker rushed round to offer support and to hear the full story. 'He said the police at Scotland Yard had behaved admirably. I am sure that in any other country the police would have played up Malatesta's political beliefs in such a way as to implicate him in the affair.'[11] But Malatesta was not off the hook. Two significant threads of evidence linked him to a gang responsible for the most grievous shooting in the history of the London police. Malatesta was required to attend the initial court proceedings in early March and then was called by the prosecution to give evidence at the Old Bailey trial in May 1911.

It must have been a deeply uncomfortable experience for such a prominent anarchist to appear in the witness box in England's Central Criminal Court. The focus of the questioning was on his relationship with Gardstein:

> I met him in a club in Jubilee Street; it was a working men's club – an Anarchist club. He asked me if I could give him the use of my tools because he had an invention to develop. He used to turn and file pieces of metal, but I did not see him often as I was not working in the workshop much then. I did not pay him anything nor he me. He could only speak a few words of English or French, so we talked very little. I used to leave the key with my landlord to give him.[12]

But Gardstein was dead, and Malatesta's evidence did not directly implicate any of the defendants. It's difficult to escape the impression that he was summoned to court simply to associate the accused in the minds of the jury with an apostle of anarchism.

A Devilish Kind of Courage

Although he was never charged, nor indeed formally questioned beyond his initial encounter with the police, Malatesta was regarded with deep, almost pathological, suspicion by senior police officers. Whereas Kropotkin, with his patrician and scholarly demeanour, was viewed with respect, Malatesta, more ramshackle in appearance and a working man, was seen as the embodiment of the anarchist menace. A history of the Metropolitan Police went so far as to state that Malatesta was an *'ex officio'* member of the Houndsditch gang, and that seems to have been the received wisdom at Scotland Yard.[13] One of the more outlandish police memoirs chronicled Malatesta's 'meteoric career of devilry'. It alleged that, in need of money, he was behind the robbery that became known as the Tottenham Outrage of 1909. 'Though Malatesta's connection with the crime was known, there was not sufficient evidence to arrest him, and he continued in his career of wholesale villainy.' According to this account, he went

Errico Malatesta outside a London court, 1912.

on to plan the Houndsditch robbery. 'All the members of this gang were aliens, murderers, sodden with vice and every kind of devilry from white-slaving to blackmail, and Malatesta and Cardstein [sic] ruled them with an iron hand.'[14] This alarmist nonsense would be of little consequence but for the senior police rank of detective inspector to which the author, Harold Brust, rose and his role in the surveillance of anarchists and other perceived security risks.

Brust simply set down in sensationalist language what other police officers expressed a little more cautiously. Another former detective inspector at Scotland Yard, Herbert Fitch, was also at one point put on Malatesta's trail and described him as having a 'striking face. Swarthy, black-haired, black-bearded, tall, with burning dark eyes, he was handsome, sinister and menacing.'[15] The assumption of Malatesta's culpability was shared by some of the country's most senior police officers. William Nott-Bower, Commissioner of the City of London Police at the time of the Houndsditch shootings, was convinced of the Italian's complicity. 'Undoubtedly, he procured for Gardstein the cylinder of acetylene gas used at Houndsditch. Undoubtedly, too, it was upon his premises that Gardstein made, or fashioned, the burglars' tools also used there. But there was insufficient evidence to prove guilty knowledge of the premeditated burglary.'[16]

A year after the Houndsditch trial, Malatesta was back at the Old Bailey – and this time in the dock. He was accused of defaming and libelling a fellow Italian anarchist, Ennio Bellelli, by circulating a leaflet alleging that Bellelli was a police spy in the pay of the Italian government.[17] The two men had been close friends but Bellelli told the court that they had fallen out bitterly: 'my wife broke the friendship [with Malatesta] at the time of the Houndsditch affair because the police were calling at my house asking me if I knew persons who participated in the murders.' They also took differing views over the Italian invasion of Libya, then part of the Ottoman Empire, and the resulting war between Italy and Turkey. In the slanging match between the two men, there were suggestions that Bellelli publicly alleged that Malatesta had been involved in the Houndsditch robbery attempt, as well as labelling him a Turkish spy.[18]

When the case got to court, Malatesta's defence was that the allegation was true. He was almost certainly justified in accusing Bellelli of being a police spy but it couldn't be proved. The jury found against Malatesta. Before sentence was passed, evidence was heard about his character, including a damning account from a police inspector. He said that the prisoner

> was known to the police as an Anarchist of a very dangerous type for a great number of years. He has been imprisoned in his own country and has been expelled from France. He has visited Egypt, Spain, France, Portugal, and, I believe, America, in the interests of Anarchy, and wherever he went there was a great deal of trouble. He is known as the leader of militant Anarchists in this country – in fact, in the world. Many of his former colleagues have passed through this court and had penal servitude for coining [making counterfeit money].[19]

The police officer also pointedly reminded the court of Malatesta's association with Gardstein, 'one of the Houndsditch assassins'. The judge got the message. Malatesta was sentenced to three months' imprisonment for criminal libel and, of much greater moment, was recommended for expulsion from Britain under the Aliens Act. The police clearly believed that Malatesta had got what he deserved.

Malatesta was a political émigré and to deport him under the terms of the 1905 Aliens Act seemed to stretch the legislation's purpose, as well as fighting with the instincts of many Liberals. A legal challenge was made against the judge's ruling, and a Malatesta Release Committee launched a vigorous campaign opposing both the prison sentence and the proposed deportation. Demonstrations were held in central London supported by an energetic publicity campaign and behind-the-scenes lobbying. Peter Kropotkin approached his old ally John Burns, who in the 1880s had been a prominent socialist and was now a Cabinet minister in Asquith's Liberal government. While anarchists led the campaign, it attracted support from prominent figures in the Labour Party and the radical wing of Liberalism. A local newspaper in North London, not noted for its radicalism, rallied to the cause of the adopted Islingtonian. 'Are we to tolerate in our country the methods of policemanism that are prevalent in the most backward of Continental countries such as Russia!' it argued.[20] A month after the initial verdict, Malatesta lost an appeal heard by the Lord Chief Justice. But while the courts disappointed Malatesta, the government came to his aid. A few days after the appeal judgment, the Home Secretary told Parliament that he would not after all issue an expulsion order against Malatesta, but neither would there be any remission of his jail sentence. The campaign had succeeded in upholding the right of asylum and preventing the deportation, but a few months after his release from jail Malatesta left Britain of his own accord after thirteen years in exile in London.

In the wake of the Sidney Street siege, evidence surfaced suggesting that another prominent European anarchist had had a role in the Houndsditch affair. Jules Bonnot, a Frenchman, was a little-known figure at the time of the robbery attempt but he achieved notoriety shortly afterwards as the leader of a gang responsible for a spate of armed robberies and murders in France. The Bonnot gang became known as the 'motor bandits' because of their propensity for stealing cars and – an innovation in the world of serious crime – using them as getaway vehicles. They operated on a scale, and with a recklessness, that far exceeded that of the Latvian émigrés in London. Bonnot himself was besieged and shot dead in April 1912 and most of his associates were either killed, guillotined or jailed. As with the Houndsditch gang, there was much discussion as to whether Bonnot and his accomplices were in any way political or simply armed criminals; and again echoing the London shootings, there was clear evidence that some of the gunmen had seen themselves as anarchists and had links with the anarchist movement.

In July 1912, three months after Bonnot's death, Scotland Yard wrote to the City of London Police to share new evidence about the Houndsditch shootings. Earlier that month, two police officers had travelled to the Isle of Wight to interview an unnamed prisoner at Parkhurst prison. The prisoner recounted how, in 1909, he had met

Bonnot – who was already making a living by burglary, stealing cars and counterfeiting – at an anarchist club in the French city of Lyons. The following year, the informant moved to England and several months later got a letter from Bonnot asking for help in arranging accommodation for a forthcoming trip to London. He subsequently met Bonnot at a pub in Soho: 'he told me that he had come to London at the request of several Russian anarchists to assist them in a criminal enterprise in the East End of London.' He met Bonnot again about ten days later:

> I remember particularly it was the morning after the tragedy at Houndsditch. He was standing at the corner of Old Compton Street and Charing Cross Road about 9 a.m. I spoke to him and noticed he was very excited. I said, 'What is the matter, Bonnot.' He said, 'We were at work last night but the men who were with me were blunderers ... The Police came on the scene but we served them right. It is a very bad business indeed, you will soon see it in the papers. I am going away by train to Lyon at once.'
>
> I am quite certain that he was the leader in the Houndsditch Tragedy.[21]

This account may be behind the outlandish suggestion rehearsed in a police memoir that Jules Bonnot was another pseudonym for Peter the Painter.[22]

Testimony provided by a prisoner who perhaps was seeking special privileges or a remission of sentence is inherently unreliable. There is no supporting evidence that Bonnot had any involvement in armed crime in London and the implication that he was on the scene at Houndsditch is simply wrong. But Bonnot did spend several months in London during the course of 1910 – and, unlikely as it may seem, was said to have worked for a time as a chauffeur for the writer Arthur Conan Doyle – and the possibility that he was in touch with some of those involved in the Houndsditch robbery attempt is not that far-fetched.[23] Certainly, some of the apologists for the French 'Anarchist-Bandits' admired the example of the

London émigrés. In 1909, the young Russian revolutionary Victor Serge, writing under a pseudonym for a French-language anarchist journal, commended 'our audacious comrades who fell at Tottingham [*sic*]', expressing 'much admiration for their unequalled bravery', which demonstrated that 'anarchists don't surrender.' Two years later, using a different pseudonym, Serge offered extravagant praise for the two gunmen who died at Sidney Street. 'The magnificent resistance of the Russian comrades killed in London', he wrote, 'has stirred the enthusiasm of rebels everywhere.'

> It constitutes an example of courage and determination from which all the tramps have drawn strength, and all the undisciplined will draw profit.
> They did well to defend themselves until death. They acted as every rebel should act in the same circumstances.[24]

It is feasible that the example of armed Latvian émigrés in London encouraged French desperadoes similarly equipped with semi-automatic weapons in their crime spree. The evident futility of the violence on both sides of the Channel and the fate of the individuals concerned heralded the end of any sympathy within the revolutionary left for armed robbery as a supposedly political act. Whatever myth-building there was about Peter the Painter and his associates, whatever burnishing of their memory, it wasn't generally the work of anarchists.

UNDER RUDOLF ROCKER's tutelage, the Jewish anarchist movement in the East End of London weathered tolerably well the loss of the Jubilee Street Club and then what he called the 'nightmare period' of the shootings at Houndsditch and Sidney Street.[25] Indeed, they continued to grow in influence. In 1912, the anarchists were at the forefront of concerted strike action in the trade in which Jewish workers were most numerous, tailoring, to challenge the 'sweating' system of subcontracting which immiserated many of those caught up in it. This was widely remembered as the high point of Rocker's London years. The *Arbayter Fraynd* appeared daily for the duration of the walkout and the outcome was seen as a victory for the strikers. The dispute coincided with a strike in the London docks. Rocker and his comrades saw this as a common struggle and organized joint strike meetings.

When the tailoring strike was over, the *Arbayter Fraynd* campaigned for active support for striking dockers. The most practical form this took was Jewish families taking dockers' children into their homes to ease the strikers' hardship. Rocker's partner, Milly Witcop, was one of a group of women activists who organized the billeting of children in East End Jewish homes – several hundred youngsters were temporarily rehoused. Some came to live with Naomi Ploschansky and her family. She remembered coming across Milly Witcop with one of the children, 'a real toughie', who was not happy in his new home:

> She said she'd taken him to several houses where he could stay, but he had run away. And so I asked him: Why didn't you stay? Oh, he wasn't going to stay with those Jews, you know. So maybe I don't look very Jewish, but I said: Would you come and stay with us? And he said: Yes, I'll stay with you. So I took him home. We had already taken care of three or four youngsters, of the dockers' children, and so he was another one.[26]

This was one of the most concrete expressions of solidarity between Jewish leftists and the established labour movement in the East End.

'The period between the successful strike of 1912 and the outbreak of the war in 1914 was the peak of our movement,' Rocker recalled. 'We were kept busy in every direction. The Jewish trades unions grew and increased their memberships and their activities. We had big meetings every day. Our organizations expanded.'[27] The First World War changed everything. It was, in the words of the foremost historian of the Jewish East End, 'a death blow to East End Anarchism'.[28] The international anarchist movement fractured when Kropotkin expressed support for the allied war effort against

Rudolf Rocker with dark hair and glasses and Polly Witcop (Milly Witcop's sister) in front of him, with comrades including Millie Sabelinsky, 1912.

a militaristic and expansionist Germany while Rocker, Malatesta and most other anarchists of prominence advocated outright opposition to war. Wartime measures included the internment of enemy aliens. In December 1914, Rocker, a German, was arrested at his home at Dunstan Houses in Stepney Green and remained in detention until the war was almost over. In 1916 the *Arbayter Fraynd*, already much reduced in size and readership, was closed down and its printing equipment seized. Milly Witcop, who had been at the forefront of keeping the paper going, was interned.

The revolutions in Russia in 1917 were initially celebrated enthusiastically by East End anarchists. Many Russian émigrés – among them Peter Kropotkin – travelled home. Both Rudolf Rocker and Milly Witcop were keen to move to Russia, but only if they could do so together. That wasn't permitted. In March 1918, the month of Rocker's 45th birthday, the British authorities sought to repatriate him to Germany via the Netherlands. He managed to stay in the Netherlands and later in the year was reunited there with Milly Witcop and their young son. They abandoned plans to head for Russia. 'The rule of the Bolsheviki is a new system of tyranny,'

Rocker wrote to Witcop in August 1918. 'In order to remain in power they are sacrificing the real revolutionists.'[29] In the 1930s, the family settled in the United States.

The anarchist movement that sought to re-establish itself in London's East End after the war was a pale shadow of its earlier incarnation. The *Arbayter Fraynd* resumed publication, but it had become an anachronism and by the mid-1920s it was all but dead. Leah Feldman first came to London from Warsaw towards the end of 1913. She was fifteen and found work in the fur trade. She was impressed by Kropotkin's pamphlet *An Appeal to the Young*, became involved in the East End movement when anarchism was at its zenith, and gave money each week to the *Arbayter Fraynd*. In 1917, swept up in the excitement about the revolution, she moved to Russia and stayed there for ten years. When she returned to London, she found that the anarchist movement had changed beyond recognition. 'No young people, only a few old people. And I was so depressed. It was so monotonous. Terrible ... I said England now is [stagnant] water. It don't move. It soon will be smelling.'[30] By far the most vibrant anarchist movement ever seen on British soil had shrivelled to almost nothing.

The tradition of Jewish East End radicalism survived, however. The Battle of Cable Street in October 1936 witnessed a mass political mobilization in the East End to frustrate plans by Oswald Mosley's black-shirted British Union of Fascists to march through the area. It has entered political mythology – and was indeed a remarkable and inspiring moment. Some activists saw this as a rekindling of the alliance between Jewish leftists and non-Jewish labour movement militants evident a generation earlier. After the Second World War the hard left achieved a remarkable series of local electoral successes. In the 1945 general election, Phil Piratin won the Stepney Mile End seat as the Communist Party candidate by a clear margin over the sitting Labour MP, who was also of Jewish heritage. He was the only communist returned in that election from an English constituency. Later that year, communists won ten seats on Stepney Borough Council. The following year, communists took both Stepney Mile End seats on London County Council. The local electoral performance of the Communist Party soon faded, and both anarchists and communists would insist that there was no link between their brief periods of political prominence in the East End. But both flourished on the Jewish immigrant striving for education and empowerment, the quest for social justice, the outsiders' need to bypass less-than-welcoming established political movements and the imperative to challenge antisemitism.

13
Legacy

At the time of the Siege of Sidney Street, William Hitchcock was a fishmonger on Salmon Lane in Limehouse. He and his family lived above the shop. They were less than a mile away from the shoot-out. His eleven-year-old son, Alfred, retained a memory of that drama – two decades later, he turned to those events in Stepney for the final scene of his 1934 noir movie *The Man Who Knew Too Much*, regarded as one of the best films of Hitchcock's early, London-based, years as a director. The plot is fanciful – starting on the ski slopes of St Moritz and revolving around a secret plan to assassinate a European diplomat while he's visiting the Albert Hall in London. This in turn leads to the kidnap of a teenage girl. The denouement is in a dingy house in Wapping, a dockside district of the East End, which is the refuge of an armed gang tied up with a religious cult. The most sinister member of the gang is played by Peter Lorre, an actor who was Hungarian-born and of Jewish descent and had only recently fled Nazi Germany. Lorre's spoken English was still poor, much like the gunmen whose desperate endeavour to stave off police and army a generation earlier Hitchcock was seeking to represent.

The finale is closely modelled on Sidney Street, though with a dramatically higher death toll. The house is besieged and a crowd of onlookers gathers as a firefight develops. Several minor incidents in the movie are lifted directly from the Stepney battle: a woman housekeeper is reduced to her bloomers to stop her fleeing, much as Betsy Gershon was at 100 Sidney Street; a lone policeman goes to knock on the door of the house that the gunmen are occupying and is straightaway shot in an echo of the fate of Sergeant Leeson; and a postman tries to complete his delivery round in spite of the incessant gunfire, a much-repeated but probably apocryphal part of the Sidney Street narrative. Hitchcock had some difficulties with the censors, who didn't want the London police to be depicted as if they were expert shots or habitually used firearms. As a compromise, in the film a truckload of rifles from a nearby gun shop is distributed to the otherwise unarmed police. There are no Scots Guards in the movie version and there is no top-hatted Home Secretary, and the house doesn't catch fire. The police storm the building after a protracted shoot-out, and one of the gang – who is menacingly on the roof of the house with the kidnapped girl – is killed by the girl's sharpshooter mother. Although the film was a success, Hitchcock doesn't seem to have liked the ending. He remade the film in the 1950s, the only movie he revisited, but without the closing gunfight.

Another cultural giant of the twentieth century was drawn to the echoing resonance of Sidney Street. In 1930, Georges Simenon introduced Inspector Maigret in a serialized novel entitled *Pietr-le-Letton*, or 'Peter the Latvian', the first of more than a hundred novels and stories featuring the famed Paris-based detective. The name of the villain is clearly borrowed from Peter the Painter and, like his model, Peter the Latvian has a bewildering array of aliases. Simenon's Peter is from Pskov in Russia, close to the Baltic states, which at one time was believed to be Peter the Painter's home town. But he is portrayed in the novel as 'a capo of [a] major international ring mainly involved in fraud' rather than as a revolutionary exile.[1] And while the novel includes plenty of guns and shootings, there is no jewellery robbery and nothing similar to the Stepney shoot-out, and none of the action takes place in London.

Alfred Hitchcock's film and Georges Simenon's novel were not the first renditions in popular culture of Latvian exiles and the violence they perpetrated. As early as 1912, Clarendon released a seven-minute (and of course silent) spy film featuring a fictional arch-villain and entitled *Dr Brian Pellie and the Secret Dispatch*. This was one of the earliest films made by Wilfred Noy, who went on to direct more than eighty movies. In this short film, Dr Pellie steals a letter that the hero, a British secret service agent, has been instructed to guard with his life and take to Russia. The resulting chase sees Pellie and his girlfriend jump on a tram to escape their pursuers, who then stop another tram and order it to reverse and join the trail. Pellie and his allies barricade themselves in a house and open fire on the troops and armed police surrounding it. The building catches fire and the master criminal, who has already sustained a bullet wound, is arrested on the roof.[2] Some of the action sequences are clearly based on the shoot-outs at Tottenham and Stepney and would immediately have been recognized as such by the audience.

The most substantial feature film based on the incident came almost half a century after the events it depicts. *The Siege of Sidney Street*, released in 1960, was directed by Robert S. Baker and Monty Berman, the latter an East Ender who was born two years after the siege. This benefited from the collaboration on the storyline and screenplay of two established writers, Jimmy Sangster (who makes a cameo appearance as Churchill) and Alexander Baron.[3] The film is in the noir style with lots of night-time scenes and shadowy gaslit rooms. It takes in the Tottenham robbery attempt as well as Houndsditch and Stepney. The Jubilee Street Club features repeatedly and there are some good touches in the dialogue. When a policeman asks at a pub opposite the club what happens over the road, the publican responds, 'They say there's anarchists, and atheists, and vegetarians. Vegetarians!' It boasts an impressive cast. Donald Sinden plays the main character, a police detective who infiltrates the gang and falls for the female lead, who is played by Nicole Berger, complete with French accent – her character is named Sara Trassjonsky, and is depicted as in love with Peter the Painter (played by Peter Wyngarde).

Although much of the film is melodrama, the screenwriters took trouble to incorporate authentic detail. The film opens with a lone policeman walking at first light along Sidney Street and throwing a stone at a window, to be greeted by gunfire from within the house. The layout of the Peter the Painter 'wanted' poster matches the original; there's a publican selling access to the vantage point on his roof; and the commercial sign over 11 Exchange Buildings, 'Ch. Inwald', is precisely correct. The film acknowledges the help of the City of London Police. The plot and dialogue offer at least some understanding of the motivation of the gunmen. At one point Sara confides in Peter the Painter that she saw Cossacks raid her village and kill her parents and other members of her family – a reflection of what impelled the Latvians towards taking up arms. Peter the Painter declares to Sara, 'We steal because no one will give. We steal so there won't be any more refugees. So people like your parents will not be massacred. Any sacrifice is worth that.'

In the film, Peter the Painter is inside 100 Sidney Street during the siege. The Donald Sinden character manages to extract Sara from the building. When the fire starts, she dashes through the police line to seek to save her lover from the flames. She is accidentally shot by one of the men in the building, but Peter the Painter manages to get out through the loft and into a neighbouring house. As Sara is close to death on the street, she catches a glimpse of Peter slipping into the crowd. So plenty of liberties are taken, but the film certainly added to an East End legend. 'Peter the Painter: Anarchist, artist, assassin', the trailer proclaimed. 'A fanatic with a cause who made time to kill and found time to love ... A terrifying portrait of a man who shot his way into world headlines and earned immortal infamy.'

As was sometimes the fashion at the time, the film led to a paperback book, again entitled *The Siege of Sidney Street* and written by Frederick Oughton. This proclaimed on its cover that it was 'based on the screenplay by Jimmy Sangster'. The book presented itself as 'a sensational story with a scaffolding of truth – of the gaslit, gin-soaked era when marauding anarchists took whatever they could grab'. It was a hastily written potboiler, and it's easy to see why Alexander Baron – who had family roots in the East End and three years later wrote *The Lowlife*, one of the classic London novels – wanted to keep his distance.

A little over a decade later, another writer immersed in the Jewish East End, Emanuel Litvinoff, wrote a much more successful and ambitious novel based on Houndsditch and Sidney Street. *A Death Out of Season* – the first part of Litvinoff's Faces of Terror trilogy, which extends to encompass the brutality of Stalin's Russia – achieves some success in re-creating the revolutionary underworld in Russian-ruled Warsaw and in depicting the drama and anguish of the stand-off in Stepney. It is less adept when introducing an entirely fictional character, Countess Lydia Alexandrova, a young Russian aristocrat turned revolutionary. She is at the centre of a love triangle – she loves the Gardstein character and is loved by Peter the Painter. Peter is depicted as an agent in the Okhrana, the Russian secret police, and as a provocateur – but also as a double agent who is a revolutionary at heart. At the core of the plot is an attempt to encourage revolutionary émigrés to blow up King George v at his coronation procession – so revisiting one of the more alarmist angles of the newspaper reporting of Gardstein's modest stock of chemicals and weapons – which, according to the book's plot, the Russian authorities believe will prompt the British authorities to expel political exiles and end the right to asylum. That bomb plot gets sidelined when the attempt to rob the Houndsditch jewellers goes wrong. A brief outline doesn't do justice to a powerful novel, which is of course fiction with a 'scaffolding' of fact.

At around the same time as Litvinoff was starting work on his trilogy, the German film director Peter Lilienthal made *Malatesta*, which turns to aspects of the Italian anarchist's life and political activism while in London to explore the attraction of political violence to some on the revolutionary left. This was an urgent concern in West Germany: some student radicals were moving towards a more insurrectionary style of politics and the Baader–Meinhof Group (or Red Army Faction) was established in the year that Lilienthal's film was released, 1970. It depicts Malatesta as, at least initially, the leader of the group that becomes embroiled in the Siege of Sidney Street – though he seeks, unsuccessfully, to restrain his fellow anarchists from violence. At one point, Malatesta chides Gardstein: 'You are a rebel not a revolutionary. A rebel cannot wait for the right moment.' Peter the Painter is mentioned, but not depicted. The film has an impressive cast, with Eddie Constantine as Malatesta, Christine Noonan as Nina Vassileva and the writer and activist Heathcote Williams both acting and contributing to the screenplay. *Malatesta* won film awards in West Germany and was nominated for the Palme d'Or at the 1970 Cannes Film Festival.

The drama played out on the streets of the East End has continued to attract the interest of novelists. Jon Stephen Fink's *A Storm in the Blood*, published in 2009, is based explicitly and precisely amid the police murders at Houndsditch and the armed encounter in Stepney. As with Litvinoff, he foregrounds a woman character, Rivka, and he allows Peter the Painter a mistress. His publishers emphasized the corollaries with contemporary events, describing the book as 'a gripping thriller filled with echoes of violence, ethnic unrest and terrorism which recall the ominous atmosphere of London in the weeks after the bombings of July 2005'. Those suicide bombings were the 7/7 attacks – four explosions in central London targeting commuters and carried out by Islamist radicals that claimed more than fifty lives.

Fink's novel appeared in time for the centenary of Houndsditch and Sidney Street. That anniversary saw the first memorial plaques put up to those in uniform who had been killed. Until then, there was nothing to mark the site of these dramatic and tragic encounters. A plaque on Cutler Street commended the 'courage and sense of duty' of the three City of London policemen killed nearby. On Wexford House in Sidney Street, a smaller plaque commemorated the fire brigade officer who suffered fatal injuries in the aftermath of the siege. Both are inconspicuous and hidden away. It's as if those responsible felt an obligation to mark the centenary, but in a manner that would neither attract attention nor in any way make heroes out of the gunmen.

Of the media coverage of the anniversary, a standout piece by Richard Brooks in the *Sunday Times* looked back on the life of his maternal grandfather, Mendel Himmelfarb, then a Latvian leftist in the East End.[4] He wasn't involved in the violence, but in the closed world of Latvian émigrés in London he must have known or known of those who were. Himmelfarb was from the Baltic port of Liepaja (then Libau). He was arrested as a teenager for calling for the overthrow of the tsar, escaped and took the boat to Tilbury. Although Jewish by birth, he was an atheist. Liepaja now has a memorial wall to remember the many thousands of Jews shot dead there by German troops in 1941.

Brooks recounted that his grandfather was a successful businessman, setting up a chain of tobacconist shops, but remained a communist until his death in 1970. For many émigrés from across Russia and Eastern Europe, the success of the Bolshevik Revolution was a moment of hope. For some, that sense of hope quickly sputtered and died; for others, it lasted a lifetime. Among the Latvians in London, it wasn't only Jacob Peters, a Marxist rather than an anarchist, who returned to Russia to aid the revolution. Kristaps Salnins, who also had a battery of assumed names, including Grishka and Jacob Fogel, went back in 1917. He had been active in the 1905 Revolution and in exile was a prominent social democrat and, perhaps briefly, an anarchist sympathizer. On his return, he was promptly recruited as a Soviet intelligence agent and deployed as an evangel of revolution, including a spell as a Soviet military adviser and trainer in Spain during the civil war. In 1939, he suffered the same fate as Peters. He was shot during Stalin's terror.[5] Yourka Dubov, whose real name was Juris Laivins, returned to Latvia the year after his acquittal in the Old Bailey. He was jailed for a political offence but released amid the revolutions of 1917. He was still living in Riga in the mid-1920s.[6]

The Liesma anarchist group in London didn't long survive Sidney Street. Some of its members were dead. Others were on the run. There was no attempt to regroup. The policy of revolutionary expropriation had been shown to be a dead end. Whatever justification might be put forward for armed robbery in the heat of a struggle against a vicious dictatorship, it could hardly apply in a country that was neither the enemy nor particularly oppressive. In three armed incidents in London, the revolutionaries had lost five men from their own ranks. They had also been condemned by many whom they might have regarded as political allies. The conspicuous propriety with which the émigrés had been treated by a police force pursuing the murderers of three of their colleagues must – or should – have given cause for reflection. Aspects of both the police investigation and the criminal prosecution arising from the Houndsditch shootings were flawed, but there is nothing to suggest that any of those arrested on suspicion of involvement were tortured, threatened or abused. The trial was broadly fair and the verdict gave the defendants the benefit of the doubt, as it should. The question remains whether the stand-off at Sidney Street could have been resolved without loss of life, and whether indeed the fire that engulfed 100 Sidney Street was started deliberately, but there's no doubt who opened fire first.

The most direct legacy of Sidney Street lay in the moves to ensure that London's police had access to modern and powerful firearms so that they would never again be comprehensively outgunned by criminals. Winston Churchill took steps to test and commission new police weapons almost immediately, though it was some months before the guns were available to be used. The official response to Houndsditch and Sidney Street was most notable for what didn't happen. In spite of the shrill demands from the popular press and from the opposition, and indeed the immediate instinct of Churchill and the Home Office, the Liberal government did not rush through new anti-immigrant legislation. The Aliens Act remained unchanged, with the right of political asylum undiminished. It was the First World War, not the acts of Latvian émigrés, that prompted the move to a much more regulated and restrictive regime of immigration and residence rights. And it was war, rather than repugnance of the likes of Peter the Painter, that led to the eclipse of East End anarchism. The pull of post-tsarist Russia, the rival attractions of communism and Zionism and the increasing acculturation of East End Jewry all chipped away at the movement. The three great anarchist intellectuals who lived in or near London at the time of the Sidney Street siege – Peter Kropotkin, Errico Malatesta and Rudolf Rocker – had all left the country by the close of 1919. The number of anarchist émigrés in London was much diminished. Within a decade, the political street culture of the East End had changed utterly.

In spite of the material, political, social and demographic change the East End has witnessed in the long passage of time since members of the Liesma group and their friends gathered at

59 Grove Street, the Siege of Sidney Street still has contemporary resonance. 'The anxieties it dramatised – over immigrants, extremism and the welcome both receive in London – remain acute today,' in the words of *The Economist*.[7] The venom directed at East European migrants more than a century ago found an echo more recently in the run-up to Brexit. The antisemitism that the Houndsditch police murders and the Siege of Sidney Street provoked bears comparison with the Islamophobia fuelled by acts of Islamist terror. Many of the Latvian activists lived in streets where families of Bangladeshi Muslim heritage now make their homes. Shamima Begum, who as a fifteen-year-old travelled with two young friends to Syria and became a 'jihadi bride' to an Islamic State fighter, went to school close by in Bethnal Green. Her fate in becoming in effect stateless and barred from returning to Britain mirrors that of May Peters almost a century earlier, who was pilloried because her Russian ex-husband was mistakenly believed to be Peter the Painter.

The analogies between then and now are not precise. The Latvian émigrés were cruel and reckless in their use of guns, but they resorted to them to evade arrest, not to instil terror. Whatever their creed, it was not religious. Just as the Jewish East End disowned armed robbery and expropriation, so the Bengali East End repudiates violence in the name of religion. But Peter the Painter's footsteps echo through some of the unresolved issues that still stalk our streets.

There's a curious aftermath to the tale of Peter the Painter. In 2008, a row broke out over the decision of a housing association to name two newly built blocks of flats at the southern end of Sidney Street as Peter House and Painter House. Plaques placed on the buildings explained that they had been 'named after Peter Piaktow, who was known as Peter the Painter, the antihero of the nearby Sidney Street Siege in 1911'. It was a curious move. Anti-heroes associated with violent crime aren't usually celebrated in this way. There was no local lobby group arguing that Peter the Painter should be commemorated. And there's nothing to suggest that Peter ever set foot inside 100 Sidney Street. A local councillor said that rather than take the name of a 'murderer', it would have been better if the flats had honoured the memory of the police officers who were killed. The Metropolitan Police Federation was also understandably angry. 'This was a long time ago, but these people were anarchists who killed police officers,' commented a representative of the federation. 'It's very disappointing that the local housing association has chosen to honour them in this manner when, once again, terrorism is at the forefront of people's minds.'[8]

In response, the chief executive of Tower Hamlets Community Housing argued that as there was no evidence that Peter the Painter was involved in the killing of the three policemen at Houndsditch, the blocks were not being named after a murderer. 'There is some doubt as to whether he existed,' he asserted, 'but he is the name East Enders associate with the siege and Sidney Street.' The row died down as quickly as it flared up, and the names of the blocks remain unchanged, as do the plaques explaining them. But it demonstrates the power the name Peter the Painter still possessed, a century after it started to circulate, to arouse strong emotions.

TIMELINE

23 January 1909   A wages robbery in Tottenham results in a two-hour chase and shoot-out; a policeman, a boy and one of the two robbers, Jacob Lepidus, suffer fatal gunshot wounds

29 January 1909   Public funeral of Police Constable William Tyler and ten-year-old Ralph Joscelyne

12 February 1909   The second armed robber, Paul Hefeld, dies in hospital

16 December 1910   Police interrupt an attempt to rob Harris's jewellery shop on Houndsditch in the City of London: the robbers shoot their way out, killing three police officers and seriously wounding two others

17 December 1910   The body of one of the robbers, George Gardstein, is found in a first-floor room on Grove Street in Whitechapel

19 December 1910   Peter the Painter and Fritz [Svaars] are named by the police as suspects in the Houndsditch police murders

Timeline

22 December 1910 — Funeral services at St Paul's for the three police officers: Sergeant Robert Bentley, Constable Walter Choat and Sergeant Charles Tucker

3 January 1911 — Police and soldiers lay siege to 100 Sidney Street in Stepney, where two of the Houndsditch suspects have taken refuge. The shoot-out lasts six hours before the house catches fire; the bodies of Fritz Svaars and William Sokoloff are found in the rubble

18 January 1911 — Home Secretary Winston Churchill gives evidence at the inquest into the two men who died at 100 Sidney Street

1 May 1911 — The Old Bailey trial begins of four people charged in relation to the Houndsditch killings and attempted robbery

12 May 1911 — Nina Vassileva is the only person convicted and is sentenced to two years in jail; she is cleared on appeal the following month

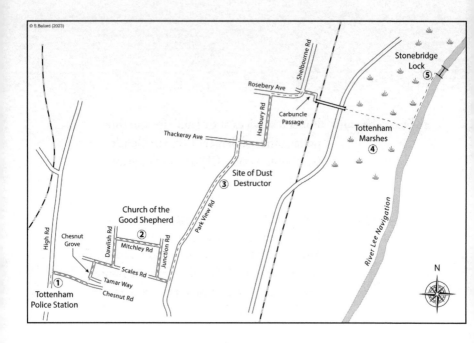

WALK:
FROM TOTTENHAM POLICE STATION
TO THE MARSHES

This walk doesn't traverse the entire route taken by the two armed robbers, Paul Hefeld and Jacob Lepidus, as they sought to escape with the wages money from Schnurmann's rubber factory in Tottenham. We follow them until they cross the river Lee (or Lea), by which time they had killed two of their pursuers but still believed, forlornly, that they could make good their getaway.

Our starting point is Tottenham Police Station at 398 High Road, N17 9JA [1]. The station was rebuilt a few years after the Tottenham Outrage but on the same site. It's a forbiddingly imposing building replete with outsize Union Jack, giving the impression of some viceregal mansion in a colonial outpost. That can't have been the intention. Can it? On the Chesnut Road side of the police station, there's a plaque in tribute to the policeman shot dead during the robbery:

> In memory of William Frederick Tyler Police Constable 403 of 'N' Division Metropolitan Police Service Fallen while bravely serving the community on the 23rd January 1909
>
> Erected by the officers of Haringey Borough Police and the community on the centenary of 'The Tottenham Outrage'.

The site of the rubber factory is almost immediately opposite – much of it is now a car park.

Once they had got their hands on the bag with the wages money, the robbers ran east on Chesnut Road away from the High Road, and then zigzagged through the backstreets along Chesnut

Grove, Scales Road, Dawlish Road and then Mitchley Road. It was here that the Schnurmanns' car caught up with the two Latvians, prompting the bullets which both disabled the car and killed young Ralph Joscelyne. On what is now the Church of the Good Shepherd [2] on Mitchley Road, with a foundation stone dating from 1891 – reopened for worship in 2010 and part of St Mary's Tottenham – there's a recent memorial plaque:

> In memory of RALPH JOSCELYNE 1899–1909 who was shot on this spot during the Tottenham Outrage on Jan. 23rd 1909
> May he rest in peace
> Justorum animae in manu Dei sunt

The Latin translates as 'the souls of the righteous are in the hands of God'.

At the end of Mitchley Road, we need to take a slight detour to get back on the path taken by the robbers and their pursuers: right onto Junction Road, left on Scales Road, and left onto Park View Road, with Down Lane Park on the right. A lifelong Tottenham resident told me that as a child she was taken down Park View Road by her grandfather to be shown bullet holes on the walls that were said to be a legacy of the outrage. Whatever the truth of that story, there's no obvious bullet holes evident today.

Beyond the park on the right lay what was then called the Dust Destroyer [3], a refuse incinerator. Until recently, it remained a civic amenity site and the sturdy brick walls which were probably already in place in 1909 are still evident. This was where PC Tyler managed to head off and challenge the two gunmen. He was shot and carried into a house on Thackeray Avenue. The householder submitted a compensation claim for the bloodstains on his carpet. Much of the terraced housing in this area would have been there when Hefeld and Lepidus raced past. If we go to the eastern end of Thackeray Avenue, then follow the road round as it becomes Hanbury Road, then turn right onto Rosebery Avenue, that takes us out onto Shelbourne Road. Opposite there's a footpath with the rather sinister name of Carbuncle Passage. Its appearance isn't entirely welcoming either. This leads to a long footbridge which takes you over railway lines and a main road and onto Tottenham marshes [4]. This area is smaller and perhaps better drained than it would have been back then, but still much the same.

If you go straight ahead, so due east, towards the Lee, then head left towards a parking area, just beyond there's a bridge over Pymmes Brook, the first of three parallel watercourses. You are then on the banks of the much more considerable River Lee Navigation, and you'll see the Waterside Cafe (check opening hours; it has a toilet with disabled access as well as good-value food), which is a great place to sit out with a cuppa and a snack. It was here at Stonebridge Lock [5] that the Latvians crossed the Navigation – the desultory river Lee lies just beyond – and made their way southwards on the east bank. There's lots of residential moorings here, but no public access along this section of the robbers' route, and that's where we will leave them, fleeing towards Walthamstow, firing on those pursuing them, and heading towards their deaths.

Take the path along the west side of the Navigation, a nice walk when the weather is good, and after fifteen minutes you will hit Ferry Lane, the busy road route across the marshes. If you turn right onto Ferry Lane, in a few minutes you will get to Tottenham Hale train and tube station. But do consider heading left, towards the Ferry Boat Inn and opposite it the Walthamstow Wetlands (again, please check opening hours), a very special place for Londoners who love wildlife and which is blessed by an excellent café. A few minutes further on along Ferry Lane, at the far side of high-rise student residences, is Blackhorse Road tube and rail station. From High Road to marshes to station, the walk is about 3 kilometres (2 mi.).

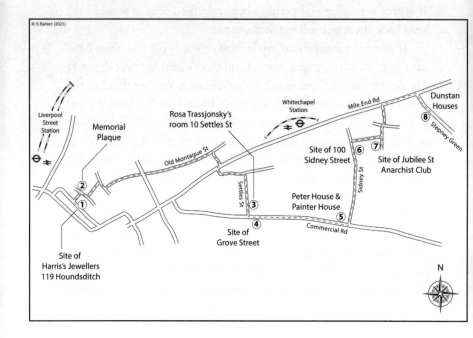

WALK:
FROM HOUNDSDITCH TO SIDNEY STREET

This 3-kilometre walk takes you from the site of the shootings at Houndsditch, where three policemen were killed when they interrupted an attempt to rob Harris's jewellery business, along the route taken by members of the gang as they took their wounded comrade, George Gardstein, away from the scene and then beyond to the site of the Siege of Sidney Street and of the nearby anarchist club on Jubilee Street. It's a stroll through what was, in the first half of the last century, the Jewish East End, an area which has been transformed beyond measure but where there are still some pockets of housing that those whose stories are recounted in this book would have walked past regularly.

Houndsditch is close to Liverpool Street Station and easy to get to – EC3A 7BT is the best postcode to use. The street has changed utterly since 1910 and there's hardly a building from that time still standing, but the street layout is little-changed. The section we are heading to is immediately opposite a 21-storey high-rise opened in 2019 colloquially known, because of its curved shape, as the 'Can of Ham', and more formally as 70 St Mary Axe – it's not as immediately recognizable as the nearby 'Gherkin' but in much the same spirit. As you walk along Houndsditch from Bishopsgate heading east, you come to the junction with Cutler Street. Harris's jewellers was a couple of doors down from here on the left at 119 Houndsditch [1]. At the time of writing in the spring of 2023, a coffee shop marks the spot.

At the far end of Houndsditch you can see the distinguished eighteenth-century church of St Botolph's. This is St Botolph's, Aldgate; there is another church to this distinctly obscure seventhcentury English abbot at the other end of Houndsditch on Bishopsgate. Aldgate is traditionally regarded as where the East End begins, and for those involved in the robbery attempt, the East End was home ground. But we're not heading that way. Go back a few paces and turn onto Cutler Street and then, a few yards up on the right, take a pedestrian entrance into what's marked as Clothier Street. It's little more than a yard and all the buildings here are modern, but this was once Exchange Buildings – the spot where the would-be robbers sought to burrow into the back of Harris's shop and where the three policemen were shot dead. The back of the coffee shop stands exactly where the gang tried to break through the wall. One side of Exchange Buildings backing on to these Houndsditch premises would have stood on the small adjoining parking area, with another row opposite – all three-storey. And the yard was then a cul-de-sac. You can get a sense of how tiny the floor area of the buildings would have been and how constricted was the space in which the drama played out.

Head back to Cutler Street and turn right, away from Houndsditch. You then get to a T-junction and opposite is a disappointingly anonymous black plaque [2] put up by the Corporation of the City of London in 2010, a hundred years after the shooting. The inscription reads,

> Near to this spot on the 16 December 1910 three City of London Police Officers were fatally wounded whilst preventing a robbery at 119 Houndsditch. In commemoration of Sgt Robert Bentley, Sgt Charles Tucker, PC Walter C. Choat, whose courage and sense of duty will not be forgotten.

This is close to the spot where the wounded Gardstein and his accomplices ran into Isaac Levy, the tobacconist heading home, and warned him away at gunpoint.

Follow Cutler Street to the right, and then turn left on Harrow Place. When you get to Middlesex Street, turn right, then left on Wentworth Street, where for the first time we come to a handful of buildings that would have been standing as the gang went past. They were seen a couple of times as they made their way along Wentworth Street, which is at the heart of the Petticoat Lane street market, one of the oldest surviving markets in the country. It's not clear exactly what route they took from here, but they seemed intent on avoiding main roads – making their way, in the words of the *Daily Chronicle*, 'through dark and little frequented by-ways' – and we'll do the same. And we know their destination: the rooms a mile away in Grove Street where Peter the Painter, Fritz Svaars and Luba Milstein lived. Gardstein's own room, on Gold Street in Stepney, almost another mile to the east, was too far away given the bullet wounds he had sustained. Neither Grove Street nor Gold Street have survived.

When you get to Commercial Street – one of the main arteries through the East End – cross straight over onto what is still Wentworth Street. You'll walk past a side entrance to Toynbee Hall, a philanthropic endeavour that has been working for self-improvement and social justice in this area since 1884. On the left-hand side, Flower and Dean Walk marks the site of Flower and Dean Street, where in the 1880s two of Jack the Ripper's victims lived. Cross over the bottom of Brick Lane and carry straight on along Old Montague Street, once at the heart of the Jewish East End – though you wouldn't guess it now. Reuben's grocery shop, a gathering point for several of the group, was along here.

At Greatorex Street – once Great Garden Street, where Nina Vassileva, Fritz Svaars and George Gardstein briefly had lodgings – turn right. Then head across Whitechapel Road onto Fieldgate Street and along the side of the Whitechapel Bell Foundry. This was where the Liberty Bell, so iconic of American independence, was made and where Parliament's Big Ben was recast; the company was established in 1570 and these premises date from 1670, but sadly the foundry closed in 2017. Follow Fieldgate Street as it turns sharply, and rather confusingly, to the left. We're now at the back of the huge East London Mosque, which has extended to include a small synagogue – it still bears a Star of David and the signage of the Fieldgate Street Great Synagogue. This opened in 1899 and was, when it stopped holding regular services in 2009, the last working synagogue in Whitechapel. A little further along, the seven-storey building with the striking tower is – surprise! – Tower House, built in 1902 as a Rowton House providing very cheap accommodation for single working men, and now turned into upmarket apartments.

Turn right on Settles Street, the left side of which is very much as it would have been in 1910. At the far end on the left is one of the few buildings with a connection to Houndsditch still standing. Rosa Trassjonsky lived at 10 Settles (or Settle) Street [3], in the back room on the second floor, paying a weekly rent of 3*s* 6*d*. Many of the photographs and letters seized by police were found here. Luba Milstein got a couple of hours' rest in this room amid the shock and confusion of the Houndsditch shootings and Gardstein's fatal injuries. Grove Street [4], where Gardstein was brought and where he died, was on the other side of Commercial Road – Ropewalk Gardens meets Commercial Road much where the junction with Grove Street once stood. It was, according to a newspaper reporter, 'a narrow sordid thoroughfare, with small two-storied [*sic*] houses, chiefly occupied by foreigners'. From Houndsditch, it's a long way to support a severely wounded man.

Carry on heading east – so that's a left turn from Settles Street – onto Commercial Road and you pass streets where several of the Houndsditch defendants lived. On the left is Turner Street, where Jacob Peters had a room – the house has gone though some nineteenth-century housing remains. Further along Commercial Road, on the south side, Buross Street is now simply a stub of a road. Nina Vassileva lived along here. And on the other side of the road is Philpot Street, a broad street which served as an outdoor speaking venue for Yiddish-speaking activists and others.

Another couple of hundred yards along Commercial Road, you come to Peter House [5], social housing built in 2006 and, as a plaque explains, named after 'the anti-hero of the nearby Sidney Street Siege'. As you turn left on Sidney Street, there is its twin, Painter House. It is striking to find public housing named after a suspected gunman, and it need hardly be said that even almost a century after the event, the London police were not best pleased.

Just beyond Painter House is Siege House and you might be forgiven for thinking that you have reached the site of 100 Sidney Street. Not so. That's still a quarter of a mile away towards the street's northern end.

As you head up Sidney Street, there are pockets of elegant mid-nineteenth-century housing – notably around Sidney Square, where some of the houses still have wooden shutters. Just beyond on the left between Ashfield Street and Newark Street there's a full block of red-brick Edwardian tenements, almost identical to Martin's Mansions of which 100 Sidney Street was part. The besieged house [6] had four floors, including a mansard roof, and was built in 1900. This is where Svaars and Sokoloff took refuge – and where they died. The building was burnt out on 3 January 1911. Three months later, when the ten-yearly census was conducted, the building was listed as 'demolished', though the neighbouring properties were still occupied. This row of houses was pulled down in the 1950s. It was on the right between Wolsey Street and Lindley Street, where Wexford House now stands – if you look carefully, you'll spot a tiny plaque on the front of Wexford House put up by the London Fire Brigade and the Jewish East End Celebration Society. It reads,

> In Memory of District Officer Charles Pearson of the London Fire Brigade who died from injuries received at 100 Sidney Street near this site
> During the siege of Sidney Street on the 3rd of January 1911

It's a pity that the lettering is so small as to be almost unreadable. This is the only marker of the location of one of the most dramatic episodes in London's history.

The Rising Sun, which provided a vantage point for journalists, was on the street corner opposite the junction with Wolsey Street. The Home Secretary, Winston Churchill, looked on from the junction with Lindley Street, and from a yard entrance by a beer shop at 131 Sidney Street, across the road from the besieged building. Turn right onto Lindley Street – this is where Karl Hoffman lived, in a room in which Fritz Svaars and Peter the Painter planned their next move after their hurried departure from Grove Street. The only building from that time still standing is Lindley House, at the end on the left. It dates from 1910 and the Virgin Mary it displays indicates that this was a church initiative. At the end stands Jubilee Street – and a wonderful row of early nineteenth-century Victorian two-storey terraced housing which is among the most charming in the East End. The buildings on the west side of the street are listed. The ironwork on the balconies is glorious, and many houses still have boot scrapers.

If you turn right onto Jubilee Street and walk past the two-storey terrace, the anarchist club was on the right – the site [7] is buried underneath sturdy blocks of social housing. It's striking how close the club was to the site of the Sidney Street siege. Turn round to head north again and follow Jubilee Street through the arch where it becomes simply a footpath. You will get to Rinkoffs, one of the very few surviving Jewish bakeries and confectioners in the East End and still a family business. It has seats outside and is well worth a stop. The business was established by Hyman Rinkoff, who was born in Ukraine in 1895. He opened his first shop on Old Montague Street in 1911, the same year as the Siege of Sidney Street.

A few yards further on, you come to Whitechapel Road. Turn right for Stepney Green tube or left for the much-extended and modernized (it's on the Elizabeth Line) Whitechapel tube and overground station. Opposite Whitechapel station is the brand new Tower Hamlets Town Hall, a spectacular repurposing of the listed Royal London Hospital building. But if you still have the energy, there is a final stop worth a visit. Turning right onto Whitechapel Road, you walk past a modern slate plaque declaring that Captain James Cook once lived here (yes, that Captain Cook!) and a little before you get to Stepney Green station, there's Stepney Green on your right. Head down here a short way, taking in what looks like one of London's most splendid ghost signs ('DAREN BREAD Best for Health') – alas it's not the original but was restored about twenty years ago, which means aficionados of this sort of thing regard it as a fake.

Just beyond, clearly signed, is five-storey Dunstan Houses [8], built in 1899, which still has a central staircase open to the elements. This is where Rudolf Rocker and Milly Witcop and many of their comrades lived. The Rocker home was No. 33, facing Stepney Green. It's where Rudolf and Milly's son, Fermin, grew up. 'Dunstan Houses, though hardly an abode for the affluent, nevertheless had its own class distinctions, and offered a scale of accommodations for the poor, the poorer and the poorest,' Fermin Rocker wrote in a memoir of his childhood:

> The finances of my parents must have looked up a little after I arrived on the scene, for No. 33 was in what might be termed the luxury wing of the building. We had such conveniences as a private kitchen and a private lavatory in contrast to the flats in the adjoining sections, some of which had kitchens but no private toilets and others which had neither and whose occupants had to draw their water from a communal tap.

Dunstan Houses was the intellectual epicentre of East End anarchism in the years before the First World War, by far the most vibrant and significant anarchist movement Britain has ever seen. Lest we forget!

REFERENCES

INTRODUCTION

1 Winston Churchill, 'The Battle of Sidney Street', *Nash's Magazine*, March 1924, pp. 16–18, 98.
2 'A Stand-Off in London's East End in 1911 still Echoes Today', *The Economist*, 16 December 2020.
3 V. I. Lenin, 'Guerrilla Warfare', 1906, www.marxists.org/archive/lenin/works, accessed 1 October 2023.
4 'A Year in Film: 1911', www.screenonline.org.uk, accessed 23 February 2023.
5 George Dangerfield, *The Strange Death of Liberal England* (London, 1935).

1 THE TOTTENHAM OUTRAGE

1 *Tottenham and Edmonton Weekly Herald*, 29 January 1909.
2 Report by Police Superintendent W. Jenkins, 7 February 1909, MEPO 3/194, The National Archives (TNA). This is the most substantial official account of the robbery and pursuit.
3 *Tottenham and Edmonton Weekly Herald*, 27 January 1909.
4 Ibid.
5 *The Times*, 27 January 1909.
6 MEPO 3/194, TNA.
7 *The Star*, 23 January 1909.
8 MEPO 3/194, TNA.
9 *Daily Chronicle*, 30 January 1909.
10 MEPO 3/194, TNA.
11 Ibid.
12 *Daily Mirror*, 30 January 1909; *The Star*, 29 January 1909.
13 Mourning card, Bruce Castle Museum.
14 *The Times*, 26 January 1909. A garbled account by an MI5 informant more than twenty years after the event suggested that a Latvian using the name Jacob Vogel, who was better known by another pseudonym, Grishka, and whose real name was Kristaps Salnins, was involved. KV 3/39, TNA.
15 *Daily Mirror*, 26 January 1909.
16 *The Times*, 26 January 1909.
17 Notes relating to the Tottenham Outrage, Bruce Castle Museum.
18 *Daily Chronicle*, 30 January 1909.
19 *The Star*, 25 January 1909.

2 THE 'ALIEN INVASION'

1 Letter from the consul general in London of imperial Russia, 1 February 1909, MEPO 3/194, The National Archives (TNA).
2 Jerry White, *London in the Nineteenth Century: A Human Awful Wonder of God* (London, 2008), p. 154.
3 Quoted in David Feldman, *Englishmen and Jews: Social Relations and Political Culture, 1840–1914* (New Haven, CT, and London, 1994), p. 167. The title of Sholem Aleichem's novel translates as *Adventures of Mottel, the Cantor's Son* and it was unfinished at the time of the author's death in 1916.
4 *Daily Chronicle*, 5 January 1911.
5 MEPO 5/110, TNA. The letter with the abusive comments about Charles Martin was passed on by the Home Office to the committee examining compensation claims. Martin claimed £600 in compensation, mainly for the rebuilding of 100 Sidney Street; he was awarded £175.
6 Saskia Sassen, *Guests and Aliens* (New York, 1999), p. 81.
7 David Glover, *Literature, Immigration, and Diaspora in Fin-de-Siècle England: A Cultural History of the 1905 Aliens Act* (New York, 2012), p. 1.
8 Anatol Lieven, *The Baltic Revolution: Estonia, Latvia, Lithuania and the Path to Independence* (New Haven, CT, and London, 1993), p. 30; Toivo U. Raun, 'The Revolution of 1905 in the Baltic Provinces and Finland', *Slavic Review*, XLIII/3 (1984), pp. 453–67.
9 Mihails Hazans, 'Emigration from Latvia: A Brief History and Driving Forces in the Twenty-First Century', in *The Emigrant Communities of Latvia: National Identity, Transnational Belonging, and Diaspora Politics*, ed. Rita Kasa and Inta Mieriņa (New York, 2019), pp. 35–58.
10 V. I. Lenin, 'Guerrilla Warfare', September 1906, www.marxists.org/archive/lenin/works/1906/gw.
11 This account of the political activity of Peter the Painter in Latvia is based on the groundbreaking research of Philip Ruff in his book *A Towering Flame: The Life and Times of the Elusive Latvian Anarchist Peter the Painter* (London, 2019).
12 Ibid., p. 18.
13 Ibid., pp. 35, 61–2.
14 Ibid., p. 59.
15 Ibid., p. 69.
16 Raun, 'The Revolution of 1905', pp. 465–6.
17 Prince [Peter] Kropotkin, *The Terror in Russia: An Appeal to the British Nation*, 8th edn (London, 1911), p. 55.
18 Ibid., p. 2.
19 Ruff, *A Towering Flame*, p. 90, has identified the author as Hermanis Punga.
20 Ramsay MacDonald, *The Revolution in the Baltic Provinces of Russia* (London, 1907), pp. v–xi.

3 THE WORKER'S FRIEND

1 *The Star*, 25 January 1909.
2 *Daily Mirror*, 26 January 1909.
3 *The Times*, 26 January 1909.

References

4 Herbert T. Finch, *Traitors Within: The Adventures of Detective Inspector Herbert T. Finch* (London, 1933), p. 35. The purported brother in question appears to have been Nikolai (or Vladimir) Striga, who also went by the name Vladimir (or perhaps Peter) Lapidus and was at one time a prominent anarchist in Ukraine. He is said to have moved to Paris and died when he stumbled while carrying a home-made bomb, though both the family connection and the manner of his death are open to question.
5 *Daily Mirror*, 27 January 1909; *The Times*, 27 January 1909.
6 *The Star*, 28 January 1909.
7 *Tottenham and Edmonton Weekly Herald*, 17 February 1909.
8 'The Tottenham Outrages', *Jewish Chronicle*, 29 January 1909.
9 *Daily Telegraph*, 5 January 1911.
10 Jerry White, *London in the Nineteenth Century: A Human Awful Wonder of God* (London, 2008), pp. 343–4; Jerry White, *London in the Twentieth Century: A City and Its People* (London, 2001), pp. 259–63.
11 CLA/048/CS/01/03/004, CLA/048/CS/01/01/025, London Metropolitan Archives (LMA).
12 CLA/048/CS/01/01/004, LMA. The photos are at CLA/048/CS/01/03/013/9–10. I am very grateful to members of the Police History Society for their help in identifying the type of pistol shown in these photographs.
13 Jonathan Ferguson, *The 'Broomhandle' Mauser* (Oxford, 2017), pp. 68–9.
14 *Evening Times* (Glasgow), 10–11 April 1908; Philip Ruff, *A Towering Flame: The Life and Times of the Elusive Latvian Anarchist Peter the Painter* (London, 2019), pp. 70–72.
15 'Police Alert in Alien Colony in Scotland', *Daily Chronicle*, 7 January 1911.
16 *Tottenham and Edmonton Weekly Herald*, 27 January 1909.
17 CLA/048/CS/01/03/014, LMA. Confusingly, information shared with MI5 more than twenty years later suggests that Sokoloff was the robber who escaped after the Motherwell incident, though it attributes an assumed name to him, Jacob Vogel, which was actually used by another Latvian political exile. KV 3/39, TNA.
18 Vlad Solomon, *State Surveillance, Political Policing and Counter-Terrorism in Britain, 1880–1914* (Martlesham, Suffolk, 2021), p. 208.
19 Ruff, *A Towering Flame*, pp. 60, 73.
20 The membership card had been issued in London in July 1910 to 'Grunbergs', not an alias Gardstein appeared to use, so it may not have been Gardstein's card. CLA/048/CS/01/01/004, LMA.
21 There were also two exceptionally interesting novels written by anarchists and depicting the London movement of which they were part, John Henry Mackay's *The Anarchists* (first published in German in 1891) and *A Girl among the Anarchists* (1903) written by Helen and Olivia Rossetti under the pseudonym 'Isabel Meredith'.
22 *La Révolte*, 1–24 March 1891, cited in Richard Bach Jensen, *The Battle against Anarchist Terrorism: An International History, 1878–1934* (Cambridge, 2014), p. 18.
23 Jensen, *The Battle against Anarchist Terrorism*, p. 36.
24 Ibid.
25 This was the incident that formed the basis of Joseph Conrad's novel *The Secret Agent*.
26 Cited in Jensen, *The Battle against Anarchist Terrorism*, p. 311.

27 Rudolf Rocker, *The London Years*, trans. Joseph Leftwich (London, 1956), p. 204.
28 Jensen, *The Battle against Anarchist Terrorism*, p. 315.
29 Robert Anderson, 'The Problem of the Criminal Alien', *Nineteenth Century and After*, LXIX (February 1911), pp. 217–24.
30 Haia Shpayer-Makov, 'The Reception of Peter Kropotkin in Britain, 1886–1917', *Albion*, XIX/3 (1987), pp. 373–90.
31 Mina Graur, *An Anarchist 'Rabbi': The Life and Teachings of Rudolf Rocker* (New York, 1997), pp. 76–7.
32 Casimir Pilenas, an interpreter, in his evidence at the Old Bailey, cited the titles of some of the books which Nina Vassileva gave to her landlord for safekeeping. He commented, 'they are all revolutionary books,' and it would probably have been an offence to possess them in Russia. Two of these items appear to be pamphlets in Russian by Peter Kropotkin, *Revolutionary Government* (1892) and *The State: Its Historic Role* (1897). Old Bailey Proceedings Online, 5 May 1911, www.oldbaileyonline.org; *The Times*, 6 May 1911.
33 Lillian Wess, 'Opening of a New Club in the East End', *Freedom*, March 1906, p. 8.
34 Jonathan Moses, 'The Texture of Politics: London's Anarchist Clubs, 1884–1914', RIBA, published online 2016 at www.ribaj.com/intelligence.
35 Ibid.; architectural plans of 165 Jubilee Street, GLC/AR/BR/07/1361, LMA; Pietro Di Paola, *The Knights Errant of Anarchy: London and the Italian Anarchist Diaspora (1880–1917)* (Liverpool, 2013), p. 180.
36 Rocker, *The London Years*, p. 179.
37 John Pether [Andrew Whitehead], 'A Conversation with Nellie Dick', *Raven*, VI (1988), pp. 155–66.
38 Naomi Ploschansky (Nellie Dick) interviewed by Andrew Whitehead, 6 January 1993.
39 Rocker, *The London Years*, pp. 178–9.
40 *Freedom*, April 1906.
41 Guy A. Aldred, *No Traitor's Gait: The Autobiography of Guy A. Aldred* (Glasgow, 1955–63), pp. 298–9, 313.
42 Rocker, *The London Years*, pp. 191–3.
43 Naomi Ploschansky (Nellie Dick) interviewed by Andrew Whitehead.
44 William Nott-Bower, *Fifty-Two Years a Policeman* (London, 1926), p. 231; Rocker, *The London Years*, p. 204.
45 CLA/048/CS/01/02/019, LMA.
46 Undated cutting from the *Evening News* in scrapbook of Detective Inspector Fred Wensley, Wensley Family Archive, Bishopsgate Institute.
47 'Die Ende fun Arbayter Fraynd Klub' (The End of the Arbayter Fraynd Club), *Arbayter Fraynd*, 2 December 1910.
48 *Daily Telegraph*, 5 January 1911; *Daily Chronicle*, 5 January 1911; *The Times*, 25 February 1911.
49 *Morning Post*, 7 January 1911.

4 COMRADES AND LOVERS

1 Charles Perelman statement, CLA/048/CS/01/01/005A, ff. 278–80, London Metropolitan Archives (LMA). In the 1911 Census, he was listed as Charles Pearlman and his birthplace given as Minsk in Russia, now the capital of Belarus.
2 Philip Ruff, *A Towering Flame: The Life and Times of the Elusive Latvian Anarchist Peter the Painter* (London, 2019), pp. 130–31.
3 Ibid., pp. 18–19.
4 A Security Service document from 1932 suggests, rather elliptically, that 'Jacob Vogel' was involved in the Tottenham robbery – KV 3/39, The National Archives (TNA).
5 Isaac Perelman statement, CLA/048/CS/01/01/005A, f. 281, LMA.
6 A detailed police plan of the layout of 59 Grove Street is at COL/PC/01/090/B/6, LMA.
7 The most revealing statements in this regard are those of Luba Milstein, CLA/048/CS/01/01/005B, ff. 204–29, LMA, and Esther Goodman, CLA/048/CS/01/01/022, LMA.
8 Yourka Dubof statement, CLA/048/CS/01/01/005A, ff. 54–5, LMA. The translator was Dubof's landlady, Elsa Petter.
9 Luba Milstein statements, LMA, and her signed depositions, CRIM 1/121, ff. 562–85, TNA.
10 Nicholas Tocmacoff statement, CLA/048/CS/01/01/005A, ff. 353–60, LMA. In later statements Tocmacoff identified John Rosen and Karl Hoffman as among the men he could not initially put a name to who were at Grove Street on 16 December 1910. The 'tall, slim man' was probably 'Joseph' or Sokaloff. When he gave evidence at the Old Bailey, Tocmacoff said he was present at 59 Grove Street for an hour (rather than twenty minutes).
11 Lonnie and Theodore Janson statements citing Hoffman, CLA/048/CS/01/01/005A, ff. 133–40, LMA.
12 Max Nomad, *Dreamers, Dynamiters and Demagogues: Reminiscences* (New York, 1964), pp. 146–50.
13 CLA/048/CS/01/01/004, LMA; Ruff, *A Towering Flame*, p. xiv.
14 *The Times*, 6 May 1911; *Morning Leader*, 6 May 1911.
15 'Houndsditch Murders, Notes of Evidence Given at Guildhall Police Court', f. 32, B16/102, LMA.
16 Edward Humphrey statement, CLA/048/CS/01/01/005A, f. 120, LMA.
17 *The Star*, 11 May 1911.
18 CLA/048/CS/01/01/012, LMA.
19 Ruff, *A Towering Flame*, pp. 176–9.
20 Karl Hoffman statement, CLA/048/CS/01/01/005A, ff. 117–9, LMA.
21 Vassileva's supposed comments to her lawyer were reported to the police by Casimir Pilenas, an interpreter – CLA/048/CS/01/03/015, LMA.
22 CLA/048/CS/01/01/020, LMA.
23 Translated letter from Brixton prison, CLA/048/CS/01/01/017A, LMA.

5 HOUNDSDITCH

1 John Thomas Mann statement, CLA/048/CS/01/005A, London Metropolitan Archives (LMA).
2 Detective Superintendent John Ottaway statement, CLA/048/CS/01/01/005B, ff. 255–8, LMA.
3 Harry Harris statement, CLA/048/CS/01/03/01, LMA. Initial press reports suggested that the haul could have been as much as £20,000 – *The Star*, 17 December 1910.
4 'Houndsditch Murders, Notes of Evidence Given at Guildhall Police Court', f. 32, B16/102, LMA.
5 Ottaway statement, LMA. A grainy photograph showing the extent of the removal of brickwork is at CLA/048/CS/01/03/010/13, LMA.
6 Police Constable Walter Piper statements, CLA/048/CS/01/01/005A, f. 291, and 005B, ff. 289–90, LMA.
7 Max Weil statement, CLA/048/CS/01/01/005A, ff. 378–9, LMA.
8 Sergeant William Bryant, signed deposition, CRIM 1/121, ff. 74–82, The National Archives (TNA). Punctuation has been amended.
9 Police Constable James Martin statement, CLA/048/CS/01/01/005A, ff. 185–6, LMA.
10 Police Constable Arthur Strongman statement, CLA/048/CS/01/01/005A, ff. 331–2, LMA.
11 Strongman statement, CLA/048/CS/01/03/015, LMA; 'Houndsditch Murders', f. 47.
12 Solomon Abrahams statements, CLA/048/CS/01/01/005A, ff. 5–18, LMA.
13 Ada Parker statement, CLA/048/CS/01/01/005A, ff. 275–7, LMA.
14 Isaac Levy statements, CLA/048/CS/01/01/005A, ff. 158–67, LMA.
15 Rosie Trasshonsky [Rosa Trassjonsky] statement, CLA/048/CS/01/01/005A, ff. 361–5, LMA; Luba Milstein statements, CLA/048/CS/01/01/005B, ff. 204–29, LMA.
16 Karl Hoffman signed deposition, CRIM 1/121, ff. 585–91, TNA.
17 *The Star*, 19 December 1910.
18 CLA/048/CS/01/03/015, LMA.
19 Detective Inspector Fred Wensley statement, CLA/048/CS/01/03/015, LMA.
20 Ibid.
21 Frederick Porter Wensley, *Detective Days: The Record of Forty-Two Years' Service in the Criminal Investigation Department* (London, 1931), p. 158.
22 Detective Inspector Ernest Thompson statement, CLA/048/CS/01/01/005A, ff. 340–350, LMA.
23 Detective Inspector Ernest Thompson statement, CLA/048/CS/01/01/005A, LMA.
24 Fourteen-year-old Solomon Abrahams told the *Daily Chronicle*, 19 December 1910, 'The woman I am certain, was one of the firing party.' No one else present, including the police officers, mentioned seeing a woman with a gun, and Abrahams's account has to be regarded as unreliable.
25 CLA/048/CS/01/01/018, LMA.
26 Casimir Pilenas's statement said to be based on comments made by Nina Vassileva to her lawyer on 20 March 1911 at Holloway jail, CLA/048/CS/01/03/015, LMA; *The Times*, 24 March 1911.

27 Milstein statements, CLA/048/CS/01/01/005B, ff. 204–29, LMA. A violin, a mandolin and a tambourine were found when police searched Peter the Painter's room after Gardstein's body had been discovered there.
28 Old Bailey Proceedings Online, 2 May 1911, www.oldbaileyonline.org.
29 Ibid.

6 100 SIDNEY STREET

1 *Daily Chronicle*, 23 December 1910.
2 Ibid.
3 *Daily Mirror*, 23 December 1910. Churchill was present when tests were carried out on more than twenty types of revolvers and pistols in mid-January, according to the *Daily Mirror*, 13 January 1911. Both the Metropolitan Police and the City of London force selected the Birmingham-made Webley & Scott .32 automatic pistol for those occasions when police were issued with firearms.
4 Ossif [*sic*] Federoff statement, CLA/048/CS/01/01/017, London Metropolitan Archives (LMA). Federoff stated that at 8 p.m. on Sunday, 18 December, Tocmacoff came round and told him, 'I have just come from the Police Station, and the Police are outside your house.' Tocmacoff's signed deposition stated that, on his release, he was 'compelled' by the police to go to Federoff's room on Romford Street – CRIM 1/121, ff. 104–23, The National Archives (TNA).
5 *Daily Chronicle*, 20 December 1910.
6 *Daily Chronicle*, 20 and 21 December 1910.
7 HO 144/19780, TNA.
8 CLA/048/CS/01/01/001, LMA; *Daily Chronicle*, 24 December 1910.
9 CLA/048/CS/01/01/005A, ff. 394–5, LMA.
10 CLA/048/CS/01/03/015, LMA.
11 Jacob and Polly Kempler statements, CLA/048/CS/01/01/005A, ff. 147–50, LMA; items found at 44 Gold Street, CLA/048/CS/01/01/004, 005B, ff. 151–2, and 015, LMA.
12 *The Star*, 28 December 1910; *Daily Chronicle*, 28, 29 December 1910. King George V's coronation was six months later on 22 June 1911.
13 *Daily Mirror*, 29 December 1910.
14 Naomi Ploschansky (Nellie Dick) interviewed by Andrew Whitehead, 6 January 1993.
15 Donald Rumbelow, *The Houndsditch Murders and the Siege of Sidney Street* (London, 1990), pp. 181–2; Philip Ruff, *A Towering Flame: The Life and Times of the Elusive Latvian Anarchist Peter the Painter* (London, 2019), p. 193.
16 Detective Constable Frederick Gunner statement, CLA/048/CS/01/03/015, LMA.
17 Luba Milstein statements, CLA/048/CS/01/01/005B, ff. 204–29, LMA.
18 Ibid.
19 KV 3/39, TNA. The key MI5 informant, himself a former Latvian revolutionary, appears to have taken the name A. B. Nelson and, to judge from a jotting on the file, he may at one time have been known as Bisseneek. He was keen to take British nationality, which is what may have induced him to provide information. See also Ruff, *A Towering Flame*, pp. 165–6.
20 Naomi Ploschansky (Nellie Dick) interviewed 6 January 1993. The census records show that in April 1911, Russia-born Solomon Mars was the

Ploschanky family's boarder at 146 Stepney Green. He was listed as a designer working on military embroidery and at 24 was seven years older than Nellie.
21 Lonnie and Theodor Janson statements, CLA/048/CS/01/01/005A, ff. 133–40, LMA.
22 Betsy Gershaw [sic] deposition, 9 January 1911. A 37-page printed collation of the depositions given as part of the inquest into the deaths of the two men at 100 Sidney Street is at HO 144/19780, TNA.
23 Rebecca Fleishman statement, CLA/048/CS/01/01/023, LMA. Luba Milstein also mentioned in court that 'Joseph' had an unusual walk: 'He did not limp, but he always carried one shoulder higher than the other' – *The Times*, 18 March 1911.
24 Frederick Porter Wensley, *Detective Days: The Record of Forty-Two Years' Service in the Criminal Investigation Department* (London, 1931), p. 171.
25 CLA/048/CS/01/03/015, LMA.
26 Jacob Fleishman statement, CLA/048/CS/01/01/023, LMA.
27 The undated letter, written in Latvian, is in an uncatalogued file, B16/102, LMA. A facsimile of the first page of the letter and a full translation are included in Rumbelow, *Houndsditch Murders*, pp. 121, 209–11. Just as this book was going to press I was able – through a remarkable coincidence – to present a copy of Svaars's letter to the intended recipients, his family in Latvia.
28 Rumbelow, *Houndsditch Murders*, p. 144, states, though without attribution, that as Perelman had helped the police to locate one of the three people mentioned in the reward poster (that is, Fritz Svaars), he was entitled to, and received, a third of the £500 reward offered.
29 CLA/048/CS/01/03/015, LMA.
30 Ibid.
31 Plans and drawings of 100 Sidney Street, Wensley 4/1/1-3. Bishopsgate Institute.
32 *Evening News*, 4 January 1911.
33 Davis Schieman statement, MEPO 5/110, TNA.

7 'A DEVILISH KIND OF COURAGE'

1 Frederick Porter Wensley, *Detective Days: The Record of Forty-Two Years' Service in the Criminal Investigation Department* (London, 1931), pp. 170–71.
2 Ibid., pp. 170–72.
3 Report of Superintendent Mulvany, MEPO 5/110, The National Archives (TNA).
4 Wensley, *Detective Days*, p. 172.
5 B. Leeson, *Lost London: The Memoirs of an East End Detective* (London, 1934), pp. 214–15.
6 Detective Inspector Fred Wensley's evidence at the inquest into the deaths of the two men at 100 Sidney Street, HO 144/19780, TNA.
7 All quotes in paragraph taken from Chief Superintendent John Stark's evidence at the inquest, ibid.
8 MEPO 5/110, TNA.
9 HO 144/19780, TNA
10 *Daily Mail*, 4 January 1911; *Daily Telegraph*, 4 January 1911. In fact, troops had opened fire during the Spa Fields riots in Clerkenwell in 1816. Soldiers were

References

also stationed on bridges across the Thames, but not used, during the Chartist demonstration at Kennington Common in 1848 and held in reserve during socialist-led demonstrations in and around Trafalgar Square in 1887.
11 *Evening News*, 3 January 1911; *Daily Mail*, 4 January 1911.
12 Wensley, *Detective Days*, p. 174.
13 C. Graham Grant, 'The Sidney Street Affair in Its Medico-Legal Aspect', *Transactions of the Medico-Legal Society*, IX (1911–12), pp. 21–33. The photograph appeared in the *Daily Mirror*, 4 January 1911.
14 Winston Churchill, 'The Battle of Sidney Street', *Nash's Magazine*, March 1924, pp. 16–18, 98.
15 HO 144/19780, TNA.
16 *The Times*, 19 January 1911.
17 Quoted in Randolph S. Churchill, *Young Statesman: Winston S. Churchill, 1901–1914* (London, 1991), p. 409.
18 *Evening News*, 3 January 1911.
19 *Daily Chronicle*, 4 January 1911.
20 *The Star*, 4 January 1911.
21 Jonathan Ferguson, *The 'Broomhandle' Mauser* (Oxford, 2017), pp. 26–9.
22 Basil Thomson, *The Story of Scotland Yard* (London, 1935), p. 182.
23 Hansard, 6 February 1911, hansard.parliament.uk/commons.
24 *The Times*, 19 January 1911.
25 Randolph Churchill, *Young Statesman*, p. 409; Leeson, *Lost London*, p. 215; Winston Churchill, 'The Battle of Sidney Street'.
26 *Evening News*, 3 January 1911.
27 *The Battle with the London Anarchists* (London, 1911), p. 13.
28 Churchill, 'The Battle of Sidney Street'.
29 'Why Ukraine's Army Still Uses a 100-Year-Old Machinegun', www.economist.com, 11 May 2022.
30 *Daily Mail*, 4 January 1911.
31 *Evening News*, 4 January 1911.
32 Written answer from R. B. Haldane, Secretary of State for War, Hansard, 16 February 1911, hansard.parliament.uk/commons.
33 C.C.B. Morris, *Fire!* (London and Glasgow, 1939), p. 35.
34 *Daily News*, 4 January 1911, cutting in LCC/FB/GEN/02/005, London Metropolitan Archives (LMA).
35 LCC/FB/GEN/02/005, LMA. See also *Evening News*, 3 January 1911, and William Henry Wilks and Walter Herbert Drew inquest evidence, HO 144/19780, TNA.
36 Letter from the Chief Officer of the London Fire Brigade to Sir Edward Henry, 5 January 1911, LCC/FB/GEN/02/005, LMA.
37 Statement by W. H. Drew, 5 January 1911, LCC/FB/GEN/02/005, LMA.
38 Statement by A. E. Edmonds, 5 January 1911, LCC/FB/GEN/02/005, LMA.
39 Statement by C.C.B. Morris, 5 January 1911, LCC/FB/GEN/02/005, LMA.
40 Winston Churchill inquest evidence, HO 144/19780, TNA.
41 Morris, *Fire!*, pp. 34–9.
42 Ibid., p. 39.
43 *Daily Chronicle*, 4 January 1911.
44 Melville L. Macnaghten, *Days of My Years* (London, 1915), p. 259.
45 *Daily News*, 4 January 1911.
46 Police Superintendent John Mulvany inquest evidence, HO 144/19780, TNA.

47 Station Officer Richard Clark, Fireman Richard Gander and Fireman Alfred Henry Colman inquest evidence, HO 144/19780, TNA.
48 Letter from Westley Richards & Co., 20 January 1911 – CLA/048/CS/01/01/025, LMA.
49 C. Graham Grant inquest evidence, HO 144/19780, TNA.
50 Coroner's inquest summing up, HO 144/19780, TNA.
51 *Daily Chronicle*, 5 January 1911.
52 *Daily Mail*, 4 January 1911.
53 *Evening News*, 4 January 1911.
54 *Constabulary Gazette*, 7 January 1911, cutting in CLA/048/CS/01/03/005, LMA.
55 Macnaghten, *Days*, pp. 264–5.
56 *The Times*, 24 January 1911; *Daily Express*, 24 January 1911; Joseph Meaney, *Scribble Street* (London, n.d.), pp. 55–6.

8 'THE COSSACKS OF BOURGEOIS JOURNALISM'

1 HO 144/19780, The National Archives (TNA).
2 Philip Gibbs, *Adventures in Journalism* (London, 1923), p. 61.
3 Sidney Dark, Harry Leatherdale and W. Holt White were the three bylined reporters in the *Daily Express*, 4 January 1911.
4 Joel H. Wiener, *The Americanization of the British Press, 1830–1914: Speed in the Age of Transatlantic Journalism* (Basingstoke, 2011), pp. 183–6.
5 Kennedy Jones, *Fleet Street and Downing Street* (London, 1919), pp. 130–31.
6 *Evening News*, 3 January 1911. The next day's *Daily Mirror* also made reference to the Gordon riots, while *The Times* and the *Daily Telegraph* drew a comparison with the Cato Street conspiracy, an attempt in 1820 to assassinate the Cabinet.
7 Adrian Bingham and Martin Conboy, *Tabloid Century: The Popular Press in Britain, 1896 to the Present* (Oxford, 2015), p. 2.
8 Six volumes of William Hartley's sketches, covering the period from 1893 to 1918, were donated to the Crime Museum at New Scotland Yard. These include sketches of at least three of the Houndsditch defendants and one of the police witnesses – see Jackie Keily and Julia Hoffbrand, *The Crime Museum Uncovered: Inside Scotland Yard's Special Collection* (London, 2015), pp. 64–7.
9 Jones, *Fleet Street and Downing Street*, p. 235, quoting from the *Daily Mirror*, 28 January 1904.
10 *Daily Telegraph*, 5 January 1911. Their reporter was probably Ellis Ashmead-Bartlett, who was later a distinguished war correspondent for the paper. Rebecca Fleishman gave her version of the encounter to the committee examining her compensation claim, MEPO 5/110, TNA.
11 *Daily Mirror*, 6 and 9 January 1911.
12 *The Battle with the London Anarchists* (London, 1911).
13 Gibbs, *Adventures in Journalism*, p. 60.
14 See www.screenonline.org.uk/film; Luke McKernan, 'The Siege of Sidney Street', https://lukemckernan.com, posted 2 January 2011; Luke McKernan tells me that the names of three of the newsreel operators are known: Bertram Brooks-Carrington and Alfred Sowerbutts for Gaumont, and I. Roseman for Pathé.

References

15 At the time of writing in October 2023, several minutes of the newsreel footage filmed at Sidney Street are available on the BFI site www.bfi.org.uk and on YouTube.
16 Alan Burton and Steve Chibnall, *Historical Dictionary of British Cinema* (Plymouth, 2013), pp. 301–10.
17 *Daily Express*, 4 January 1911.
18 Cited in Christopher Hassall, *Edward Marsh, Patron of the Arts: A Biography* (London, 1959), p. 171.
19 Churchill recalled many years after the event being greeted by catcalls of 'Oo let 'em in' when he arrived at Sidney Street on the day of the siege – Winston Churchill, 'The Siege of Sidney Street', *Men Only*, June 1936, pp. 47–54 – but that may not be a reliable memory.
20 I am grateful to Mark Huskinson for information about his great-great uncle. Edward Huskinson (1877–1940) was the editor of *The Tatler* for more than thirty years and designed posters for the Conservative Party as well as being described as a first-class cricketer and a keen yachtsman.
21 'The Lessons of Houndsditch', *The People*, 25 December 1910. The author of the poem was given as Madge St Maury.
22 'Di Hetse Gegen di Anarkhistn' [The Incitement Against the Anarchists], *Arbayter Fraynd*, 23 December 1910.
23 Gibbs, *Adventures in Journalism*, pp. 67–8. His 'Among the Aliens' articles in the *Daily Chronicle* appeared in three successive issues, 9, 10 and 11 January 1911. Gibbs also had a bylined article, 'An Evening in an Anarchists' Club', in *The Graphic*, 7 January 1911.
24 'The Anarchist Leader: interview with Mr. Rocker', *Morning Post*, 7 January 1911; Rudolf Rocker, *The London Years*, trans. Joseph Leftwich (London, 1956), pp. 209 10.
25 '"Expropriation" and Anarchists: The Movement in London', *The Times*, 7 January 1911.
26 *The Times*, 11 January 1911.
27 'The Lettish Refugees', *The Times*, 4 January 1911.
28 *Daily Mail*, 4 January 1911.
29 *Daily Express*, 5 January 1911.
30 'Aliens and the Aliens Act: Measure that Fails to Guard Our Shores', *Daily Express*, 6 January 1911.
31 *Daily Telegraph*, 5 January 1911.
32 David Feldman, *Englishmen and Jews: Social Relations and Political Culture, 1840–1914* (New Haven, CT, and London, 1994), pp. 360–62.
33 'Russia in London', *Jewish Chronicle*, 6 January 1911.
34 *Tottenham and Edmonton Weekly Herald*, 3 February 1909.
35 'The City Coroner's Summing-Up at Inquest on Sergeant Bentley', HO 144/19780, TNA.
36 Recommendation of the inquest jury, HO 144/19780, TNA.
37 Winston Churchill to H. H. Asquith, 3 January 1911, cited in Randolph S. Churchill, *Young Statesman: Winston S. Churchill, 1901–1914* (London, 1991), p. 409.
38 Hassall, *Edward Marsh*, pp. 170–71.
39 David Glover, *Literature, Immigration, and Diaspora in Fin-de-Siècle England: A Cultural History of the 1905 Aliens Act* (New York, 2012), pp. 182–9; Feldman, *Englishmen and Jews*, pp. 362–6; Bernard Gainer,

The Alien Invasion: The Origins of the Aliens Act of 1905 (London, 1972), pp. 206–7.

9 ACQUITTED

1 *The Star*, 13 May 1911.
2 Frederick Porter Wensley, *Detective Days: The Record of Forty-Two Years' Service in the Criminal Investigation Department* (London, 1931), pp. 162–3.
3 The 1911 Census showed Wensley and his family living at 98 Dempsey Street, parallel to and one street beyond Jubilee Street.
4 Fred Wensley's scrapbooks, Wensley 3/1, Bishopsgate Institute; Arthur Harding devoted a chapter to Wensley in his typescript autobiography, 'My Apprenticeship to Crime', Bishopsgate Institute.
5 William Nott-Bower, *Fifty-Two Years a Policeman* (London, 1926), p. 231.
6 City of London Police records, Macnaghten to Nott-Bower, 30 January 1911, CLA/048/CS/01/01/004, London Metropolitan Archives (LMA).
7 CLA/048/CS/01/03/014, LMA – it's not clear who underlined part of the text, but it is more likely to have been the recipient (or his 'chief') than the sender. I am grateful to members of the Police History Society for their help in establishing details of Searle's career in the Metropolitan Police.
8 HO 144/19780, The National Archives (TNA).
9 The four photographs survive: CLA/048/CS/01/03/016/1–4, LMA.
10 CLA/048/CS/01/03/015, LMA.
11 *The Times*, 22, 26 and 30 December 1910, 7 January 1911.
12 *The Times*, 24 February 1911.
13 PC James Woodward signed deposition, CRIM 1/121, ff. 233–4, TNA; John Rosen statement, 'Exhibits', ff. 33–41, CRIM 1/122, TNA.
14 CLA/048/CS/01/01/028, LMA.
15 *Daily Telegraph*, 6 January 1911.
16 See, for example, the full transcript of more than forty typescript pages from the shorthand of Luba Milstein's testimony of 10 May 1911 in CRIM 1/122, TNA.
17 *Daily Telegraph*, 1 December 1911.
18 *The Times*, 2 May 1911; Old Bailey Proceedings Online, 1 and 2 May 1911, www.oldbaileyonline.org.
19 Old Bailey Proceedings Online, 2 May 1911, www.oldbaileyonline.org.
20 *Morning Leader*, 3 May 1911; *The Star*, 4 May 1911.
21 The defence case started on 8 May 1911 and continued through the three following days, Old Bailey Proceedings Online, www.oldbaileyonline.org.
22 *The Times*, 13 May 1911.
23 Ibid.
24 CLA/048/CS/01/01/003, 023, LMA.
25 *The Times*, 21 June 1911.
26 Donald Rumbelow, *The Houndsditch Murders and the Siege of Sidney Street* (London, 1990), pp. 82–3, 162–3.

10 NINA, LUBA, ROSA

1 Philip Ruff, *A Towering Flame: The Life and Times of the Elusive Latvian Anarchist Peter the Painter* (London, 2019), pp. 91, 100.
2 Special Missions section of the Russian Interior Ministry in Paris to Superintendent Ottaway, CLA/048/CS/01/01/008, London Metropolitan Archives (LMA). This could have been a garbled reference to Nina Vassileva, who was a cigarette maker and lived not far from Sidney Street.
3 William J. Fishman, *East End Jewish Radicals, 1875–1914* (London, 1975), pp. 237–8.
4 Rudolf Rocker, *The London Years*, trans. Joseph Leftwich (London, 1956), pp. 190–91. The Baltic anarchist criticized may well have been Fritz Svaars, but while the description fits, there is no confirmation of that.
5 Nellie Dick (born Naomi Ploschansky) interviewed by Andrew Whitehead, 6 January 1993.
6 CLA/048/CS/01/01/031, LMA.
7 Bessie Jacobs statement, CLA/048/CS/01/01/005A, LMA.
8 Raphael Samuel, *East End Underworld: Chapters in the Life of Arthur Harding* (London, 1981), pp. 136–8.
9 Arthur Harding typescript autobiography, 'My Apprenticeship to Crime', ff. 161–2, Bishopsgate Institute, www.bishopsgate.org.uk/archives, accessed 1 October 2023.
10 Isaac Levy statement, 4 January 1911, CLA/048/CS/01/01/005A, ff. 158–67, LMA; *The Times*, 2 February 1911.
11 *The Times*, 15 February 1911.
12 CLA/048/CS/01/01/002, LMA.
13 Detective Inspector Fred Wensley statement, CLA/048/CS/01/03/014, LMA.
14 Fanny Gordon statement, CLA/048/CS/01/01/005A, ff. 93–7, LMA. Fanny added that Nina always spoke to her in Yiddish.
15 Old Bailey Proceedings Online, 4, 5 May 1911, www.oldbaileyonline.org; Isaac Gordon signed deposition, CRIM 1/121, ff. 347–70, The National Archives (TNA).
16 *The Times*, 20 June 1911.
17 Vassileva's comments in 1960 to a reporter, Richard Whittington Egan, are cited in Ruff, *A Towering Flame*, p. 162. Sophia Goldberg, who lived in the same house as Masha Sticking on Bromehead Street in Stepney, told the police that Gardstein had been a 'constant visitor', adding, 'After the murders, Masha was very much upset and was crying on several occasions and said she could not understand why Gardstein had not called to see her' – CLA/048/CS/01/01/018, LMA. The photo of Masha Sticking is at CLA/048/CS/01/03/011/19, LMA.
18 Joseph Da Costa statements, CLA/048/CS/01/01/005A, LMA.
19 'Houndsditch Murders, Notes of Evidence given at Guildhall Police Court', f. 149, B16/102, LMA.
20 Casimir Pilenas, an interpreter, in his evidence at the Old Bailey, gave the title of some of these books, including *History of the Revolutionary Movement in Russia*, *On Revolution and on Revolutionary Government*, *A Tale about an Unrighteous Czar* and *The Government: Its Role in History*, commenting, 'they are all revolutionary books' and it would probably be an offence to possess them in Russia – Old Bailey Proceedings Online, 5 May 1911; *The Times*,

6 May 1911. Two of these titles appear to be Russian versions of pamphlets by the anarchist Peter Kropotkin, *Revolutionary Government* (1892) and *The State: Its Historic Role* (1896).
21 CLA/048/CS/01/03/014, LMA.
22 Old Bailey Proceedings Online, 5 May 1911, www.oldbaileyonline.org.
23 Marks Lubinstein statement, CLA/048/CS/01/01/005A, LMA.
24 CLA/048/CS/01/01/018, LMA; Isaac Gordon signed deposition, 23 February 1911, CRIM 1/121, ff. 347–70, TNA.
25 Frederick Porter Wensley, *Detective Days: The Record of Forty-Two Years' Service in the Criminal Investigation Department* (London, 1931), p. 162.
26 CLA/048/CS/01/01/005A, ff. 104–6, LMA.
27 William Charles Crocker, *Far from Humdrum: A Lawyer's Life* (London, 1967), p. 44.
28 Old Bailey Proceedings Online, 12 May 1911, www.oldbaileyonline.org; *Morning Leader*, 13 May 1911.
29 *The Times*, 13 May 1911.
30 CLA/048/CS/01/03/018, LMA; *The Times*, 21 June 1911.
31 'The Liberation of Vassileva', *Freedom*, July 1911; *New York Times*, 9 July 1911.
32 *The Times*, 6 May 1911; Old Bailey Proceedings Online, 4, 5 and 11 May 1911, www.oldbaileyonline.org.
33 Rocker, *The London Years*, pp. 212–13.
34 Ibid.
35 CLA/048/CS/01/03/014, LMA.
36 James Edward Holroyd, *The Gaslight Murders: The Saga of Sidney Street and the Scarlet 'S'* (London, 1960), p. 246.
37 Christopher Andrew, *The Defence of the Realm: The Authorized History of MI5* (London, 2003), p. 128.
38 Ibid., pp. 152–8.
39 KV 3/39, TNA.
40 Holroyd, *The Gaslight Murders*, p. 245; Ruff, *A Towering Flame*, p. 176; Donald Rumbelow, *The Houndsditch Murders and the Siege of Sidney Street* (London, 1990), pp. 182–3.
41 CLA/048/CS/01/01/004, LMA.
42 Luba Milstein statements, CLA/048/CS/01/01/005B, ff. 204–29, LMA.
43 CLA/048/CS/01/01/031, LMA.
44 Police Sergeant William McKenzie statement, CLA/048/CS/01/01/005A, LMA.
45 *The Star*, 22 February 1911.
46 Luba Milstein's last and most detailed statement to police was made at Holloway prison on 17 February 1911: CLA/048/CS/01/01/005B, ff. 218–29, LMA. She was discharged at the next committal hearing on 22 February.
47 Letter written from Holloway jail, CLA/048/CS/01/03/015, LMA.
48 CLA/048/CS/01/03/015, LMA, retranslated by Roberta Newman.
49 CLA/048/CS/01/01/006, LMA.
50 Ruff, *A Towering Flame*, pp. 171–2.
51 Rosa Trassjonsky statements and notes of questioning, CLA/048/CS/01/01/005A, ff. 351–64, and CLA/048/CS/01/03/015, LMA.
52 Max Berger statement, CLA/048/CS/01/01/005A, ff. 35–7 ; Lizzie Katz statement, CLA/048/CS/01/01/005A, ff. 145–6, LMA.
53 *The Times*, 3 February 1911.

54 Personal communication from Philip Ruff, July 2022. Ruff posted the police photographs on Twitter at that time.
55 CLA/048/CS/01/03/012/9, 12, 16, LMA. The signature on the photograph from Paris is illegible.
56 Rocker, *The London Years*, p. 204.
57 J. P. Eddy, *The Mystery of 'Peter the Painter': The Story of the Houndsditch Murders, the Siege of Sidney Street and the Hunt for 'Peter the Painter'* (London, 1946), pp. 19, 27, 31–2.
58 Luba Milstein statements, LMA.
59 CLA/048/CS/01/03/015, LMA, notes retranslated by Zina Rohan.
60 Ibid.
61 Ibid.
62 Ibid. The initial translator noted that the letter was written in Yiddish but addressed in Russian. Trassjonsky seems to have imagined that she was being held responsible for Gardstein's death, though the charge against her was of being an accessory to the murder of the three policemen.
63 Colney Hatch records, H12/CH/B/03-08, LMA.
64 CLA/048/CS/01/03/015, LMA – tube feeding had at this time become a common but deeply controversial practice when dealing with imprisoned suffragettes on hunger strike.
65 Vassileva confirmed this almost fifty years later – Holroyd, *The Gaslight Murders*, p. 245.
66 Rocker, *The London Years*, p. 204.

11 WHO WAS PETER THE PAINTER?

1 Winston Churchill, 'The Battle of Sidney Street', *Nash's Magazine*, March 1924, pp. 16–18, 98.
2 The letter from Kyiv, which gave no name and a poste restante address, was dated 17 August 1912, while Ottaway's endorsement was made the following month – CLA/048/CS/01/01/009, London Metropolitan Archives (LMA).
3 Letter of 16 December 1912 – CLA/048/CS/01/01/008, LMA. An earlier letter from the Consul General, on 30 October 1911, had reported that the police in Latvia had not at that time succeeded 'in obtaining any information about Peter the Painter, whose name is Peter Pyatkoff, from his relatives who are believed to live in Kourland near Talsen' – CLA/048/CS/01/01/004, LMA.
4 Philip Ruff, *A Towering Flame: The Life and Times of the Elusive Latvian Anarchist Peter the Painter* (London, 2019), pp. 2–4.
5 Eddy's letter hasn't survived but the police's response has – CLA/048/CS/01/02/014, LMA; J. P. Eddy, *The Mystery of 'Peter the Painter': The Story of the Houndsditch Murders, the Siege of Sidney Street and the Hunt for 'Peter the Painter'* (London, 1946).
6 CLA/048/CS/01/01/016, LMA. Ruff, *A Towering Flame*, p. xx, has suggested that while in London Peter was known to some fellow Latvians as Peteris Malderis, the latter word being Latvian for a dauber or inexpert artist. Peter the Painter is known in Latvia today as Peteris Krasotajs, *krasotajs* meaning an industrial painter. It's not clear whether the Latvian name was the basis for the English usage, or is the English nickname translated back into Latvian.
7 *Evening News*, 19 December 1910 – cutting in CLA/048/CS/01/02/015, LMA.
8 *Evening News*, 4 January 1911.

9 *Daily Mirror*, 6 January 1911.
10 *Daily Mirror*, 7 January 1911.
11 *Morning Post*, 6 January 1911.
12 CLA/048/CS/01/01/002, 004, 021, LMA.
13 CLA/048/CS/01/01/004, 031, LMA.
14 Ruff, *A Towering Flame*, p. xx.
15 *The Star*, 7 January, 2 February, 7 March 1911.
16 FO 155/1643, The National Archives (TNA).
17 CLA/048/CS/01/02/024, LMA.
18 Old Bailey Proceedings Online, 2 May 1911, www.oldbaileyonline.org.
19 Melville L. Macnaghten, *Days of My Years* (London, 1915), p. 252.
20 *New York Times*, 9 July 1911.
21 Richard Deacon, *A History of the British Secret Service* (London, 1969), p. 169.
22 Basil Thomson, *The Story of Scotland Yard* (London, 1935), p. 184. William Crocker, *Far from Humdrum: A Lawyer's Life* (London, 1967), pp. 45–8, wrote that he was told by Casimir Pilenas that his brother was Peter the Painter, but if so he was misled, as the photograph he published of Peter Pilenas demonstrates. The issue is considered in Donald Rumbelow, *The Houndsditch Murders and the Siege of Sidney Street* (London, 1990), pp. 185–7.
23 CLA/048/CS/01/03/005, LMA.
24 B. Leeson, *Lost London: The Memoirs of an East End Detective* (London, 1934), pp. 217–22. The King's Head closed in the year 2000. The building still stands at 128 Commercial Road but has been much modified. Leeson's passing mention apart, there is nothing to suggest that Peter the Painter ever set foot inside this pub.
25 Ruff, *A Towering Flame*, pp. 227–37.
26 KV 2/797 and 798, TNA.
27 Rudolf Rocker, *The London Years*, trans. Joseph Leftwich (London, 1956), p. 212.
28 The report is dated January 1916 – KV 2/1025, TNA.
29 Detective Inspector John Collison statement, CLA/048/CS/01/01/005A, LMA.
30 Jectat [*sic*] Peters statement, CLA/048/CS/01/01/005A. ff. 284–5, LMA.
31 Peters's SDP membership and subscriptions cards – he joined in October 1910 – are in B16/102, LMA.
32 CLA/048/CS/01/01/006, LMA.
33 *The Times*, 13 January 1911.
34 *Daily Express*, 3 October 1918 – cutting in KV 2/1025, TNA. Ruff, *A Towering Flame*, pp. 172–5.
35 KV 2/1025, TNA.
36 R. H. Bruce Lockhart, *Memoirs of a British Agent* (London, 1932), pp. 258–9, 326–48.
37 Antony Beevor, *Russia: Revolution and Civil War, 1917–1921* (London, 2022), pp. 218–22.
38 *Daily Express*, 3 October 1918.
39 HO 45/24700, TNA.
40 Ibid.
41 Ibid.
42 Ibid.
43 Ruff, *A Towering Flame*, pp. 213–18; Rumbelow, *The Houndsditch Murders*, pp. 193–9.

12 THE ANARCHIST AFTERMATH

1. 'The Houndsditch Tragedy: Who Is Responsible?', *Freedom: A Journal of Anarchist Communism*, January 1911.
2. The leaflet was published in *Freedom*, February 1911. The notorious Dr Crippen was hanged in the grounds of Pentonville jail in November 1910 for the murder of his wife.
3. 'Di Shlakh in di Ist End' (The Battle in the East End), *Arbayter Fraynd*, 6 January 1911.
4. Errico Malatesta, 'Kapitalistn und Ganovim: Vegen di Tragedies fun Handsditch un Sidney Strit' (Capitalists and Robbers: About the Tragedies of Houndsditch and Sidney Street), *Arbayter Fraynd*, 27 January 1911. The article was subsequently published in French and in English. Malatesta probably wrote the article in French.
5. *Evening News*, 6 January 1911.
6. Malatesta, 'Kapitalistn und Ganovim'.
7. Errico Malatesta statement, CLA/048/CS/01/01/004, London Metropolitan Archives (LMA); Errico Malatesta signed deposition, CRIM 1/121, ff. 485–90, The National Archives (TNA).
8. Rudolf Rocker, *The London Years*, trans. Joseph Leftwich (London, 1956), pp. 205–6.
9. Errico Malatesta statement, CLA/048/CS/01/01/005A, ff. 173-5, LMA.
10. CLA/048/CS/01/01/005A, LMA. According to the police records of the identification parades, Malatesta was brought before a line-up that included Federoff, Peters and Dubof on 23 December, a line-up including Rosen on 3 February, and another including Hoffman on 8 February.
11. Rocker, *The London Years*, p. 206.
12. Old Bailey Proceedings Online, 2 May 1911, www.oldbaileyonline.org.
13. Douglas G. Browne, *The Rise of Scotland Yard: A History of the Metropolitan Police* (London, 1956), p. 289.
14. Harold Brust, *'I Guarded Kings': The Memoirs of a Political Police Officer* (London, n.d.), pp. 95–8.
15. Herbert T. Finch, *Traitors Within: The Adventures of Detective Inspector Herbert T. Finch* (London, 1933), p. 46.
16. William Nott-Bower, *Fifty-Two Years a Policeman* (London, 1926), pp. 232–3.
17. Old Bailey Proceedings Online, 14 May 1912, www.oldbaileyonline.org.
18. Pietro Di Paola, *The Knights Errant of Anarchy: London and the Italian Anarchist Diaspora (1880–1917)* (Liverpool, 2013), pp. 146–53.
19. Old Bailey Proceedings Online, 14 May 1912.
20. *Islington Daily Gazette*, date unknown. I am indebted to Professor Carl Levy for this reference.
21. CLA/048/CS/01/01/026, LMA.
22. Ernest Nicholls, *Crime within the Square Mile: The History of Crime in the City of London* (London, 1935), p. 117.
23. John Merriman, *Ballad of the Anarchist Bandits: The Crime Spree that Gripped Belle Époque Paris* (New York, 2017), pp. 110–11; Richard Bach Jensen, *The Battle against Anarchist Terrorism: An International History, 1878–1934* (Cambridge, 2014), pp. 348–50; Richard Parry, *The Bonnot Gang: The Story of the French Illegalists* (London, 1987), p. 69.

24 Parry, *The Bonnot Gang*, pp. 35, 50. Victor Serge set down his own account of his association with anarcho-bandits in France in *Memoirs of a Revolutionary* (New York, 2021), pp. 37–52.
25 Rocker, *The London Years*, p. 218.
26 John Pether [Andrew Whitehead], 'A Conversation with Nellie Dick', *The Raven*, 11/2 (1986), pp. 155–66.
27 Rocker, *The London Years*, p. 226.
28 William J. Fishman, *East End Jewish Radicals, 1875–1914* (London, 1975), p. 306.
29 Cited in Thomas C. Jones, 'The Rocker-Witkop Family and the Closing of Political Asylum in Britain', *Revue d'histoire du XIXe siècle*, LXI/2 (2020), pp. 123–49.
30 Leah Feldman interviewed by Andrew Whitehead, 7 October 1985.

13 LEGACY

1 Georges Simenon, *Pietr the Latvian*, trans. David Bellos (London, 2013), p. 13.
2 Details of the film are available at the BFI's Screen Online at www.screenonline.org.uk.
3 The typescript screenplay of 'The Siege of Sidney Street' is in the Alexander Baron papers at the University of Reading – MS 5126/485.
4 Richard Brooks, 'Glimpsing the Ghosts from the Siege of Sidney Street', *Sunday Times*, 2 January 2011.
5 Philip Ruff, *A Towering Flame: The Life and Times of the Elusive Latvian Anarchist Peter the Painter* (London, 2019), pp. 219–22.
6 Ibid., pp. 179–83.
7 *The Economist*, 19 December 2020.
8 *East London Advertiser*, 25 September 2008, at www.eastlondonadvertiser.co.uk; *Daily Telegraph*, 25 September 2008.

SELECT BIBLIOGRAPHY

ARCHIVES

Archives listed in order of importance

LONDON METROPOLITAN ARCHIVES

CLA/048/CS/01/01-019: City of London Police records relating to the Houndsditch murders including witness statements, official correspondence, confiscated documents and photographs, files relating to the dead police officers, news cuttings and more

B16/102: Uncatalogued records relating to the Houndsditch murders and the Sidney Street siege, including photographs, ephemera, news cuttings and bound volumes containing witness statements, proceedings at the Guildhall police court and the hearings into compensation claims

COL/PC/01/090/B/3–6: Detailed maps and plans relating to the Houndsditch attempted robbery drawn up by the police for use at the committal hearings and trial

LCC/FB/GEN/02/005: London Fire Brigade records relating to the blaze at 100 Sidney Street, Stepney, on 3 January 1911

GLC/AR/BR/19/1361: Plans relating to the use of the hall of 165 Jubilee Street in Stepney, 1904–14

H12/CH/B/03–08: Colney Hatch asylum, records relating to Rosa Trassjonsky

THE NATIONAL ARCHIVES, LONDON

CRIM 1/121: Witness depositions prepared for the trial arising out of the Houndsditch murders

CRIM 1/122: Details of exhibits prepared for the trial arising out of the Houndsditch murders, including statement transcripts, witness depositions and other items

HO 144/19780: Home Office records relating to the Siege of Sidney Street, including inquest proceedings, correspondence, claims for compensation and news cuttings

HO 45/24700: Home Office records relating to May Peters (born May Freeman)

KV 2/797–8: Security Service files relating to Peter and Anton Miller, and Soviet espionage in the UK principally in the 1920s

KV 2/1025: Security Service files concerning Jacob Peters

KV 3/39: Security Service records on anarchist activities and the political background of the Sidney Street siege

MEPO 3/191: Metropolitan Police records relating to the Siege of Sidney Street, including some witness statements and official correspondence, as well as police commendations and compensation claims

MEPO 3/194: Metropolitan Police records relating to the Tottenham Outrage, including police commendations, compensation claims and funeral and memorial arrangements

MEPO 5/110: Metropolitan Police and other records relating to compensation claims arising out of the Siege of Sidney Street

BISHOPSGATE INSTITUTE, LONDON

Wensley/3–4: Scrapbooks and news cuttings of Detective Inspector Fred Wensley; building and street plans relating to 100 Sidney Street; DI Wensley's notebooks listing serious crimes and arrests

LCM/286: 'Houndsditch Police Murders', scrapbook containing news cuttings

Arthur Harding, 'My Apprenticeship to Crime' typescript autobiography, available online at www.bishopsgate.org.uk/archives

HARINGEY MUSEUM AND ARCHIVE, BRUCE CASTLE MUSEUM, LONDON

Photographs, postcards, documents and cuttings relating to the Tottenham Outrage

BRITISH FILM INSTITUTE, LONDON

Battle of London, Pathé Frères Cinema, 1911 (about 5'30") – an edited version is available online at www.britishpathe.com

Houndsditch Murderers, Andrews' Pictures, 1911 (about 6'45") – available online at https://player.bfi.org.uk

The Great East End Anarchist Battle, Gaumont Graphic, 1911 (about 3'30") – an edited version with some extraneous content is available online at www.britishpathe.com/video/

Dr Brian Pellie and the Secret Despatch, Clarendon Film Co., 1912 (about 6'40")

COURT RECORDS

Old Bailey Proceedings Online, www.oldbaileyonline.org

INTERVIEWS

Nellie Dick (born Naomi Ploschansky) interviewed by Andrew Whitehead over the phone from Florida, 5 November 1985, and in person in Oyster Bay, NY, 6 January 1993 – recordings in the National Sound Archive (NSA), https://sounds.bl.uk

Leah Feldman interviewed by Andrew Whitehead in North London, 7 October 1985 – recording in NSA

Fermin Rocker interviewed by Andrew Whitehead in North London, 27 September 1985 – recording in NSA

FILM

The Man Who Knew Too Much (dir. Alfred Hitchcock, 1934)
The Siege of Sidney Street (dir. Robert S. Baker and Monty Berman, 1960)
Malatesta – in German (dir. Peter Lilienthal, 1970)

Select Bibliography

BOOKS AND PAMPHLETS

Aldred, Guy A., *No Traitor's Gait: The Autobiography of Guy A. Aldred* (Glasgow, 1955–63)
Andrew, Christopher, *The Defence of the Realm: The Authorized History of MI5* (London, 2003)
Barton, Geoffrey, *The Tottenham Outrage and Walthamstow Tram Chase: The Most Spectacular Hot Pursuit in History* (Sherfield on Loddon, 2017)
The Battle with the London Anarchists (London, 1911)
Beevor, Antony, *Russia: Revolution and Civil War, 1917–1921* (London, 2022)
Bennett, John, *Mob Town: A History of Crime and Disorder in the East End* (New Haven, CT, and London, 2017)
Bingham, Adrian, and Martin Conboy, *Tabloid Century: The Popular Press in Britain, 1896 to the Present* (Oxford, 2015)
Browne, Douglas G., *The Rise of Scotland Yard: A History of the Metropolitan Police* (London, 1956)
Brust, Harold, *'I Guarded Kings': The Memoirs of a Political Police Officer* (London, n.d.)
——, *In Plain Clothes: Further Memoirs of a Political Police Officer* (London, 1937)
Churchill, Randolph S., *Young Statesman: Winston S. Churchill, 1901–1914* (London, 1991)
Clarke, F. G., *Will-o'-the-Wisp: Peter the Painter and the Anti-Tsarist Terrorists in Britain and Australia* (Melbourne, 1983)
Collier, Patricia, *Secrets of the Tottenham Outrage* (London, 2007)
Crocker, William Charles, *Far from Humdrum: A Lawyer's Life* (London, 1967)
Dangerfield, George, *The Strange Death of Liberal England* (London, 1935)
Deacon, Richard, *A History of the British Secret Service* (London, 1969)
Di Paola, Pietro, *The Knights Errant of Anarchy: London and the Italian Anarchist Diaspora (1880–1917)* (Liverpool, 2013)
Eddy, J. P., *The Mystery of 'Peter the Painter': The Story of the Houndsditch Murders, the Siege of Sidney Street and the Hunt for 'Peter the Painter'* (London, 1946)
Emsley, Clive, *Crime and Society in Twentieth Century England* (Abingdon, 2013)
——, *The English Police: A Political and Social History* (Hemel Hempstead, 1991)
Feldman, David, *Englishmen and Jews: Social Relations and Political Culture, 1840–1914* (New Haven, CT, and London, 1994)
Ferguson, Jonathan, *The 'Broomhandle' Mauser* (Oxford, 2017)
Finch, Herbert T., *Traitors Within: The Adventures of Detective Inspector Herbert T. Finch* (London, 1933)
Fink, Jon Stephen, *A Storm in the Blood* (London, 2009)
Fishman, William J., *East End Jewish Radicals, 1875–1914* (London, 1975)
Gainer, Bernard, *The Alien Invasion: The Origins of the Aliens Act of 1905* (London, 1972)
Gibbs, Philip, *Adventures in Journalism* (London, 1923)
Glover, David, *Literature, Immigration, and Diaspora in Fin-de-Siècle England: A Cultural History of the 1905 Aliens Act* (New York, 2012)
Gould, Robert W., and Michael J. Waldren, *London's Armed Police: 1829 to the Present* (London, 1986)
Graur, Mina, *An Anarchist 'Rabbi': The Life and Teachings of Rudolf Rocker* (New York, 1997)
Harris, J. D., *Outrage! An Edwardian Tragedy* (London, 2000)

Hassall, Christopher, *Edward Marsh, Patron of the Arts: A Biography* (London, 1959)
Holroyd, James Edward, *The Gaslight Murders: The Saga of Sidney Street and the Scarlet 'S'* (London, 1960)
Jensen, Richard Bach, *The Battle against Anarchist Terrorism: An International History, 1878–1934* (Cambridge, 2014)
Jones, Kennedy, *Fleet Street and Downing Street* (London, 1919)
Kadish, Sherman, *Bolsheviks and British Jews: The Anglo-Jewish Community, Britain and the Russian Revolution* (London, 1992)
Keily, Jackie, and Julia Hoffbrand, *The Crime Museum Uncovered: Inside Scotland Yard's Special Collection* (London, 2015)
Kirby, Dick, *Whitechapel's Sherlock Holmes: The Casebook of Fred Wensley OBE, KPM, Victorian Crimebuster* (Barnsley, 2014)
Knepper, Paul, *The Invention of International Crime: A Global Issue in the Making, 1881–1914* (Basingstoke, 2010)
Kropotkin, [Peter], *The Terror in Russia: An Appeal to the British Nation* (London, 1909)
Leeson, B., *Lost London: The Memoirs of an East End Detective* (London, 1934)
Lieven, Anatol, *The Baltic Revolution: Estonia, Latvia, Lithuania and the Path to Independence* (New Haven, CT, and London, 1993)
Litvinoff, Emanuel, *A Death Out of Season* (London, 1973)
Lockhart, R. H. Bruce, *Memoirs of a British Agent* (London, 1932)
Macnaghten, Melville L., *Days of My Years* (London, 1915)
Meaney, Joseph, *Scribble Street* (London, n.d.)
Merriman, John, *Ballad of the Anarchist Bandits: The Crime Spree that Gripped Belle Époque Paris* (New York, 2017)
Morris, C.C.B., *Fire!* (London and Glasgow, 1939)
Nicholls, Ernest, *Crime within the Square Mile: The History of Crime in the City of London* (London, 1935)
Nomad, Max, *Dreamers, Dynamiters and Demagogues: Reminiscences* (New York, 1964)
Nott-Bower, William, *Fifty-Two Years a Policeman* (London, 1926)
Oughton, Frederick, *The Siege of Sidney Street* (London, 1960)
Parry, Richard, *The Bonnot Gang: The Story of the French Illegalists* (London, 1987)
Porter, Bernard, *The Origins of the Vigilant State: The London Metropolitan Police Special Branch before the First World War* (London, 1987)
The Revolution in the Baltic Provinces of Russia (London, 1907)
Rocker, Fermin, *The East End Years: A Stepney Childhood* (London, 1998)
Rocker, Rudolf, *The London Years*, trans. Joseph Leftwich (London, 1956)
Rogers, Colin, *The Battle of Stepney: The Sidney Street Siege, Its Causes and Consequences* (London, 1981)
Ruff, Philip, *A Towering Flame: The Life and Times of the Elusive Latvian Anarchist Peter the Painter* (London, 2019)
Rumbelow, Donald, *The Houndsditch Murders and the Siege of Sidney Street* (London, 1990)
Samuel, Raphael, *East End Underworld: Chapters in the Life of Arthur Harding* (London, 1981)
Sassen, Saskia, *Guests and Aliens* (New York, 1999)
Simenon, Georges, *Pietr the Latvian*, trans. David Bellos (London, 2013)
Solomon, Vlad, *State Surveillance, Political Policing and Counter-Terrorism in Britain, 1880–1914* (Martlesham, Suffolk, 2021)

Taylor, Antony, *London's Burning: Pulp Fiction, the Politics of Terrorism and the Destruction of the Capital in British Popular Culture, 1840–2005* (London, 2012)

Thomson, Basil, *The Story of Scotland Yard* (London, 1935)

Wensley, Frederick Porter, *Detective Days: The Record of Forty-Two Years' Service in the Criminal Investigation Department* (London, 1931)

White, Jerry, *London in the Nineteenth Century: A Human Awful Wonder of God* (London, 2008)

—, *London in the Twentieth Century: A City and Its People* (London, 2001)

Wiener, Joel H., *The Americanization of the British Press, 1830–1914: Speed in the Age of Transatlantic Journalism* (Basingstoke, 2011)

ARTICLES

Anderson, Robert, 'The Problem of the Criminal Alien', *Nineteenth Century and After*, February 1911, pp. 217–24

Churchill, Winston, 'The Battle of Sidney Street', *Nash's Magazine*, March 1924, pp. 16–18, 98

—, 'The Siege of Sidney Street', *Men Only*, June 1936, pp. 47–54

Connor, Sam, 'The Edwardian Press and Melodrama in the Aftermath of the Sidney Street Siege', www.historyworkshop.org.uk, posted March 2012

Gidley, Benjamin, 'Towards a Cosmopolitan Account of Jewish Socialism: Class, Identity and Immigration in Edwardian London', *Socialist History*, XLV (2014), pp. 61–79

Grant, C. Graham, 'The Sidney Street Affair in Its Medico-Legal Aspect', *Transactions of the Medico-legal Society*, IX (1911–12), pp. 21–33

Hazans, Mihails, 'Emigration from Latvia: A Brief History and Driving Forces in the Twenty-First Century', in *The Emigrant Communities of Latvia: National Identity, Transnational Belonging, and Diaspora Politics*, ed. Rita Kasa and Inta Mieriņa (New York, 2019), pp. 35–58

Holmes, Colin, 'In Search of Sidney Street', *Bulletin of the Society for the Study of Labour History*, XXIX (1974), pp. 70–77

—, 'The Reubens Brothers: Jews, Crime and the East London Connection, 1887–1911', in *An East End Legacy: Essays in Memory of William J. Fishman*, ed. Colin Holmes and Anne J. Kershen (London, 2018), pp. 93–116

Jones, Thomas C., 'The Rocker-Witkop Family and the Closing of Political Asylum in Britain', *Revue d'histoire du XIXe siècle*, LXI/2 (2020), pp. 123–49

Knepper, Paul, 'The Other Invisible Hand: Jews and Anarchists in London before the First World War', *Jewish History*, XXII (2008), pp. 295–315

[McKernan, Luke], 'The Siege of Sidney Street', https://thebioscope.net, posted January 2011

Moses, Jonathan, 'The Texture of Politics: London's Anarchist Clubs, 1884–1914', www.ribaj.com, posted December 2016

Moss, Eloise, 'The Scrapbooking Detective: Frederick Porter Wensley and the Limits of "Celebrity" and "Authority" in Inter-War Britain', *Social History*, XL/1 (2015), pp. 58–81

Pether, John [Andrew Whitehead], 'A Conversation with Nellie Dick', *Raven*, VI (1988), pp. 155–66

Porter, Bernard, 'Piatkoff (Piaktow), Peter (nicknamed Peter the Painter)', *Oxford Dictionary of National Biography*, published online 2005, revised 2011

Raun, Toivo U., 'The Revolution of 1905 in the Baltic Provinces and Finland', *Slavic Review*, XLIII/3 (1984), pp. 453–67

Shpayer-Makov, Haia, 'The Reception of Peter Kropotkin in Britain, 1886–1917', *Albion*, XIX/3 (1987), pp. 373–90

NEWSPAPERS

Arbayter Fraynd (Worker's Friend) (Yiddish)
Daily Chronicle
Daily Express
Daily Graphic
Daily Mail
Daily Mirror
Daily Telegraph
Evening News
Evening Standard
Freedom: A Journal of Anarchist Communism
The Graphic
Jewish Chronicle
Morning Leader
Morning Post
Pall Mall Gazette
The People
The Star
The Times
Tottenham and Edmonton Weekly Herald

ACKNOWLEDGEMENTS

Several friends went above and beyond the normal bounds of friendship in helping this book to completion and reading it in draft form. Zina Rohan offered advice on the big things and the small and this volume is much the better for her generous and wise counsel. She also guided me on Russian history and the Russian language and translated inscriptions from Russian. Nick Nugent and Susie Thomas cast a supportive and critical eye over just about every chapter, though they were sent out of sequence just to make their lives difficult. Tania Nugent was a great help with Latvian words and phrases and through her, in a remarkable coincidence, I made contact just as this book was going to press with the Latvian family of one of the men who died at 100 Sidney Street, Fritz Svaars. Martin Plaut offered support and encouragement as I got to grips with setting down the Sidney Street story. David Goodway looked over the chapters about the anarchist movement, while Carl Levy read the sections about Errico Malatesta and kindly shared a presentation he had made about the attempts to deport the Italian anarchist from Britain. Peter Rowlands helped to keep me on the right side of the law and of legal and judicial process.

I am very grateful to Roberta Newman for her skill and efficiency in translating from Yiddish articles in the anarchist journal the *Arbayter Fraynd* and to my friend and Yiddish enthusiast David Mazower for his help in identifying the key articles. I have gained from the advice and courtesy of many other friends and historians, including Nick Baron, Thomas Jones, Luke McKernan, Jonathan Moses, William Pimlott, Vlad Solomon, Jerry White, Sarah Wise and Zinovy Zinik. Members of the Police History Society were generous in response to my pleas for help and expert advice. Anuradha Awasthi, Bernard Gabony, Sara Hyson, Aman Kanwar, Rachna Kanwar and Sam Miller have been willing guinea pigs on the walks around Tottenham and across the East End.

Thirty years and more ago, I met and interviewed a small number of Rudolf Rocker's surviving *chaverim*, comrades, and others with memories of London's East End in the first two decades of the last century. I have warm memories of long conversations with Nellie Dick (born Naomi Ploschansky), Fermin Rocker, Leah Feldman and Lou Appleton. All were anarchists or brought up in anarchist households, and while none had any sympathy for politically motivated violence, their reminiscences opened a window on the political culture of the East End amid which the Latvian gunmen found shelter.

Donald Rumbelow and Philip Ruff, historians who have both written landmark accounts of Houndsditch and Sidney Street and their political context, have been welcoming to this newcomer on their patch. Dave Watkins at Reaktion first suggested that I write a book about anarchists and aliens and Amy Salter has expertly guided the title through to publication; Susannah Jayes assisted with picture selection and research. Sebastian Ballard designed the maps, which will help readers to follow in the footsteps of some of those whose stories are told in this book.

To you all, a very warm thank you!

Without the extensive City of London Police records about the Houndsditch murders at the London Metropolitan Archives (LMA) in Clerkenwell, there would be much less to say about this tragedy and the shoot-out in Sidney Street which followed from it. And we would know a lot less about the Latvian political exiles who were principally responsible. Without the courtesy and efficiency of the LMA's staff, researching this book would have been a more arduous task. I am particularly grateful to the LMA's archivists and conservators for allowing me to inspect inscriptions on the back of some of the photographs they hold and for enabling me to consult some of their uncatalogued holdings. Sally Bevan, Senior Archivist at the LMA, was of great help in securing me permission to publish many of the images in this book. At the City of London Police, Chief Inspector Rachel Bullimore, Staff Officer to the Commissioner, and Gary Brailsford-Hart, Director of Information, very kindly arranged for me to be able to include images from their archives.

At the Bishopsgate Institute, Michelle Johansen pointed me to valuable material in their archives and invited me along to one of her evening classes about these exceptional holdings. At Bruce Castle Museum in Tottenham, I was greeted by a staff member, Valerie Crosby, who shared her own family stories about the armed robbery known as the Tottenham Outrage. The YIVO Institute for Jewish Research in New York went to a great deal of trouble to provide digital copies of crucial issues of the *Arbayter Fraynd* not available in London. I am also in the debt of archivists, librarians and staff at the National Archive and the British Library, two institutions that we should all cherish.

Anu has as ever been an unfailing support and rigorous critic and this book could not have been contemplated never mind completed without her love and encouragement. It is dedicated to our children, Samira and Rohan, of whom we are very proud.

It is normal in acknowledgements to say that responsibility for errors and shortcomings lies with the author alone. But in line with the custom of the times recounted, if you want someone to blame . . . well, there's always Peter the Painter.

PHOTO ACKNOWLEDGEMENTS

The author and publishers wish to thank the organizations and individuals listed below for authorizing reproduction of their work.

Author's collection: pp. 111, 140, 141, 143, 147, 161, 183; Sebastian Ballard: pp. 270, 274; Bishopsgate Institute: pp. 11, 126 (Wensley Family Archive), 127 (Wensley Family Archive); Bruce Castle Museum (Haringey Archive & Museum Service): pp. 22, 27; *Daily Chronicle*, 4 January 1911: pp. 130–31 (Public Domain); *Daily Mirror*, 4 January 1911: p. 158 (Public Domain); Getty Images: p. 248 (Archiv Gerstenberg/ullstein bild); *Illustrated London News*: p. 89 (issue 3740, p. 999, 24 December 1910, from article 'Armed Burglars in the City: The Terrible Houndsditch Affray'/Public Domain); Jewish East End Celebration Society: p. 34; Library of Congress, Washington, DC: p. 150; London Metropolitan Archives: p. 65; London Metropolitan Archives, by kind permission of the Commissioner of the City of London Police: pp. 39, 80, 83, 84, 86, 92, 94, 105, 113, 197, 208, 215, 227, 237; *The People*, 25 December 1910: p. 165 (Public Domain); from G. R. Sims, ed., *Living London* (1902): p. 37; Andrew Whitehead: pp. 29, 65; Wikimedia Commons: pp. 163 (Public Domain), 255 (Public Domain).

INDEX

Page numbers in *italics* refer to illustrations

Abney Park cemetery 26–8
Abraham, Solomon 97–8
Aldred, Guy 65–6
Aleichem, Sholem 35
Alexander II, tsar of Russia 54–5
Aliens Act 1905 37–8, 164–5, 170–74, 219, 250, 265
All-Russia Co-operative Society (ARCOS) 207, 234
All-Russia Extraordinary Commission (Cheka) 234–5, 238
anarchism 13, 43, 52–72, 112, 114–15, 167–70, 178–80, 224, 229, 236, 238, 242–57, 264–5, 281
Anderson, Robert 59–60
anti-heroes 10–11, 221
antisemitism 12–13, 33–4, 35–6, 46–7, 164–5, 266
Antwerp 120
Arbayter Fraynd, Der (Yiddish-language journal) 63, *63*, 70–72, 167, 217, 243–5, 253–4, 256
artillery 141–2, *141*
Ashmead Bartlett, Ellis 159
Asquith, Herbert Henry 15–16, 137, 172–3
Australia 10, 82, 85, 124, 232–4

Baker, Robert S. 260
Bakunin, Mikhail 54
Balfour, A. J. 138
Baron, Alexander 35, 260–61
Battle with the London Anarchists, The 160–61, *161*
Bellelli, Ennio 249–50

Bentley, Robert (police sergeant) 95–9, 109, 111, *111*, 186, 192, 209, 276
Bermon, Monty 260
Beron, Leon 177–8
Bethnal Green 266
Bialystok 216
Bifsteks *see* Palamieks, Janis
Blind Beggar, The (pub) 11
Bodkin, Archibald 184–6
Boer War 7, 135
Bonnot, Jules 10, 251–3
Bourdin, Martial 56
British Film Institute 15, 162
Briviba (Latvian-language journal) 44, 229
Brodie, Morris 69
Brooks, Richard 263–4
Bruno, Ludwig 51
Brust, Harold 249
Bryant, William (police sergeant) 95–9, 107
Burns, John 250

Cable Street, 'Battle' of 9, 256
Campbell, Rose 82–5
Cawley, Mary Ann 25
Cheka *see* All-Russia Extraordinary Commission
Chertkov, Vladimir 38
Chesterton, G. K. 54
Choat, Walter (police constable) 96–9, 107, 109, 111, *111*, 276
Churchill, Winston 7–8, 110–11, 136–47, *143*, 151, 162–4, *163*, 173–4, 221, 260, 265, 279

311

City of London cemetery, Ilford 111, 114
City of London Police 11, 14, 104, 107, 110, 141–2, 150, 177–9, 185–6, 190, 224–5, 232–3, 276
Clapham Common murder 177–8
Colney Hatch Asylum 219–20
Communist Club 48, 238
Communist Party 236, 256–7
Conan Doyle, Arthur 252
Conrad, Joseph 54, 182
Court of Appeal 191, 204
Craigneuk 51–2
Crimea 85
Crocker, William 203

Da Costa, Joseph 200
Daily Chronicle 130–31, 160–61
Daily Express 156, 170, 292
Daily Mail 170
Daily Mirror 154, *158*, 159–60
Daily Telegraph 159–60, 171
Dangerfield, George 15
Dick, Nellie *see* Ploschansky, Naomi
Dr Brian Pellie and the Secret Dispatch (film) 259–60
Drew, W. H. (Fire Brigade sub-officer) 144
Dubof, Yourka 68, 75, 77–9, 85, 107, 109, 112–13, 120, 182, 185, 187, 189–90, 192, 198, 264
Dzirkalis, Alfreds *see* Hoffman, Karl

Eagles, Charles (police constable) 25
Eddy, J. P. 168, 223
Edmonds, A. E. (Fire Brigade station officer) 144–5
Edward VII 27, 154
Evening News 154, 156–7
Evening Standard 157
Exchange Buildings 88–100, *92*, *94*, 107, 109, 116, 184, 186, 189–92, 195–6, 199–200, 246, 261
expropriation 8, 12, 40, 43, 119, 169, 235, 244, 264

Federoff, Osip 69, 78–9, 87, 107, 113, 120, 182, 184, 192, 289
Feldman, Leah 256
Fenians 57, 151

Fink, John Stephen 263
Fitch, Herbert 249
Fleishman, Jacob 123
Fleishman, Rebecca 121–3, 126–8, 159–60
Fogel, Jacob *see* Salnins, Kristap
Foreign Office 241
Frankel, Reuben 117, 209
Freedman, Dr Mengele 201
Freedom (journal) 54, 64, 204, 242–3
Freeman, May *see* Peters, May

Gardstein, George ('Morin', 'Muronzeff', 'Puika') 50, 53–4, 68, 78–81, *80*, 86–7, 90, 93, 120, 124, 175, 177, 187–8, 190–92, 195–6, 198–9, 203–5, 229, 244, 246–7, 249
  lodgings in Gold Street 79, 87, 107, 114–15, 149
  shooting and death 99–109, 111, *113*, 117, 158, 185, 214, 218, 225, 235
George V 115, 262
Gershon, Betsy 87, 121–4, 125–7, 159, 258
Gibbs, Philip 155, 162, 168
Goldberg, Sophia 295
Gordon, Fanny 69, 198–9, 202
Gordon, Isaac 199–201, 204
Gordon, Polly 199–200
Grantham, Sir William 109, 186–91, 203, 230
Grishka *see* Salnins, Kristaps
Guildhall Police Court 182–6
guns 20–25, 49–50, 79, 102, 107, 111, 114, 129, 148–9, 265, 289

Hackney 20, 82–3
Hale End 24–5
Harding, Arthur 176, 196
Harmsworth, Alfred 156
Harris's jewellery shop 52, 88–9, *89*, 184, 187, 191, 211, 247, 275
Harris, Harry 90
Harris, Samuel 110
Hartley, William 157
Hartmanis *see* Gardstein, George
Hefeld, Paul 18–24, 31–2, 47–9, 271–2
Henry, Sir Edward (commissioner, Metropolitan Police) 58, 142, 206
Himmelfarb, Mendel 263
Hitchcock, Alfred 258–9

Index

Hitchcock, William 258
Hoffman, Karl 68, 75–6, 78, *84*, 85, 101–2, 107–8, 114, 116, 118, 120–21, 184–5, 192, 198, 213–14, 279
Home Office 15, 112–13, 115, 134, 136, 138, 154, 180, 241, 265
Houndsditch 8, 10, 13, 52, 59–60, 69, 77, 81, 86, 88–93, *89*, *92*, 110, 116, 124, 160, 164–5, 169, 184, 191–3, 230
Huskinson, Edward 165, 293

Illustrated Police News *159*
identification parades 184, 247, 299
Independent Labour Party 45
India 40, 57, 152, 230
Iranian embassy siege 7
Ireland 40, 57, 173–4

Jack the Ripper 10, 221, 224, 277
Jacobs, Bessie 184, 195–6
James, Henry 54
Janson, Lennie 120
Janson, Theodor 120
Jensen, Richard Bach 58
Jewish Association for the Protection of Girls and Women 206
Jewish Chronicle 171–2
Jewish immigration 12–13, 15–16, 32–8, 165–6, 174
Jones, Kennedy 156
Joscelyne, Ralph 21, 26–8, *27*, 272
Jubilee Street Club 13, 52, 67–9, 77, 80, 122, 154, 160, 177, 194, 196, 209, 217, 224, 242–3, 247, 260, 280
 closure of Club 69–72, 253
 opening of Club 61–7, *65*

Keyworth, Albert 20
King's Police Medal 25, 110
Kray brothers 10–11
Kropotkin, Peter 38, 44–5, 53, 55, 60–62, 64, 248, 250, 254–6, 265, 284, 295–6
Kyiv 209, 223, 228

Laivins, Juris *see* Dubof, Yourka
Latvia 19, 38–45, 169, 180, 226
 1905 Revolution 8–9, 40–44, 74–5, 242–3
Latvian (language) 75, 106, 122, 124, 132, 185, 197

Latvian (Lettish) Social Democratic and Workers Party 41, 45, 235–7
Leeson, Ben (police sergeant) 132–3, 136, 154, 233, 258
Leggatt, Ted 62
Lenin 11, 38, 40, 44, 238, 241
Lepidus, Jacob 18–25, 47–8, 51, 271–2
Lescinska, Otilija ('Tija') *39*, 193
Levi, Joe *see* Smoller, Max
Levy, Isaac 99–100, 109, 187, 189–90, 237, 276
Liddell, Guy 240–41
Liepaja (Libau) 87, 124, 263
Liesma (flame) anarchist group 12, 53–4, 179, 191, 229, 232, 264–6
Lilienthal, Peter 262
Litvinoff, Emanuel 261–2
Lockhart, R.H. Bruce 238
London Fire Brigade 142–51, *147*, 163, 279
Lord Mayor's Show 67

MacDonald, J. Ramsay 45
Maclean, Neal 239
Macnaghten, Melville (assistant commissioner, Metropolitan Police) *147*, 152, 178–9, 231
Malatesta, Errico 60–62, 68, 79, 90, 200, 244–51, *248*, 262–3, 265
Malatesta (film) 262–3
Man Who Knew Too Much, The (film) 258–9
Mann, Crossman & Paulin brewery 7, 133–4
Marks *see* Smoller, Max
Mars, Solomon 119, 289–90
Marseilles 118, 181, 226
Marsh, Edward 164, 173
Martin, Charles 35, 71, 284
Martin, James (police constable) 96–7, 107, 179, 189–90
Marx, Karl 54
Mauser pistol 50, 79, 81, 102, 107, 114, 138, 149, 190
Maxim machine gun *140*, 141–2
Metropolitan Police 12, 14, 85–6, 133, *150*, 152, 177–9, 180, 248
 Special Branch 178–9, 181, 207, 217, 221
MI5 119, 207, 234, 240

Miller, Anton 235
Milstein, Jack 210
Milstein, Luba 69, 76–9, 82, 91, 100–103, 106, 108–9, 112, 117–18, 121, 182, *183*, 185, 192, 198, *208*, 209–19, 277–8
Minsk 125
Molchanoff, Pavel 103, 118, 123, 228
Morning Post 169
Morris, C.C.B (Fire Brigade divisional officer) 145–6
Morrison, Arthur 35
Morrison, Steinie 177–8
Moscow 238–41
Motherwell 50–52
Mulvany, John (Police Superintendent) 132–5, 148
Muronzeff *see* Gardstein, George
musical instruments 77–8, 228, 289

Nacht, Siegfried 246
Nelson, A. B. 289
New York 115, 195
newsreels 15, 162–4, 292
Nomad, Max 80
Nott-Bower, William (commissioner, City of London Police) 178, 249
Noy, Wilfred 259

Old Bailey 10, 14, 81, 102, 109, 112, 120, 175, 186–91, 203–4, 230, 235, 247, 249–50, 264
Ottaway, John (detective superintendent) 89, 91, 181, 207, 212, 221
Oughton, Frederick 261

Page-Croft, Henry 239
Palamieks, Janis ('Bifsteks') 74–5, 82
Paris 47, 58, 60, 66, 118, 193, 217
Parker, Ada 98
Pearson, Charles (Fire Brigade district officer) 148, 279
People, The 164–5, *164*
Perelman, Charles 69, 73–6, 117, 125–7, 198, 287
Perelman, Fanny 73
Perelman, Isaac 75
Peter the Painter 8–12, *11*, 50, 69–70, 76–81, 100–103, 109, 116–19, 125, 149, 154–5, 160, 192, 217, 221–35, *227*, 252–3, 266–7
  in film and literature 259–63
  in France 118, 181, 209, 226–8
  in Latvia 40–43, 53, 74–5, 81, 222–3
  in the United States 43, 232
  nickname 112, 224
  real identity 222–3
Peters, Jacob 69, 75, 78, 87, 107, 109, 113, 120, 125, 182, 184, 187–90, 192, 224, 235–41, *237*, 264, 278
Peters, Maisie 238, 241
Peters, May 237–41, 266
Piatkow, Peter *see* Peter the Painter
Pilenas, Casimir 284, 295–6, 298
Pilenas, Peter 298
Pinkovski, Peter 224
Piper, Walter (police constable) 93–4, 97, 107, 109
Piratin, Phil 256
Ploschansky, Naomi (Nellie Dick) 62–3, 67–8, 119, 194–5, 213, 254
Poland 206, 216, 256
police interpreters 14, 108
popular press 14–15, 25–6, 155–62
postcards 22, *140*, *141*, 162, *163*
Pskov 226, 259
Punga, Hermanis 284

Riga 26, 31, 38–9, 41–4, 47–9, 82, 85, 174, 180, 238, 264
Rising Sun, The (pub) 155, 163, 279
Rocker, Fermin 281
Rocker, Rudolf 58–67, 69, 71, 168–9, 194, 204–5, 217, 220, 234–5, 247, 253–6, *255*, 265, 281
Rosen, John ('the Barber') 69, 75, 78, 82–5, *83*, 107, 114, 184–5, 189–90, 192, 198, 201
Royal Engineers 142
Royal Horse Artillery 141
Royal Irish Constabulary 151–2
Ruff, Philip 16, 41, 214, 233
Rumbelow, Donald 16, 192
Russia 8, 40–45, 49, 56, 70, 169, 180–81, 193
  Consul-General in London 32, 114, 181, 222–3, 297
  secret police (Okhrana) 36, 181–2, 193–4, 222, 230–31, 236, 262

Russian language 9, 13–14, 46, 69, 114, 122, 124, 132, 182, 197, 212, 218, 235
Russian Social Democrats 236
Russian Social Revolutionaries 114–15

Sabel, Millie 65, 194, *255*
St Paul's Cathedral 110
St Petersburg 33, 40–41, 171, 180, 198
Salnins, Kristaps ('Grishka') *39*, 73–4, 264, 283
Samuel, Herbert 28
Sangster, Jimmy 260–61
Scanlan, Dr J. 102–4
Schieman, Davis 128
Schnurmann, Julius 19
Schnurmann's rubber factory 18–20
Schtern, Peter *see* Peter the Painter
Schwarze, Anna 43, 228
Searle, Edward (police officer) 179
Serge, Victor 253
Scots Guards 7, 134, 136, 140–41, 151, 155, 163
Shapiro, Alexander 234
Sidney Arms, The (pub) 137
Sidney Street 7, 9, 14–15, 35–6, 59–60, 121–41, 172, 279
  drawings, map *126*, *127*, *130–31*
  fire at 100 Sidney Street 142–51, *147*
Siege of Sidney Street, The (film) 35, 220, 260–61
Simenon, Georges 259
Sitwell, Blanche 206
Sladen, Sampson (chief officer, London Fire Brigade) 143–4
Smith, Carl 51
Smoller, Max 78, 85–6, *86*, 88, 102, 108–9, 116–17, 175, 191
Social Democratic Party 236
Sokoloff, William ('Josef', 'Yoska') 52–3, 75, 78, 85–7, 101–2, 108, 116, 118, 121, 126, 128, 135, 149, 152–3, 175, 191–2, 244
Soviet Trade Delegation 207
Spitalfields 36, 66, 76, 100, 111, 196, 198
Stalin, Joseph 10, 233, 241, 262
Star, The 157
Stark, John (police chief superintendent) 133

Stepney 7–9, 13, 15–16, 33–4, 59, 61, 67, 88–9, 100, 117–18, 137, 151, 171, 176, 180, 198, 209, 256
Stepney Green 69, 75, 85, 119, 255
Stepniak, Sergius 38
Sticking, Masha 108, 199, 295
Stoke Newington 22, 26–7, 35
Strongman, Arthur (police constable) 94, 97, 107
Svaars, Fritz 12, 42–3, 52–3, 68–9, 75–82, 91, 100–103, 108, 112, 116–18, 152–4, 189–92, 198, 209–11, 213–14, 217, 224–5, 228–9, 235–7, 244
  in 100 Sidney Street 121–35, 149
  letter to family in Latvia 124–5, 290
Svaars, Lisa 210, 235

Thomas, Dr Danford 151
Thompson, Ernest (detective inspector) 104–6
Times, The 169–70
Three Compasses, The (pub) 155
Tocmacoff, Nikolai 68, 78–9, 82, 112, 223–4, 228, 287
Tottenham 8, 18–31, 46–7, 51, 59–60, 74, 90, 110, 164–5, 172, 248, 260, 270–73
Traeberg, Sima 212–13
Trassjonsky, Rosa (Sara) 78–9, 100–103, 106, 112, 182, *183*, 185, 192, 210–11, 214–20, *215*, 260, 278
Treloar, Sir W. P. 182
Tucker, Charles (police sergeant) 97–8, 109, 111, *111*, 185, 276
Turner, John 62, 65
Tyler, William (police constable) 21–3, *22*, 26–8, *27*, *29*, 32, 271–2

Ukraine 76, 141, 197
United States 33, 38, 43, 54–5, 81–2, 156, 182, 194–5, 227, 232, 235, 256

Vanoveitch, Evan *see* Palamieks, Janis
Vassileva, Nina 69, 75, 78, 81, 85, 87, 89, 91, 107–9, 114–16, 119–22, 184–5, 188–92, 196–209, *197*, 217, 220, 228, 231, 262, 284
Veldie, Victor 119
Volkhovsky, Felix 38

Walthamstow 23
Walthuis, Homme (police constable) 224
War Office 134
Weil, Max 93, 95
Wensley, Fred (detective inspector) 81, 104–6, 129, 132, 135, 175–8, 201–2
Wess, William 64
Whitechapel 35, 53, 73, 168, 179, 215–16
Wilde, Oscar 212
Wilson, James 20
Witcop, Milly 61, 69, 168, 194, 204–5, 254–6, 281
Witcop, Polly 255

Witcop, Rose 65–6, 194
Wodehouse, Major Frederick (assistant commissioner, Metropolitan Police) 134
Woodhams, Ernest (police constable) 96, 99

Yiddish 9, 13–14, 35, 41, 46, 60, 62, 66, 69, 102, 114, 150, 167, 176, 180, 182, 188, 197–8, 212–14, 216, 278, 295, 297

Zaklis, Janis *see* Peter the Painter
Zelin, Janis *see* Rosen, John